PROSTITUTION IN THE GILDED AGE

The Jennie Hollister Story

Shining Tramp Press

Dedicated to my sister-

Barbara the Doll

Contents

Cover: Oil Painting by the Author; Other Art, Pictures, & Maps by the Author, the Connecticut State Library, 231 Capitol Ave., Hartford, or old newspapers.

Published by Shining Tramp Press
2114 Harbor View Drive, Rocky Hill, CT 06067

ISBN 978-0-9749352-4-9

Library of Congress Cataloging-in-Publication Data

E660 - 664

Murphy, Kevin J., 1949-

Prostitution in the Gilded Age: The Jennie Hollister Story

Kevin Murphy. – 1st ed.

303 p.; 23.5 cm.
Includes author's notes and index.

1. Prostitution
2. Biography
3. History, Prostitution, U.S., Gilded Age
4. History, Hartford, Connecticut

Printed by Amazon
First Edition: January 2015

McGuire – McQueeney

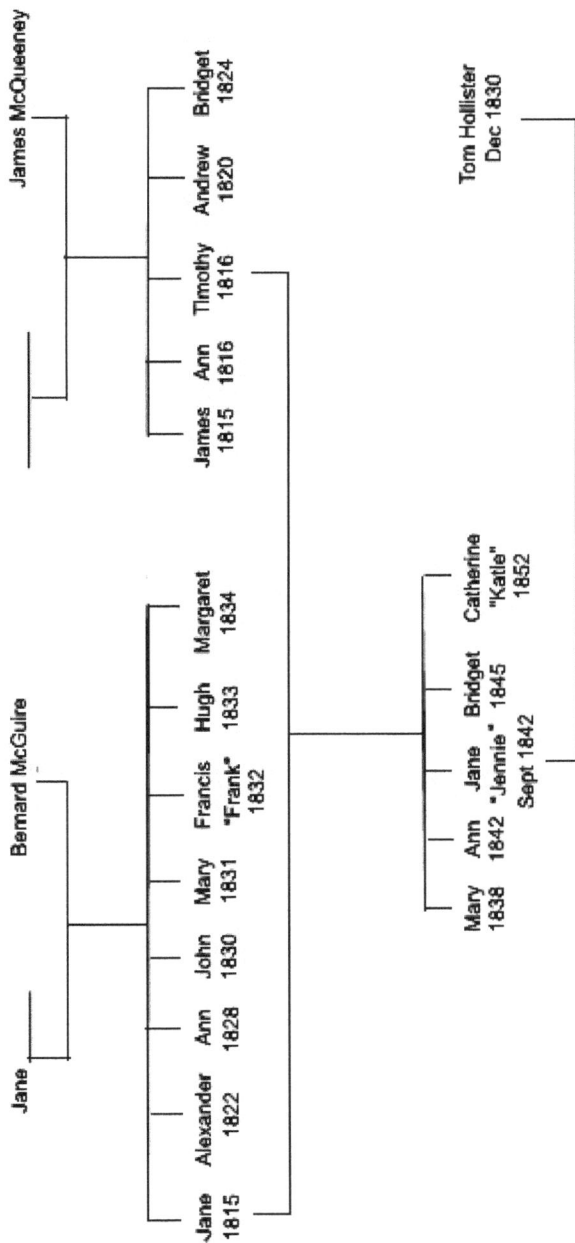

James McQueeney

- James 1815
- Ann 1816
- Timothy 1816
- Andrew 1820
- Bridget 1824

Jane — **Bernard McGuire**

- Jane 1815
- Alexander 1822
- Ann 1828
- John 1830
- Mary 1831
- Francis "Frank" 1832
- Hugh 1833
- Margaret 1834

- Mary 1838
- Ann 1842
- Jane "Jennie" Sept 1842
- Bridget 1845
- Catherine "Katie" 1852

Tom Hollister Dec 1830

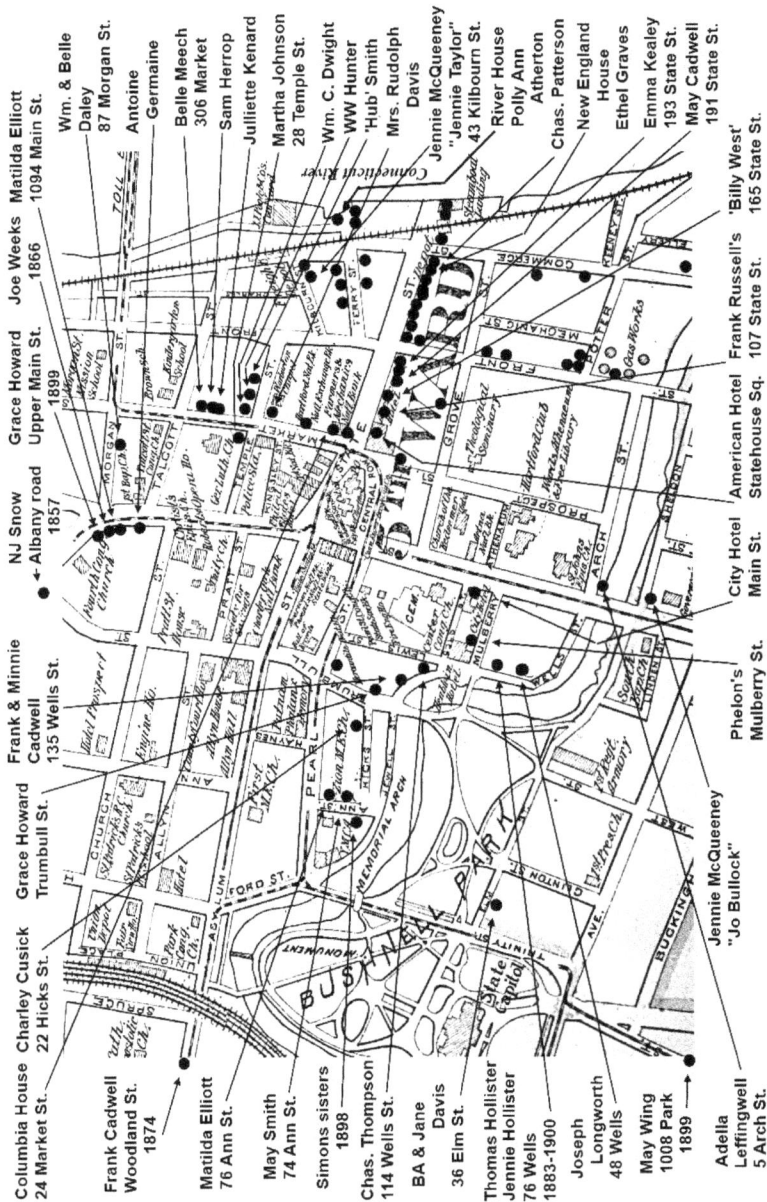

Matilda Elliott 1094 Main St.
Wm. & Belle Daley 87 Morgan St.
Antoine Germaine
Belle Meech 306 Market
Sam Herrop
Julliette Kenard
Martha Johnson 28 Temple St.
Wm. C. Dwight
WW Hunter
'Hub' Smith
Mrs. Rudolph Davis
Jennie McQueeney "Jennie Taylor" 43 Kilbourn St.
River House
Polly Ann Atherton
Chas. Patterson
New England House
Ethel Graves
Emma Kealey 193 State St.
May Cadwell 191 State St.

Joe Weeks 1866
Grace Howard Upper Main St. 1899
NJ Snow Albany road 1857
Frank & Minnie Cadwell 135 Wells St.
Grace Howard Trumbull St.
Charley Cusick 22 Hicks St.
Columbia House 24 Market St.

Connecticut River

'Billy West' 165 State St.
Frank Russell's 107 State St.
American Hotel Statehouse Sq.
City Hotel Main St.
Phelon's Mulberry St.
Jennie McQueeney "Jo Bullock"

Frank Cadwell Woodland St. 1874
Matilda Elliott 76 Ann St.
May Smith 74 Ann St.
Simons sisters 1898
Chas. Thompson 114 Wells St.
BA & Jane Davis 36 Elm St.
Thomas Hollister Jennie Hollister 76 Wells 1883-1900
Joseph Longworth 48 Wells
May Wing 1008 Park 1899
Adella Leffingwell 5 Arch St.

Introduction

Jennie Hollister was one of the most successful madames of the Gilded Age—that curious period from about 1870 to 1910. Every city in the land had a duplicate copy of Jennie Hollister. Fannie Porter's San Antonio, Texas brothel was a frequent stop for outlaws, including Butch Cassidy and the Sundance Kid. In San Francisco, Sally Stanford outshone the other madames and eventually became the mayor of Sausalito. Josie Arlington of New Orleans's "Storyville" opened her first bordello on Customhouse Street in 1895. Eleanora Dumont had bawdy houses in gold and silver boomtowns all over the Rockies. Annie Wilson, Queen of Omaha's Underworld, eventually bequeathed her twenty-five-room mansion to the city for a hospital. Dorothy Parker ran Dorothy's Rooms at the Last Chance Gulch in Helena, Montana. The differences between these women, and their houses of ill fame, could be etched on a ladybug's nose. By following the highs and lows of Jennie Hollister's life in Hartford, Connecticut, the lives and careers of all other prostitutes and madames come clearly into focus.

Jennie Hollister seemed the perfect madame—very attractive, stately, overflowing with personality, and possessed of a strong native intelligence.

Jennie's home—and parlor house—rested elegantly on the east side of Bushnell Park, the central park of the city. This 6,000-square-foot Second French Empire mansion sat at 76 Wells Street and it was as beautiful and luxurious as any home in town.

The Gilded Age represented the only time in American history when prostitution was *virtually* legal. The Civil War proved such a grizzly affair that, afterward, the average citizen were unmoved by a little vice. By the turn of the twentieth century, even small cities had dozens of bawdy houses and countless houses of assignation. In addition, there were plenty of saloons and cigar stores with backroom operations.

Eventually, America regained its social conscience and, almost overnight, the houses of ill repute disappeared. The truly lucky madames were the ones who didn't live to see the end of an era. Jennie Hollister passed away in 1900, just a few years before the houses of ill fame were closed forever. Though Jennie ran a luxurious and orderly parlor house, it would never have survived society's social reforms and return to righteousness.

Jennie Hollister's seventeen-room parlor house was almost as roomy and comfortable as Governor Morgan Bulkeley's Italianate mansion on Washington Street or Mark Twain's huge "steamboat" manse—both just a few blocks away. The Hollister place glistened with white clapboards and phallic red brick chimneys atop a Pennsylvania gray slate mansard roof. The property enjoyed almost a hundred and ten feet of frontage on Wells Street, and the back and side yards accommodated lush and charming gardens. The Hollisters' home at 76 Wells Street, with its aristocratic clientele, brought out the envy in all the city's other madames.[1]

A leafy collection of elms, oaks, and maples shaded the house from the noonday sun. Looking west, Jennie Hollister could see the great expanse of

Bushnell Park, with its lazy Park River, miles of bridle paths, and acres of well-manicured lawns. What had originally been the lifeless "city park" became such a huge attraction that, on Sunday afternoons, families from miles around took leisurely carriage drives through this verdant playground.

Just to the west of Bushnell Park, and fairly touching the clouds, stood Connecticut's mammoth new State Capitol—the working venue of some of the Hollisters' best patrons. Jennie and Tom Hollister entertained the finest collection of lawmakers and businessmen of money and property. Men of the highest station, from all over the state, spent their spare time at the Hollisters' house of ill repute. Jennie and Tom Hollister bought the place in early 1882, and spent a fortune on lavish improvements, including steam heat. Jennie Hollister was twelve years younger than her husband, who passed away in 1894. When Jennie died in 1900, she had been in business for eighteen years—and her arrest record for keeping a house of ill repute featured only one smudge—in 1899. All those years, when wary clients broached the subject, Jennie replied reassuringly, "We have never been bothered by the police during the many years of our existence."[2]

Tom's father, Joseph Hollister, had been a New York City policeman and as a courtesy, the local police gave the Hollisters extensive latitude. In turn, the Hollisters made sure that each January the chief of police received about the same as a saloonkeeper would pay for his license—$450 in cash. (That's why bordellos weren't usually raided in early January, as police waited for proprietors to do the right thing.) The Hollisters also made sure that the chief, captains, lieutenants, and beat cops all received Christmas gifts. Lastly, Jennie and Tom ran 76 Wells Street in an orderly manner. The police had no trouble leaving the Hollisters alone.

Far more important in the calculus of Gilded Age prostitution, were the "bishops"—not the religious sort, but the city father type—who felt that prostitution was a necessary evil. As a result, houses of ill fame operated freely while the police kept a careful—albeit distant—watch. The police knew every house: the proprietors, proprietresses, madames, inmates, runners, and patrons. (Runners were business solicitors.) Yet they rarely raided the orderly houses. When they did perform raids, revenue drove the incursions. Without these houses of sin, streetwalkers would overrun the city, creating a terrible atmosphere for respectable women and businessmen alike. Elected officials, merchants, bankers, professional men—and even clerics—felt it best to allow the houses of ill fame to operate, as long as the businesses were orderly.

Cities across the country set up red light districts to corral the vice. Bawdy houses were allowed to operate freely. After a fashion, the scheme worked well. When Mark Twain first visited Hartford in 1868, he wrote a letter to his editor at *Alta California* magazine and gushed, "Of all the beautiful towns it has been my fortune to see, [Hartford] is the chief . . . [it] seems to be composed almost entirely of dwelling houses—not single-shaped affairs . . . but massive private hotels, scattered along the broad, straight streets. . . . Some of these stately dwellings are almost buried from sight in parks and forests. . . .You do not know what beauty is if you have not been here. . . .The morality of this locality is . . . marvelous. . . .Young ladies walk these streets alone as late as ten o'clock at night, and are not insulted. . . . I see the whole female element of the community . . . turn out about eight o'clock in the evening and swarm back and forth through Main Street. . . . It is said that ladies of the highest respectability go freely to lectures and concerts at night in this city of 40,000 souls, without other escort than members of their own sex. . . ."[3]

Could Jennie Hollister's place have been one of those that Mark Twain walked by when he lived in Hartford? We'll never know for sure, but it might have been. If keeping prostitution behind closed doors made Mark Twain think so highly of the city, perhaps the bishops knew what they were doing.

Throughout the 1890s, as wilder and bawdier characters of the demimonde poured into the wide-open Capitol City of Connecticut, vice of all sorts ran on borrowed time. In 1895, the wooden, covered bridge to East Hartford burned until the river swept away the few remaining charred splinters of wood. Naturally enough, the common council appointed a new bridge commission. At the helm of this new body was ex-Gov. Morgan Bulkeley who had been mayor of the city from 1880 to 1888. When it came to individuals, Bulkeley had no prejudices of any kind, but he loathed the demimonde. In the end, as Bulkeley sweated over the cost of the longest stone arch bridge in the world, he made a fateful decision: there would be no houses of ill repute on the streets that led to the new bridge.

Bulkeley bought up huge sections of the tenderloin, including vast stretches of the waterfront along the Connecticut River, and bulldozed buildings with abandon. Gone were the flophouses, the flag taverns, tumbledown shacks, and the houses of ill fame that had plagued the city from the earliest times. The toughs and the prostitutes had lost their homes and their haunts. Meanwhile, just before traffic flowed over the new bridge in late 1907, Judge Edward Garvan of the city's police court sent ten madames to jail for three months. Up to that time, the madames only paid fines. The tenderloin trembled, as the city closed down around them; soon they would have to leave.

One last note: When Jennie McQueeney began working in the roadhouse of her friend and mentor, Angeline Prentice, she took the name

Jennie Taylor. Around 1870, when she started her own house, in a failed attempt to remain in the shadows, she became Josephine "Jo" Bullock. Lastly, after she married Tom Hollister in 1878, Jennie Hollister emerged. The name stuck until her death in 1900. If your storyteller has done his job correctly, these changes will be fairly smooth and almost imperceptible.

Chapter 1

Jennie McQueeney of Dublin

In late September of 1842, Jennie Hollister was born Jane "Jennie" McQueeney in Dublin, Ireland. (The names McQueen and McQueeney derive from McSweeney.) The infant, Jennie, bore her mother's name, Jane (McGuire) McQueeney. As a toddler, young Jennie McQueeney was an absolute doll, with blonde hair, blue eyes, fair skin, and a sharp little mind. The barbaric Celts, the Viking plunderers, the Norman invaders, the alternating Anglo-Norman rulers, and the English Kings spent thousands of years enslaving the Irish people—their blood and sinew spilling into Ireland's ever-evolving cauldron of brains, talent, bone, and bowel. In the end, these disparate forces combined to create divine little creatures like Jennie McQueeney.[4]

The Irish have always been famous for naming children after parents and relatives, forcing a new identity upon the younger generation. Little Jane became Jennie; the girl, Bridget, became Delia; the son, Denis, became Dinny; and so it went. All her life, Jennie McQueeney used the formal name, Jane, only on important occasions: penned in the ship's manifest before her voyage to America; on mortgage papers; affixed to her marriage license; and engraved on her impressive tombstone in Cedar Hill Cemetery, Hartford. All other times, Jennie sufficed.[5]

Timothy McQueeney, Jennie's father, was an illiterate laborer in Dublin—on the eastern shore of Ireland. The McQueeneys, with their four girls; and the McGuires, with eight children, lived just north of what was then called the River Anna Liffey—a substantial body of water that ran west to east across the center of Dublin. Both families were Roman Catholic. The McQueeneys worshiped at St. Michan's on Church Street, while the McGuires prayed at St. Mary's Pro-Cathedral on Marlborough Street. The name St. Mary's Pro-Cathedral suggests a painful history. The Church of Ireland—Anglicans—own St. Mary's Pro-Cathedral, but it has always acted as the seat of the Roman Catholic Archdiocese of Dublin. Ireland's history brims with thousands of these historical curiosities.[6]

For Jennie McQueeney, 1842 proved a monumentally bad time to enter the world. From 1700 to 1841, Ireland's population quadrupled to 8.2 million residents. The island had become painfully overcrowded and the stress cracks of an economic disaster were already beginning to show.[7]

The Great Famine, though officially bracketed between 1845 and 1851, plunged Ireland into at least seven decades of suffering. The Irish died and emigrated in record numbers, and the population of Ireland kept falling until 1926, when it leveled off just above 4.2 million. A common phrase during this long and painful period was "deserted Ireland," for there were empty cottages all over the countryside and Ireland had no young adults. Old folks and small children seemed the only inhabitants for a long time after the Great Hunger.[8]

Cottier farmers, who owned nothing and lived completely on potatoes, overran Ireland by the time the blight brought Ireland to ruin in 1845. The

Irish had seen famines before and told themselves that the following year would be different. However, in July 1846, a Relief Commissioner sent the following report to England: "I am sorry to state that. . . . The prospect of the potato crop this year is even more distressing than last year—that the disease has appeared earlier and its ravages are more extensive." Truth told, in 1846, the potato harvest was only 20 percent of pre-Famine levels. To make matters worse, much of that paltry crop rotted in storage.[9]

As Ireland's economy crumbled, emigration levels climbed, especially in far western Ireland where people were hungry and destitute. In Counties Mayo, Galway, Clare, Cork, and Kerry, emigration was the highest in the land. So was crime. In Dublin, crime rose only about 50 percent above pre-Famine levels. But in the far western counties, it went up more than 100 percent.[10] It could hardly be helped; people were fighting, stealing, and killing for food.

With few options, many of the hungry, evicted Irish farmers were descending on the cities, looking for relief. Life in cities like Dublin deteriorated fast, and the economic collapse extended far beyond the shores of Ireland. In cities all over western Europe—London, Glasgow, Edinburgh, and Paris—tradesmen and artisans gathered at large, hot-blooded rallies to air their grievances, and more importantly, to demand jobs.[11]

Trinity College and the Irish Parliament had been built just south of the Liffey, in Trinity Ward and the South City Ward. All along the river, quays berthed ships carrying goods and raw materials of every description. These ships were loaded and unloaded by a massive collection of poor, illiterate Irishmen, living just north of the Liffey in the dilapidated tenements of the North City Ward. The poor, uneducated residents of these dilapidated buildings, of course, included Jennie McQueeney, her parents, siblings, aunts, uncles, and cousins.

As illiterate laborers, the McGuires and McQueeneys didn't have a chance in such a desperate economy. Both families had been on the lookout for something better. At length, Timothy McQueeney got encouraging news from relatives in America. They lived in Providence, Rhode Island, but thought Timothy McQueeney and his family would find work and a good life in Hartford, Connecticut. Around 1850, a familial connection existed between Hartford and Providence that has been lost over time. Just as the Dublin and Kingstown railroad had come to Ireland in 1834, the Hartford, Providence, and Fishkill railroad came to Hartford in 1839—and connected to New York a decade later. The workforce shifted to the cities as steam power replaced Connecticut's 200 water powered mill towns, a trend that grew mightily throughout the Gilded Age.

As a stellar example, Pliny Jewell of Vermont came to Hartford in 1845 and began a leather tanning business on the banks of the Park (Little) River. Three years later, he opened a shop on Trumbull Street, and in a few short decades, P. Jewell & Sons became the largest producer of industrial belting in the world. Hartford burgeoned with businesses, from saddlers to printers, who started small in the mid-1830s and built their firms up into world-beaters by the 1850s. After an ill-fated handgun-manufacturing venture in Patterson, New Jersey, Samuel Colt returned to Hartford in 1847 to produce ever more sophisticated revolvers. To cap his enormous success, in 1855, Colt built the largest private armory in the world, Colt Patent Fire-Arms Company, on the banks of the Connecticut River in the city's south meadows. In the same vein, Christian Sharps had been issued a patent on a unique breech-loading rifle in 1849. The orders for this one rifle began the Sharps Rifle Manufacturing Company on Rifle Row (later

Capitol Avenue). All of this doesn't even touch upon Case, Lockwood & Brainard, the largest printer in Connecticut; Plimpton Manufacturing Company, the largest government envelope printer in the United States; and a dozen other major concerns that originated in Hartford around the middle of the nineteenth century. It seemed that the city couldn't help itself as it blossomed into a vast manufacturing hub and the demand for skilled mechanics and immigrant Irish laborers grew with the businesses in this supercharged town on the shores of the Connecticut River.

Twenty-nine-year-old Timothy McQueeney and his eighteen-year-old sister-in-law, Ann McGuire, were the first to emigrate. Dublin connected to Liverpool with a small fleet of steam vessels—mostly paddle side-wheelers. The Dublin and Liverpool Steam Packet Co. led this trade, carrying sometimes 100,000 passengers a year. Crossing the Irish Sea proved traumatic for many passengers, as there were no cabins. Beyond that, the animals wedged in below decks gave off an overpowering smell. These overcrowded ferries offered only deck steerage service, so passengers were exposed to the elements and arrived at Liverpool suffering from complete exhaustion.

At the end of September 1846, Timothy McQueeney and Ann McGuire spent fourteen hours aboard one such Dublin steam ferry, crossing the Irish Sea to Liverpool. From there, they booked passage on the square-rigged packet ship *New York* for the voyage across the North Atlantic to America. Before the Famine, virtually all of the Irish who emigrated did so through the Cove of Cork—called Queenstown after 1849—or through Liverpool in England. However, the famine forced many Irish to sail from small, little-used ports such as Ballina, Westport, Tralee, Sligo, Kinsale, Killala, Newry, and Waterford. Sadly, these desperate exiles had no choice but to take ships of questionable seaworthiness. It spelled disaster in 1847—Black '47—when thousands died trying to get to America in these "coffin ships."

The packet ships out of Liverpool offered the safest passage and the cheapest ticket prices of the Famine years, making the harrowing trip across the Irish Sea worth the risk. Since 1838, when the steam packet *SS Sirius* successfully crossed the Atlantic, it was only a question of time before the wooden sailing ships slipped into obsolescence. In 1840, Samuel Cunard's steamer *Britannia* won him a Royal Mail contract, and his company went on to become a legendary maritime success. These early steamships were primitive side-wheelers and averaged only ten knots. However, they could cross the Atlantic in fourteen to seventeen days while sailing vessels needed forty days. From New York to Liverpool, many of these sailing vessels eventually managed a record fifteen days, but the east to west run seemed the real stump puller. In 1846, the *Yorkshire* finally bested her competitors by sailing into New York Harbor after only sixteen days at sea. Ships set these records with crews that worked the North Atlantic regularly. Wind and weather being such fickle mistresses, another ship might not get so favorable a slant in a lifetime. The packet ships that the McGuires and McQueeneys boarded at Liverpool could average twelve knots in a twenty-four hour period under favorable conditions, and over time, the journey settled into a six-week voyage.[12]

After suffering a month and a half of bad food and boredom, Timothy McQueeney and Ann McGuire sailed into New York Harbor on November 6, 1846. A small steam ferry brought the port physician out to the vessel to examine the 308 steerage passengers. The doctor didn't bother the 38 passengers in cabin class, a common practice. Soon thereafter, steam tugs pushed and pulled the *New York* to Manhattan's South Street Seaport on the East River. The passengers were at last released to get about their new lives in America. Timothy McQueeney and Ann McGuire caught the train from New York to New Haven and then another north to Hartford. (This may explain why so many McQueeneys settled in New Haven.)[13]

When he first arrived in Hartford in 1846, Timothy McQueeney set up housekeeping in rented rooms on Pleasant Street. Soon thereafter, he landed a job as a stable worker at the United States Hotel in Statehouse Square. James M. Goodwin—J. P. Morgan's uncle, and one of the wealthiest men in the city—had purchased the hotel in 1838. The Goodwin family could trace its roots back to the founders of the city. Over the centuries, they earned a reputation as gimlet-eyed businessmen, but also as world-class tightwads. So said, Timothy McQueeney's wages for tending the hotel's horses and carriages wasn't much. He quickly worked himself up to coachman, a job where tips from guests of the hotel helped with his household expenses. Even so, immigrants have always expressed shock at the cost of living in America and Timothy McQueeney's weekly wage must have been problematic from the get-go.[14]

Back in Dublin, Jane and the children made plans for passage to America. While it hardly seems possible, in the two years that it took the McQueeneys to arrange the finances and details of the trip, life in Dublin deteriorated further. The English had been building workhouses for the poor all over Ireland since 1838, but now the whole Poor Law Union teetered on the verge of collapse. One officer in a South Dublin Union, in tendering his resignation, explained his dilemma, "With the knowledge of the poor house being full . . . feelings are created revolting to a Christian mind. . . . Here I would beg to call your attention to the case of Martin Murray . . . whom I found, with a family of seven, in a starving state. . . . [I] gave them an order for admission, which order, like many others, was returned to me, endorsed 'no room.' I gave the family relief . . . and when my book came to be reported on, the rations I had given them would not be sanctioned!"[15]

To make matters worse, the Poor Laws were reduced. "The commissioners deem it desirable . . . to suspend, on 18 March [1848], all orders under the . . . Irish poor relief extension act, authorizing 'outdoor relief' to able-bodied men."[16]

As the 1848 February Revolution in France played out, British officials became more and more concerned. After the overthrow of Louis Phillipe, the French Second Republic came to life. Instability reigned until the end of the year, when the French people elected Louis Napoleon who organized the Second French Empire. In Ireland, the 1848 French uprising gave hope to Irishmen like John Mitchel, publisher of *The United Irishmen*. Mitchel felt that the French experience would be the catalyst for revolution and home rule in Ireland.

The British were taking no chances. On Tuesday, March 21, 1848, at the Head Office, the police arrested John Mitchel "for the publication of three seditious articles."[17] (Later convicted on charges of felony-treason, the court exiled him to Bermuda and then Tasmania, Australia.)[18]

In May, life in Dublin took another bad turn. On Sunday, May 21, the rights of Dubliners to pass peaceably through the streets ended. The police blockaded a popular thoroughfare and a military regiment buttressed the decision. Even professional people, on their way to their homes and offices, were hindered from passing along one of the most crowded thoroughfares of Dublin. The tension was explosive.[19]

The time had come to leave Ireland. Jane McQueeney took her four daughters and left for America just as the British chose to use the Coercion Act against Dubliners. As *The Irish Felon*—the successor of *The United Irishman*—wrote "We are soon . . . to live under the severe law, which . . .

transfers . . . rights to the constitutional mercies of police and detectives. From the day named in the proclamation . . . no person whatsoever shall carry or process arms elsewhere than in his own dwelling house. The contraband instruments include guns, pistols or other firearms, or parts of such—likewise any sword, cutlass, pike or bayonet. . . . Any open carrying of such arms to be a misdemeanor and punishable with two years imprisonment. . . ."[20]

Just as Timothy McQueeney had done, Jane and her four young daughters took a steam ferry across the Irish Sea bound for Liverpool—and ultimately America. Jane McQueeney, aged thirty-two, must have suffered the trials of Job during the passage to America because her daughters were so young. At nine, Mary could conceivably have offered some help with her siblings. Ann, at six, couldn't do much; Jennie and Bridget, at five and three, respectively, probably had all they could do just to hold back tears and sit still.

The steamers from Dublin put into the Clarence Dock in Liverpool. Most of the emigrants already had their tickets and, if Jane McQueeney timed it right, she and the children could board the ship early. However, sailing vessels were notoriously bad at maintaining schedules. Oftentimes, passengers were required to put up at a boarding house for a few days—if not weeks. During the day, emigrants spent their time strolling between the Waterloo Dock and the Clarence Dock—and "more especially about Denison, Regent, Carlton, Porter, Stewart, and Great Howard Streets."[21] Though nothing could deter those in transit from walking about the city, this could be a dangerous pastime. Before boarding their vessels, emigrants were forced to deal with ship's brokers, runners, boarding-house keepers, thieves, hustlers, and pickpockets—each trying to separate them from their money. Lastly, they had to pass a medical inspection.

Most emigration vessels departed from the Waterloo dock and it presented a scene from a lunatic asylum—

> Men, women and children were scrambling up the sides of the ship. One could see hundreds of people confused, screaming. Luggage and boxes were flung aboard, followed by the passengers. When they or their luggage missed the ship and fell into the water, a man in a rowboat rescued them and got a reward. But sadly, there wasn't always someone there to rescue the clumsy passengers and, consequently, some drowned. Those who did not manage to get onboard at the dock-gate had no choice but to hire a rowing boat to catch up to the ship on the River Mersey. . . . Boarding a ship wasn't easy, even for the cabin passengers.[22]

Jane McQueeney and her four daughters traveled on the *Richard Alsop,* a three-masted square-rigger built in 1847 by J. C. Given at Bath, Maine for Grinnell & Co. of New York. The *Richard Alsop* measured 157 feet and featured thick, oak planking, but still fell into a class of ships that were considered slightly built.

A clerk at the quayside offices of the ship's owners composed the *Richard Alsop's* passenger list—the only lasting item from the whole voyage. Throughout the many decades of the Irish emigration, most female passengers gave their occupations as domestic, dressmaker, servant, or milliner. When asked, Jane McQueeney said "coachman." Since the Irish subsistence farmers and cottiers never could afford horses or coaches, this "coachman" entry raises eyebrows. The McGuires and McQueeneys lived near each other and had more children than they could afford.[23] Jane's husband, Timothy, worked as a "hostler" and "coachman"—as did others in the McGuire and McQueeney families. Still, one might wonder why Jane McQueeney knew more about horses and coaches than the average woman; or was she just trying to elevate her status among the millions of female Irish emigrants?

The answer is not recorded anywhere, but the "coachman" entry points out another character trait in these two families. True, they were poor and couldn't read or write, but they had an enormous amount of fight in them. Call it stubbornness, pugnacity or belligerence—whatever fits the bill. As we shall see, the McGuires and McQueeneys had a natural scrappiness in their blood that remains difficult to quantify.

On July 28, 1848, tugs towed the *Richard Alsop* from the Waterloo Dock, with the McQueeneys probably on deck and the children's eyes bugging out. After a short trip down the River Mersey, the crew set the sails and navigated for New York. Conditions, even on a new ship like the *Richard Alsop,* were appalling. There wasn't enough space, and the passengers almost completely ignored the simplest hygiene. The food couldn't have been worse. Meals were "a concoction of barley, rye, and peas, which became saturated with moisture onboard ship."[24]

Berths were wooden bunks built into the ship's timbers. Passengers had to bring their own bedding; comfort and decency were at a minimum. Vessels were "compelled to carry livestock. Cows and calves, sheep, goats, pigs and hens were carried in the larger vessels and the noises and smells of the animals did nothing to improve conditions."[25] Passengers remained on the deck as much as possible to escape the cramped space and the wretched smell. In bad weather, they had no choice but to remain in steerage all day.

Jane McQueeney and the other passengers on the *Richard Alsop* sailed into New York Harbor on Friday, September 8, 1848. It is unlikely that Timothy McQueeney met his family in New York. He would have had no way of knowing of the ship's arrival and couldn't lose a day's pay—plus travel money—in the effort.

After the harbor physician examined the passengers, tugs jostled the *Richard Alsop* to South Street Seaport and the McQueeneys were off to the train depot. A few hours later, they pulled into Hartford's Union Station.

Jane and Timothy McQueeney were obsessed with the education of their daughters. As illiterates, they knew discrimination firsthand from their time in Ireland and expected no better in America. They were determined to do better for their four girls. Toward that end, Timothy McQueeney left Pleasant Street and rented a place at 12 Market Street. The new rooms were in the heart of the city and only one door away from the Centre Schoolhouse—the best primary school in the city.

In late 1848, when the McQueeney family reassembled in Hartford, the city had eleven school districts and a total of twenty-five schools. Far and away, the Centre School—at 16-18 Market Street—had the best reputation of all the common schools. The two-story stone building with a brick front had been in use since 1816 and featured separate playgrounds for boys and girls on the north and south sides of the building. However, the schoolhouse's "situation was unfortunate, being a few rods south of City Hall, in a narrow street, and surrounded by buildings unfavorable to the beauty and cleanliness of the grounds."[26] Sad to say, only a part of the school enjoyed any shade, and that came from the large blacksmith shop to the south.

Though there were 1,890 children in all twenty-five of the city's public grade schools, 808 students registered at the Centre School and another 118 registered at the two colored schools of the First School District. In other words, close to 50 percent of all the children in Hartford attended school in the First District and 43 percent were registered in the Centre

School. However, because so many children were needed on the family farm, the highest average attendance at the Centre School annually was 633 pupils. The school term lasted twelve weeks, with four weeks of vacation scattered throughout the year. As farm work slowed in the wintertime, school attendance skyrocketed.

The Centre School was divided into four sectors, with the youngest pupils in the 4th Department and the oldest students in the 1st Department. The children ranged in age from four to sixteen and they were assigned to classes according to their ability, not their age. Therefore, in 1848, when Jennie McQueeney started school at five, she would have been grouped in the basement classroom with children from ages four through seven. (The average daily attendance in the 4th Department was only thirty children.) Perhaps when Jennie got into the 3rd Department, she would have been in a classroom on the first floor with other students, aged five through nine. Later, she would rise to the 2nd Department—in a classroom on the first or second floor—with pupils aged eight to twelve. When Jennie McQueeney reached the 1st Department, she would have been seated in a 37' by 60' classroom on the top floor of the building, with her classmates spaced between the ages of twelve and sixteen. (In the upper grades, average daily attendance was 130.)

In any New England town of only 13,555 souls, the school system would have been highly centralized, as the Centre School shows. As such, many future physicians, lawyers, judges, mayors, governors, and U.S. senators—some extraordinarily wealthy, some only moderately wealthy— were in the Centre School when Jennie McQueeney and her sisters attended. Just as an example, County Court Judge Samuel Huntington's son, Sam, was in class with Jennie McQueeney. So were Mary and Davis Ellsworth, children of the wealthy farmer and businessman John Ellsworth.

Horse breeder and businessman, Henry Beckwith—worth over a million dollars in 1850—had a daughter, Charlotte, who was in Jennie's class. Arthur Allyn, son of future Hartford Mayor Timothy Allyn, was in Jennie's class. U. S. Congressman James Dixon's children, Clementine and James, were also in this class. While Jennie learned her abc's in the basement, James and Frankie Goodwin, sons of the largest taxpayer in the city, James M Goodwin, were in the 1st Department on the top floor, finishing their primary educations. Future mayor of Hartford, governor of Connecticut, and U. S. senator, Morgan Bulkeley, sat in the same class. Rounding out this group was future lieutenant governor of Connecticut, Billy Bulkeley.

Not to carry this too far, but the children of the most prominent men in the city—physicians, dentists, bank presidents, insurance company chiefs, brokers, merchants, and commodities dealers—filled many of the seats at the Centre School. The education at the Centre school was so superior to the other grade schools that families like the Goodwins and Bulkeleys postponed moves to the more desirable western side of the city until after their children had finished up their studies at the Centre Schoolhouse. In the fullness of time, Judge Bulkeley moved from Church Street to Washington Street and the Goodwins moved from Asylum Street to Woodland Street. Lest the message get lost, this shows the educational strategy of only two of Hartford's wealthiest families. Others, of course, followed suit.

Students studied reading, writing, grammar, spelling, composition, arithmetic, geography, history, philosophy, and the statutes of Connecticut. At the end of the common school report, the School Visitors included this note: "We cannot refrain from congratulating the Centre District upon the possession of this excellent school. . . . In all the elements of usefulness, the institution, which is the subject of this report, cannot well be surpassed."[27]

Jane and Timothy McQueeney had to have their children in this school, so they rented rooms just south of the blacksmith shop near the school property. In isolation, this decision appeared sound, but the 1850s were a time of explosive growth and great changes in all the cities of the eastern United States—particularly port cities. Since its beginnings, Hartford depended on sailing vessels to bring in rum, molasses, and other goods from foreign ports. Meanwhile, the city exported produce, cattle, lumber, and finished goods. The constant traffic in schooners, barks, and brigantines meant unending exposure to sailors from all over the world. This translated into cheap flag taverns, fleabag flophouses, and houses of ill fame on the waterfront.

New London, Connecticut is a good example of one single industry pulling a town into disrepute. Sailors involved in the whaling business often put to sea for years at a time. When these lusty sailors hit land again, they needed plenty of sleep and the companionship of some hopelessly indiscriminate women. The flophouses and brothels on Bradley, Potter, Water, Prison, and Bank Streets supplied these needs. New London's tenderloin district held to these streets for more than a century. Another port city, Norwich, Connecticut—resting at the nexus of the Yantic and Shetucket Rivers—and at the headwaters of the Thames River—supported a red light district on Water, Commerce and Market streets, along with a few houses west of the harbor on "Hardscrabble Hill."[28] Bridgeport's prostitution crept all around the harbor—Bank, Clinton and Water Streets on the west side and around Pierpont Street in East Bridgeport. New Haven's prostitution also favored the harbor. To the south and east of Yale College, Chapel, Crown, Worcester, State, Union, Fair, and Prindle Streets were notorious for well-established houses of ill fame during the Gilded Age.

Almost a universal rule before 1850, prostitution remained in these depraved areas by the waterfront, but also in roadhouses beyond the incorporated limits of cities. Modern police forces were not organized in the cities and towns of the United States until after the mid-1850s. Municipalities depended on constables and night watches. A constable, Samuel Wakeman was hired in April 1636, only six months after the earliest colonists settled at Hartford. The constable system remained in effect until the summer of 1860 when an organized police force began operations. The watch system began as a voluntary service that able-bodied men were expected to perform without pay. Later, the watch morphed into a service whereby townsmen were paid $1 a night to walk the streets from ten p.m. until four a.m. The thinly spread constables were called police, but as stated above, cities and towns did not have actual police forces until after the era of the constable came to a close.[29]

For the young McQueeney girls, living so close to the Centre Schoolhouse proved a great blessing and they received good primary educations. Jennie McQueeney could read and write well, and always had books in the places where she lived through the years.

Market Street offered one serious drawback. The McQueeneys were only two blocks from the waterfront, where prostitutes lived in large numbers and their comings and goings could not be ignored. At 12 Market Street, the McQueeneys' rooms in a small, wooden tenement were only one door from State Street. Achingly poignant, Jennie McQueeney grew up watching prostitutes openly flaunting their expensive clothes and sparkling jewels on State Street, the busiest thoroughfare in Hartford and fast becoming the core of the city's tenderloin district. The madames in particular loved to display their diamonds as they sashayed along State Street. As one might expect, the young prostitutes dressed ostentatiously, an obvious but effective means of advertising. According to the Hartford native, Dr. William W. Sanger, who wrote the original groundbreaking study on prostitution while working on New York's Blackwell's Island in 1858, the length of time that his patients were prostitutes averaged only two years. In a similar 1913 study of prostitution in Hartford, the girls claimed to have been in prostitution on average for four years. Either way, when they were active, the madames and inmates could make it look attractive—especially the madames. Common wisdom says that we spend our whole lives living out our childhood dreams. For a young girl like Jennie McQueeney, the madames' lives undoubtedly seemed glamorous and, sadly, this childhood impression had a lasting effect.[30]

Along the same lines, the Lafayette House—built in 1851 and two doors north of the Centre Schoolhouse—did business at 22-28 Market Street. Its proprietor, Mark Wheeler, tried to run a respectable hotel, but fought a losing battle. Each year, the number of houses of ill repute around State and Market Street increased, as did the dissolute characters of the half-world, bound for ruination. By the beginning of the Civil War in 1861, eighteen-year-old Jennie McQueeney watched as the hotel lost the war. As if to punctuate the obvious, Woodruff Cadwell—arrested for keeping a bawdy house two years earlier on Upper Main Street—purchased the Lafayette House with his nephew, Dorrance Cadwell. A few months after Samuel Colt died in January of 1862 at Coltsville, his one-mile-square manufacturing village in the south meadows, the police arrested Dorrance for keeping a sporting house on the Albany road. Dorrance Cadwell was destined to become the new manager of the Lafayette House.[31]

If ever there was a shining example of prostitution starting in the remote areas on the outskirts of town and later migrating to the heart of the city, this was it. As the Civil War claimed an ever-increasing number of the healthy, vital young men, people grieved endlessly. Their sensibilities were so numbed by tragedy that they lost the ability to care about a little prostitution, gambling, or drinking. With all this suffering as a backdrop, people like the Cadwells, Connecticut men by birth but illiterate nonetheless, thought nothing of ruining young girls' lives for profit. Slowly, they crept into the heart of the city and established a solid foothold. The average citizen—if they gave the matter any thought at all— figured that bordellos, gambling halls, and illegal liquor sales wouldn't last. They were right, but it took more than a half-century for the pendulum to correct.

Lafayette House / Columbia House
22-28 Market Street - Hartford

A nasty example of the type of places the Cadwells and their ilk ran was the "Bull Run" on the Windsor Locks-Granby road in northern Connecticut. The Bull Run House was a typical roadhouse sitting at the four corners created by the intersection of the aforementioned Windsor Locks-Granby road and the Suffield-Poquonnock road. The Bull Run was another squalid roadhouse with the obligatory saloon, and a backroom operation for customers with an itch. The saloon sat two miles west of Windsor Locks—a village of only 2,332 residents—and four miles south of Suffield, another small hamlet. On the night of Sunday, January 2, 1881, two illiterate half-brothers from Feeding Hills, Massachusetts, David Scott and Mitchell Cherest, tried to rob the place. During their clumsy attempt to snatch some easy cash, they killed the owner, Timothy Billings, his wife Delia, and an inmate, Julia Harris. Eventually, Scott and Cherest were apprehended, convicted of second-degree murder, and sentenced to life in the Connecticut State Prison at Wethersfield. Scott hanged himself a year later, while Cherest served forty-four years and was paroled when he was sixty-two.[32]

Roadhouses were popular because they operated far enough outside of town to obviate police intervention, but they had their own problems. Sad to say for society in general, bringing vice into the cities brought down the most egregious violent crime, while prostitution, gambling, and drinking skyrocketed. The social evil could be thought of as society's Gilded Age balancing act.

In 1850, Jane McQueeney's brother, Alexander, emigrated from Ireland and settled in Hartford near the McQueeneys. Jane and Bernard McGuire birthed eight children, and even though Alexander was fourteen years younger than Jane, the two got on well. Young Jennie did not always get along with her mother, but she did manage to cement a strong bond with her uncle, Alexander McGuire. Like so many of the McGuires and McQueeneys, he was a hostler, working all day with horses in livery stables. Alexander didn't stay in Hartford long though. Instead, he joined other McGuire family members in Providence. Just like his brother, Frank McGuire, he never married, drank too much, and died in his late sixties.[33]

While Jennie and her sisters were in school, Timothy McQueeney continued his work as a coachman at the United States Hotel. At the beginning of March 1852, McQueeney got into a scrap with another hackman, Hooker Clapp. Timothy McQueeney could "get his Irish up" faster than most and Hooker Clapp was just the type of person to start something with a snide remark or a crude gesture.

Hooker Clapp had carved out a niche as one of Hartford's most outrageous characters. Clapp was a morbidly obese giant whose only exercise was the lifting of a food-laden fork. Hooker's weight usually hovering around 375 pounds. How he ever got up into the driver's seat of a coach presented as a great mystery to everyone. While passengers were counting out bills to pay their fare, Clapp had the obnoxious habit of snatching the bill he wanted. On one occasion, Samuel Tuttle, a bald-headed Hartford seed dealer with a flowing white beard, stood in front of the Allyn House on Asylum Street counting bills, when Hooker Clapp grabbed a $5 note for his tip. Tuttle wasn't amused and had Clapp arrested. In court, Clapp pleaded guilty to "extortionate charges while 'plying his vocation as a hack driver,' and agreed to pay back the money illegally obtained." He also received a fine of $3 plus court costs.[34]

Hooker Clapp claimed that he was the only Democrat in his family, so when New London Democratic attorney, Tom Waller, outpolled Lt. Gov. Billy Bulkeley—Judge Bulkeley's son—in the November 1882 gubernatorial race, Clapp headed a huge post-election parade, smoking a big fat cigar and hungrily gobbling up the kind of excitement designed for a much slimmer man. At the height of the festivities, Hooker Clapp suffered a massive coronary and died within the hour. Even if Clapp had not passed away in the early going, he would never have survived Billy Bulkeley's resurrection after the election, as 7,000 illegal Democratic "black ballots" were tossed out in New Haven. However, instead of accepting this incredibly lucky break, in January 1883, Billy Bulkeley did the unthinkable. He handed it all to the Democrat Tom Waller, by sending a letter to the Republican legislature, averring "he would not take the office on a technicality, when clearly the voters had chosen another."[35]

Timothy McQueeney wasn't one of Hooker Clapp's admirers, and after one of the obese man's little stunts, McQueeney "jumped onto Hooker's hack, and made an aggravated attack on him." The stolid constable, Charles Nott, arrested Timothy McQueeney for assault and battery on a complaint from the city attorney. The court, "to learn him [McQueeney] better fashions and make an example of such conduct, fined him the snug little amount of $35, which together with court costs . . . amounted to $42.74. He paid it over and was discharged from custody."[36] (In 2014 dollars, Timothy McQueeney's fine and court costs would be over $4,000.)

The way the McQueeneys ran their lives, saving a little money for a rainy day wasn't possible. Many of Hartford's immigrants never had a run-in with the police, but the McQueeneys drank too much and never sidestepped trouble; they were a fight looking for a place to happen.

That same year, Jane McQueeney had a fifth child, a girl named Catherine. Everyone called her Katie. By this time, Jane McQueeney's drinking was out of control. Since it could never be said with a straight face that Jane McQueeney did a good job raising her children, one would have to conclude that she didn't pay much attention to little Katie. It's also clear by future events that Jennie McQueeney did an extraordinary amount of work in rearing her kid sister. Jennie and Katie developed a powerful bond. That said, while in the care of her parents, Katie died in 1875 at the age of twenty-two. Jennie hired a Hartford artist to paint an oil portrait of Katie, which she kept hanging in her bedroom until her own death in 1900.

Jennie never forgave her parents for Katie's death, and her mother's name does not appear on any of Jennie McQueeney's documents after Katie passed away. Even after Jennie McQueeney outlived all the members of her family and died at the turn of the century, her friends knew enough not to include her mother's name on Jennie's death certificate. "Timothy" is written as her father's name, but there is no "Jane" on the document.[37]

The 1850s were a difficult time in America. In the great manufacturing centers like Hartford, the population more than doubled during the decade, but pre-war tensions constantly undermined financial stability. As the general public searched for someone to blame for the bad economy, blacks and immigrants quickly became objects of scorn. Slavery consumed more newsprint than could be imagined and Irish immigrants became scapegoats for the great downturn in the economy—particularly the Panic of 1857. Even the *Hartford Courant*— rudderless by the mid-1850s after the Whig Party went into an irreversible death spiral—became the organ for the Know-Nothing Party. The Know-Nothing Party represented institutionalized bigotry and prejudice of the worst sort. Later, the former Whigs slowly drifted into the Republican Party, but only after Gideon Welles, Joe Hawley, and seven fellow travelers organized the Connecticut chapter of the Republican Party in February 1856.[38] The movement toward Republicanism was a slow but steady shift, aided by the fact that the merchant-banker class had no alternative.

As the economy limped along, Timothy McQueeney lost his job as a coachman at the United States Hotel. In the years that followed, he had to settle for jobs as a day laborer, further jeopardizing the family's finances. The McQueeney girls did not attend Hartford Public High School after they finished their studies at the Centre Schoolhouse. The high school—in a two-story, wooden structure at the northwest corner of Ann and Asylum Streets—represented a merger between an English Course of Study, and the Classics Department of the private Hartford Grammar School. The city's leaders and educators dedicated the new high school in late 1847, planning to educate 250 students from the city's finest families. The McQueeney girls did not qualify.

Jennie McQueeney's lack of a high school education, considering the era, should not be seen as a significant factor in her entering the world of prostitution. In *Commercialized Prostitution in New York City,* a 1913 publication of the New York Bureau of Social Hygiene, author George J. Kneeland introduced some very important statistics. Of 1,106 street cases, approximately 12 percent were illiterate and only about 5 percent had a grammar school education. Kneeland also found that, generally, the first sex offense was between the ages of fourteen and twenty-two years, with the average at seventeen. This suggests, as have many other reports, that the most dangerous stage of a girl's life is in late adolescence. In almost 40 percent of these cases, the first sexual encounter was with a stranger.[39]

July 1858 played out as a particularly bad time for the McQueeney family. On Sunday July 4, about 10 o'clock in the evening, Jane McQueeney and a slovenly woman, Celia Webb, were arrested for fighting and "trying to tear each other's clothes off on the corner of Pearl and Trumbull Streets." Celia Webb lived on Charles Street in the "old red house" and ruled as matriarch of the notorious Webb family. These people were so completely out of control that the newspapers began calling Celia "one of a renowned web-footed-family." Strangely enough, though her family represented bedlam of epic proportions—and Celia's offspring didn't seem to stand a chance in life—none of her children ever went to prison. They likely did short stretches in the county jail, as did Celia, but were spared the state prison.[40]

Jane McQueeney and Celia Webb passed the night in the lockup and on Monday appeared before the court, showing a more dignified demeanor. They were each fined $1 and costs, plus a short stay in the county jail. The court suspended judgment, however, when it was learned that each of the women had half a dozen children to support.

Thieving ran through Celia Webb's bloodstream. The *Courant* once wrote, "if Celia Webb, the mother of the Webb family, hasn't got stealing on the brain, no person ever had. She was bound over to the superior court for theft and was just discharged last week. Last evening, Mr. Cornelius O'Neill, who lives on Front Street, detected her carrying a dress away from his premises. In her company was Mrs. Kathryn Shea. Mr. O'Neill notified the police and an officer soon had the females in custody. On their way to the station house, Mrs. Webb remarked to Mrs. Shea, 'Now you know if it hadn't'a been for you, I shouldn't be in this scrape.' 'That's a lie,' said Mrs. Shea. 'No it isn't a lie either,' responded Mrs. Webb. 'And what's more, you don't do anything else but steal. *I* know. Didn't you steal a tub from Humphrey & Seyms, and a pair of shoes from Chapin & King?. . . And a bag of buckwheat flour from Owen & Parker? . . . And five bars of soap from Charles Burton? *There!* Don't you talk to me about not getting me into this scrape.' And all this was interesting to Officer Wright, who, after securing his charges in the lockup, went in search of the different articles enumerated by Mrs. Webb, and found them at various places where Mrs. Shea had disposed of them."[41]

The following morning Celia Webb and Kathryn Shea, for theft, were fined $1 each and sent to jail for fifteen days. . . .[42]

Trouble followed Celia Webb everywhere. In March 1864, Deputy Provost Marshal Fenn "found a deserter from the 5th Regiment, John Rafferty, staying with the Webb family. Fenn proceeded to arrest Rafferty, but the deserter resisted with the aid of Celia Webb and her daughter Eliza. The two women were furious, and in their rage, assaulted the officer with all sorts of weapons within reach—knives, forks, kettles, and chairs; they even threw hot water at him. In desperation, Eliza seized a butcher knife. . . . Once Rafferty was in handcuffs, Celia Webb and her daughter were arrested and taken before U. S. Commissioner Erastus Smith, charged with harboring a deserter, to which they pleaded not guilty and were imprisoned to await trial. More degraded women . . . do not exist in this city and Eliza's conduct gave evidence of it . . . cursing vehemently. . . . If the military authorities succeed in putting these women where they can do no mischief, it will be a great relief to the civil officers, who have some of the family under lock and key most of the time."[43]

In this case, Celia Webb and her daughter were in serious trouble. They were brought before U. S. Commissioner Erastus Smith the following morning. . . and were bound over for trial . . . in May. . . . Failing to procure bonds, they were remanded to jail.[44]

Jane McQueeney's arrest for fighting with Celia Webb seems to brand her as a woman of easy virtue, but this isn't necessarily so. In the second half of the nineteenth century, when a woman turned to prostitution, almost without exception she adopted an alias. Almost universally, prostitutes chose names like Lillie, Jennie, Tillie, Lottie, Nellie, and Dottie; never Jane. Since Jane McQueeney did not alter her name, it seems most likely that she was not a prostitute. Instead, it seems that rum was her problem. A meatier matter is the effect that Jane and Timothy McQueeney's alcohol consumption had on their children. Not to argue that young Jennie

McQueeney was driven into prostitution solely because of a bad home life, but it amounted to a serious contributing cause.

The following Saturday, July 10, Constable Charles Nott arrested fifteen-year-old Jennie McQueeney for vagrancy on the grounds of Trinity College. "Squire" Gibbs, the black superintendent at the school, noticed that Jennie McQueeney "had been a frequent visitor of late upon the grounds and that 'she sometimes brought a female companion, but more often one of the masculine gender, with her, all of which did not come up to his ideas of respectability.' On Saturday, Gibbs 'saw the young lady conducting herself with great impropriety . . . and he made great haste to warn her off the grounds.' Jennie's young male friend, who had been hiding in the bushes, emerged and took to his heels. Meanwhile, Jennie McQueeney remained on the grounds for some time." Gibbs was angered by Jennie's brazen behavior and made a complaint to the police, who quickly arrested her. At length, the police discharged Jennie because of her age and the fact that the evidence against her was flimsy at best.[45]

This incident is fraught with questions. Obviously, Jennie McQueeney wandered onto the Trinity College campus to meet boys. Was this a legitimate attempt to find a boyfriend above her station in life, or was her behavior as questionable as "Squire" Robert Gibbs thought? Jennie McQueeney would turn sixteen in late September, and considering that she behaved with great impropriety, was this her first clumsy attempt to trade sex for money? Perhaps she was willing, but couldn't figure out the language or the maneuverings of the trade?

Furthermore, her refusal to leave the grounds when asked seems troublesome. Perhaps Jennie acted in the confrontational way that the McGuires and the McQueeneys always attacked life's little problems. Did she hold Mr. Gibbs in low regard because he was just a grounds keeper or a black man—or both? Lastly, to what end? Did Jennie McQueeney lose respect for law enforcement, or at the very least, learn to keep the constables at arm's length? The answers to these questions will unfold as we examine Jennie McQueeney's choices in the years ahead. Interestingly enough, many of the answers are hidden in this little incident.

Helping us with these probing questions is Dr. William Sanger's study of prostitution, a text that was published the same year that Officer Nott arrested Jennie McQueeney on the grounds of Trinity College. Dr. Sanger's 2,000 questionnaires became the *History of Prostitution*. In it, Sanger came to some surprising conclusions. If one can accept Sanger's results, 26 percent attributed their entry into prostitution to "Inclination," while another 26 percent adjudged that it was "Destitution." Only 13 percent blamed it on "Seduction or Abandonment," and a final 9 percent claimed that "Drink" was the problem. Given the chance to comment, Jennie McQueeney would probably have attributed equal amounts of "Inclination" and "Destitution."

When Howard Woolston asked the same question of 1,000 prostitutes in 1921, fully 25 percent of his sample blamed the "Influence of a Procurer." Another 21 percent pointed to "Bad Home Conditions," and 18 percent and 17 percent, respectively, laid it to "Bad Company" and "Love of Finery. . . . " Jennie McQueeney undoubtedly fell under the diabolical influence of Angeline Prentice, a prostitute and madame, who we will meet shortly. That said, in Jennie's case, "Bad Home Conditions" seemed a strong contributor and Jennie's deprived childhood made her a natural for the "Love of Finery" category.

One last curiosity is children. Virtually all prostitutes deal with pregnancy, abortion, and children in their lives. The Morals Efficiency Commission of Pittsburgh in 1913 reported, "Out of 558 prostitutes, 406 had never had any children. Of the 152 who had, there was but one living child." The report continued, "The sentimental delusion that many women entered upon prostitution after betrayal, in order to provide for their child, is almost utterly unfounded."[46]

On Friday night, July 30, Jennie McQueeney's mother, Jane, got drunk again and disturbed the whole neighborhood with her boisterous and obscene language. The watchmen picked her up about midnight and put her in the watch-house until morning. In police court, Judge George Gilman found Jane McQueeney guilty of breach of the peace and fined her $1 plus court costs. He also gave her fifteen days imprisonment at the workhouse. Aloud she snapped, "And what's to be done with the children, Judge? His honor shot back, "They will go along with you if they can't be taken care of without your help. You will learn to let rum alone after a while, I reckon." Jane McQueeney countered, "I'm drunk without tasting rum at all, Judge; I get drunk on water, so I do." The *Courant* reporter mused, "Mrs. McQueeney will have a chance to try the "rum," which will be furnished to her gratuitously for the next fifteen days."[47]

The bad economic times forced the McQueeneys to move to a cheaper rent in the old Lafayette Hotel at 22 Market Street on the north side of the Centre Schoolhouse. At the time, city officials were purchasing buildings on the opposite side of Market Street so the tenements could be razed and Market Street widened. This street continued as a bizarre collection of tenements and businesses—everything from cheap hotels, livery stables, blacksmith shops, fish dealers, and billiard halls.

At a meeting of the common council in December 1856, the men of the night watch demanded a raise. They were up to $1.25 a night, but in Waterbury the going rate was $1.50, and in New Haven, $1.75. With rents and fuel costs rising, the men of the night watch couldn't wait any longer.[48]

In other business, the city fathers gave permission for a businessman to open a billiards parlor north of the Centre Schoolhouse, allowing the children to gaze out the window and watch billiards all day instead of learning their lessons. Meanwhile, in early 1858, three black men—John Bowen, George Brown, and Sampson Eaton—broke into the Market Street smokehouse of Joseph Woodruff and stole thirty to forty wood-smoked hams. Woodruff testified, "a little later, on January 28, someone entered the smoke house using a false key and stole eighty hams; moreover, on February 8, the door was broken open and another six to eight fancy hams disappeared." All of these men lived in the disgusting tenements on Ferry Street near the Connecticut River.[49]

The Panic of 1857 hit Hartford particularly hard and Timothy McQueeney—on the bottom rung of the socio-economic ladder with loads of other laborers, porters, hostlers and hackmen—was affected badly. The *Courant* took stock in 1860, "The scarcity of money, as well as credit, still hangs heavily over this fair country. A merchant in this city, who for forty-two years has been a purchaser of goods from the southern market . . . tells us that never before in spring or fall has he found it so difficult to promptly forward his goods. . . . Moneyed men, with large available means, and who have in days past been able to lend their money at 12 to 15 percent per annum, find it difficult to know what to do with it; and in the matter of other investments, it is still more difficult to suit this class."[50]

The McQueeneys were out of options. They decided to join their relatives in Providence where jobs might be more plentiful. By June 1860, the McQueeneys were en route to Rhode Island. Jane McQueeney and four of the five girls left first. Three of the girls found lodging with Timothy McQueeney's brother, James, a forty-five year old bachelor, while Jane and another daughter found a small place nearby. Timothy McQueeney remained behind, living with his widowed sister, Bridget McQueeney Mahon, and her children—a few doors north on Market Street.

Not surprisingly, Jennie McQueeney broke with her family and started a life of her own in Hartford.

Chapter 2

Entering the Oldest Profession

Eighteen-year-old Jennie McQueeney did not go to Providence. She remained in Hartford determined to chart her own course. Jennie's trouble with her parents has already been mentioned and this abrupt break with her family—including eight-year-old Katie—showed an iron will, but how would such a young girl survive?

While Jennie McQueeney's parents and siblings began anew in Rhode Island, this stubborn teenager met another Irish immigrant five years her senior, Angeline Prentice (nee Bridget Creed), who became a lifelong friend, in spite of the fact that she was a terrible influence—no matter how her life was scored. Many decades later, in an effort to break Jennie's will, Angeline claimed that she and her husband at the time, Billy Prentice, met Jennie in 1861 and started her in the prostitution business. Jennie lived with the Prentices in a roadhouse on the New Britain road just outside Hartford. Angeline also claimed that she met Jennie's future husband, Tom Hollister, in 1863 and gave him his start too![51]

Angeline's generosity knew no bounds when she was telling the story. As we shall see though, Angie was a prostitute, a madame, a thief, a liar, a home-wrecker, and had every ugly trait a person could possess. Strangely enough, Jennie called her a friend right up to the end—though she seems to have purposely left Angeline out of her 1893 will. Most probably, Angeline's scheming ways proved too much for Jennie as the younger woman ran her 76 Wells Street parlor house alone and endured serious illness in the last six years of her life. Taking care of her husband, Tom, in the years before he passed in 1894, simply added to her burden.

Jennie worked for Angeline for a few years, until she could open a bawdy house in her own name. While she made plans, she got to know Tom Hollister quite well and he helped her get away from Angeline.

Tom Hollister came from a big family, in part, because his father, Joseph Hollister, had two wives. Joseph Hollister had been a New York City policeman, but eventually turned to farming in Amenia, New York, just across the line from Kent, Connecticut. In New York, three children were born before his first wife died. Later, Joseph Hollister found a young widow, Louisa (Phinney) Waters, living in Farmington, Connecticut. He quickly arranged the proper introductions and the couple began a new life in Farmington.

Louisa was originally from Hartford. In 1825, the couple resettled on Washington Street in the Charter Oak City. Joseph Hollister first worked in Hartford as a laborer. He eventually bought a small farm on Hudson Street where he raised vegetables and three- and four-year-old prize-winning milch cows. Since Joseph Hollister's new father-in-law, Ebenezer Phinney, worked as a wholesale produce dealer, the younger man never had any trouble unloading his crops at good prices. Despite the farm, Joseph Hollister always considered himself a policeman. (Joseph Hollister may have worked the city's night watch or some other supernumerary function, but there are no records to back this up.) In the mid-1850's, he became a messenger of the city court, a job that lasted until his death in 1857. Joseph and Louisa Hollister, at length, had eight children. Thomas Adams Hollister, born on December 17, 1830, came into the world sixth in line. Counting his three half-siblings, Tom Hollister was ninth in a string of eleven children.[52]

After Joseph and Louisa Hollister were settled in Hartford, Trinity College—called Washington College until 1845—had just completed Jarvis and Seabury Halls, but still didn't have enough dormitory space. Louisa Hollister organized a student boardinghouse on Lafayette Street in 1836 and continued in the business for the next seventeen years. During Louisa Hollister's last five years in business, her establishment housed only faculty members. From 1848 to 1853, Trinity's Rev. President John Williams made his home at Mrs. Hollister's boardinghouse.

Tom Hollister always had an agreeable personality and possessed an exceptional baritone voice. When young, he sang in concerts. After completing a rudimentary education, he drifted into laboring jobs until he saw Drake, Brown & Company's advertisement in the *Courant* for an apprentice bookbinder. Though he wasn't the "16 year old . . . country boy" that Sidney Drake had in mind, Tom Hollister applied for the job at Drake, Brown's High Street offices and quickly became Hartford's newest apprentice in the book binding business. Four years later, Sidney Drake and John Parsons formed a partnership based on the stock and customers of the hard-working, wiry bookbinder, Silas Andrus, on Asylum Street near Union Station. In the early months of 1858, Drake & Parsons took wing in Silas Andrus's new building at 254 Asylum Street (Andrus block).[53]

After Tom Hollister finished his apprenticeship, he relocated to New York in an effort to parlay his newfound training into something of real value. But New York proved a tough place to rise in the business and Tom Hollister only stayed a year. When he returned to Hartford, around the time of his thirtieth birthday, he resumed his career binding books. Tom Hollister always referred to himself as a bookbinder, but when he returned home just before the shelling of Fort Sumter, he began a slow drift into the prostitution business. As stated, Angeline Prentice took credit for getting Tom Hollister started in the business of running brothels in 1863. Since Billy and Angeline Prentice were running a roadhouse beyond the incorporated limits of Hartford and Tom Hollister's first house of ill fame was on State Street, Angie's boast seems improbable. However, in the absence of hard evidence, perhaps it could be allowed that Angie did offer some help.[54]

When the police arrested Jennie McQueeney on the Trinity College campus, the public and the constables saw prostitution as a necessary evil; they also thought that keeping it behind closed doors was the best course. Armed with this general consensus, the elected officials at the highest levels of government were loath to close down houses of ill fame in one mighty raid, only to expose the citizenry to the curse of streetwalkers. Men would be propositioned many times each day, and their wives and daughters would not be able to leave home for fear they would be taken for streetwalkers as well.

As a bizarre example of a city hobbled by streetwalkers, consider the case of Jennie Crane of Hartford's lower East Side. Jennie was quite a curiosity in her way. She stood before the police court on Friday, February 14, 1900, for the fiftieth (50th) time! Her face had become as familiar as family.

Jennie had been arrested for nightwalking. She got hilariously, gloriously drunk and then walked the streets in search of a man to share her joy. The police and the court officials had gotten so used to seeing Jennie hauled into court that they missed her if she failed to return after completing her thirty days in jail.[55]

Between the streetwalkers and the shorthanded and ill-trained police force, the decision to leave bawdy houses alone didn't require much thought. Obviously, the proprietors of these houses had to maintain a certain level of decorum, but the scofflaws had no trouble working within such simple strictures.

In larger cities of the Northeast, like Boston and New York, police courts had been in place since the early 1800s. Smaller towns still relied on justices of the peace to deal with minor infractions of the law. All civil cases, for example, were tried before a justice of the peace. Criminal cases went directly to superior court. This produced a system where miscreants were brought before justices of the peace instead of bona fide judges. The system cried out for improvement.

So said, a number of different proposals were discussed at common council meetings in the 1840s, dealing with all aspects of crime and punishment. In December 1845, the council passed a resolution appointing a committee to examine the duties of watchmen, with an eye toward abolishing the system altogether. Another proposal suggested the abolishment of the watch warden, spreading his duties among the other watchmen. After much consideration, the council had misgivings and tabled the motion.[56]

After a decade of *veronicas* and *half veronicas* by the common council, the dry goods merchant, Albert Day, and a number of other men, asked the common council to petition the legislature for the right to organize a police court. In July 1851, the General Assembly granted the motion and as one councilman noted, "The legislature yesterday, passed an act authorizing this city to have a police court. . . . We now [have[the anomaly of arresting offenders by city constables, trying them before state officers, and committing them to town or county prisons."[57]

Buried in the legislature's act were some specifics: The clerk of the police court must post a $2,000 bond; judges were to serve one year; and the court had jurisdiction over all crimes and misdemeanors punishable by a maximum fine of $200 or six months imprisonment in the common jail, watch house, or city penitentiary. Meanwhile, the common council agreed that judges should be paid $400 per annum and court clerks would receive $300. The police court would transact business six days a week at City Hall—on Market Street between Kingsley and Temple Streets—and justices of the peace would surrender their powers to the new city police court judges.[58]

Eliphalet Bulkeley accepted the first appointment to the police court. Judge Bulkeley eventually founded Aetna Life Insurance Company and fathered four children, including Morgan Bulkeley, a man who later served as mayor of the city for eight years, acted as governor of the state for four and, lastly, served as one of Connecticut's U.S. senators for six—from 1905 to 1911. Morgan Bulkeley became the most powerful Republican politician in the state, and after he had served as governor, he was instrumental in building the new Hartford Bridge and ridding the city of all types of vice in the first decade of the twentieth century.

Now that Hartford's police court was up and running, one lawman summed up the prostitution dilemma succinctly, "The inmates of a house of ill fame are arrested, tried, and sentenced to the workhouse for thirty days . . . and, yet, in less than a week's time, the same individuals are again in the city, pursuing their old avocations . . . and the police have been foiled in their attempts to make our city more respectable and peaceful. . . .The police don't want to be party to such child's play. . . .When gambling saloons, with their attendant evils, are permitted to be kept on every corner . . . and when houses of prostitution are allowed to be opened in the very heart of the city . . . within the toss of a biscuit of the residences of our most respected and influential citizens, it is time that we should awake from the lethargy. . . . With an increase of population as rapid as that which we have experienced for the past few years, there will necessarily come an increase in vice and our citizens will be wise if they make provisions at the outset to keep it in check."[59]

Immediately after Hartford established a city police court in 1851, Judge Bulkeley prosecuted Julia Ann Harlow "for keeping a house of ill fame on Ferry Street."[60] This particular street, along with Kilbourn, State and Commerce—the streets closest to the Connecticut River—supported flop houses and flag taverns for decades before prostitution really blossomed in Hartford after 1850. However, Judge Eliphalet Bulkeley was not known for the hardness of his heart and simply discharged Julia Ann Harlow—ostensively because she did not have an established reputation as a madame. Though not always the case, sometimes a single close brush with jail saved a young woman from a life of vice and degradation.

The Julia Ann Harlow case, contrasted with similar cases of the time, highlights an enormous change that took shape in the last part of the Gilded Age. In the early 1850s, these cases were rare and disposed of quickly without even a Jonathan Edwards-style tongue-lashing. Prostitution had been around forever and its effect on society or the development of the city did not present a case of vile and intolerable criminality. A dozen years later—after Judge Bulkeley's oldest boy, Capt.

Charles Bulkeley, died in the Civil War—undoubtedly the judge would have cared even less about prostitution or petty vice. Charles's passing left the judge a broken man and hastened his departure from this world in 1872. As with Judge Bulkeley, the nation cared little about vice in the aftermath of the War of the Rebellion. It would be the judge's second son, Morgan—coupled with an entirely different city and social milieu—who brought an end to the city's prostitution. However, even as Morgan marched around Suffolk, Virginia, with a Springfield musket on his shoulder in 1862, he hadn't a clue that the city's battle with vice would ultimately wind up in his lap.

Gov. Morgan G. Bulkeley

It wasn't just in Connecticut that vice became an implacable force embedded deep in the social fabric of the land. During the Gilded Age, every city and town in America employed some type of armed truce with the social evil. As the nation grieved its Civil War losses, vice continued to blossom. At long last, in the first decade, or so, of the new century, "legalized" prostitution—thanks mostly to civic pride and the twin horrors of white slavery and social disease—disappeared from the American landscape forever.

Following the new police court system, the time quickly arrived for Hartford to establish a real police force. Most towns around the country had some combination of constables, sheriffs, marshals and night watchmen. Hartford's network of constables grew out of its first officer in 1636 and its night watch system took wing in 1815. The huge move forward—where a legitimate police force actually had uniforms, badges (and, surreptitiously, guns)—came in July 1860.[61]

The new city police force rented space on the second floor of the Union Hall building in Statehouse Square, a location that lawmen enjoyed because of its centralized location. By 1865, they were forced to move to the first floor of a building on Pearl Street, near Main. Unfortunately, a few years later, Connecticut Mutual bought the whole neighborhood for its new headquarters, so the police moved again to the corner of Main and Kingsley Streets—above Talcott Brothers market. At last, in 1898, the city built a new police station on Market Street and the police enjoyed a permanent headquarters for the next few decades.[62]

The men who brought Jennie McQueeney to the police rooms at City Hall in 1858 were not members of an organized police force. They were merely constables—men hired to keep the peace. The constables took the day shift, and while citizens slept, a night watch patrolled the streets on the lookout for criminal activity. Someone arrested during the night wound up in the watch-house until morning when the courts could dispose of the matter.[63]

The decade from the mid-1850s to the mid-1860s set public opinion, state statutes, police responses and the general intrigues of the prostitution business until about 1910. The methods and practices of the sex industry varied in the United States, but were influenced profoundly by the advent of organized police forces and the inability of these new departments to gain a solid footing at the outset.

As one would expect, the largest cities in America were the first to organize police forces. In New York, a municipal police department—closely allied with the Democratic Party and the Tammany Hall political machine of William Magear "Boss" Tweed—came together in 1845. However, the state legislature at Albany was Republican and itched to gain power over Boss Tweed and his political puppets. To crush New York City's Democratic government, the General Assembly forced a Metropolitan Police Department on the city in 1857. Thanks to New York's 7th Regiment, the denizens of New York learned to love the Metropolitan Police apace.

Chicago's first police department came together in 1855 under Captain Cyrus P. Bradley. After a nasty political fight, Mayor John Wentworth fired the entire force. When cooler heads finally prevailed, the officers were rehired and the police department began to function well. By 1861, a detective division was added and Cyrus Bradley was returned as superintendent of the whole department.

San Francisco and Los Angeles had similar stories of organization, missteps, and finally, a uniformed police force in 1856 and 1869, respectively. San Francisco got the jump on Los Angeles due to the madness created by the 1849 gold rush.

These early police forces had a number of things in common: manpower shortages, lack of training, poor understanding of the law, a certain amount of public distrust—and, in some cases, poor leadership and corruption.

After Hartford's new police court had been in operation for almost a decade—and considered a well-oiled machine—the time came to eliminate the constables and watchmen. The new Hartford Police Department was composed of Chief Walter Chamberlin, Captain Charles Nott, Lieutenant Charles Brewster, and five patrolmen—Clinton, Peck, Butler, Keegan, and Brown. The real standout, Officer John Butler, was a huge, powerful man—and completely without fear.

Chamberlin and Nott were both Vermonters, who as $10-a-month raftsmen, found their way down the Connecticut River in 1831 and 1843, respectively. Both men planned to build new lives in Hartford, but their plans were vague. For a first job, Walter Chamberlin ran the engine at Burgess's Sawmill in the Dutch Point shipbuilding area. To make extra money, Chamberlin joined the night watch. In those days, the watch warden, Normand Granger, supervised only four watchmen—Walter Chamberlin; Henry Moore; and two brothers, Westell and William Russell. For $1, the night watchmen went on duty at ten p.m. and finished up at four a.m. the following morning.[64]

CHIEF WALTER CHAMBERLIN

At the time, most of the town's mercantile trade transpired in the river district. At night, the raftsmen and sailors gathered in the streets in large numbers. Because stagecoaches handled so much of the town's business, on Saturday nights at least fifty stage drivers roamed about town, making noise and spoiling for trouble. The raftsmen and stage drivers rarely agreed on anything and fights were the usual outcome. In sum, the night watch had its hands full just preserving order.[65]

Walter Chamberlin, a wonderfully imaginative character, accepted an increasing amount of work as a constable over time. He left town regularly to work up cases and transfer prisoners. Chamberlin loved disguises and used them extensively to amuse himself. In 1859, Chamberlin went to New York to collect Samuel Jones, the Colchester bank defaulter, and deliver him to Norwich. Chamberlin and Jones changed trains several times and Sam Jones continually introduced Walter Chamberlin as his prisoner! Of course, Chamberlin loved it, and with his head bowed in mock shame, played it to the full.[66]

After Charles Nott found his way to Hartford, he worked on farms for a couple of years. Then, during the period of legendary fires, Nott got a job on the night watch. During Charles Nott's time as a watchman, there were major conflagrations at Pittsburgh, Milwaukee, New York, Toronto and Quebec. Half of London, England, burned to the ground. In July 1845, a conflagration consumed 300 buildings in Rochester. A fire in Brooklyn destroyed more than 300 houses and 3 churches. Fire wiped out half of Saint Louis. San Franciscans witnessed a fire that destroyed 1,500 buildings—three-fourths of the city![67]

In New England, there were large conflagrations at Bridgeport, Providence, Boston, and New Haven. Aside from a few small warehouse fires and a vandal who tried to burn down the ancient Charter Oak tree in the late 1840s, Hartford survived. Thanks to inspired planning by the state legislature and the vigilance of the night watch, the Charter Oak City—

albeit deeply irritated by the assault on its historic symbol—still managed to get by virtually unscathed.

During this distinctively bad time—when municipalities grew out of control and water systems were still futuristic fantasies—a city's only real hope lay with its night watch. It was a race against time. Could a few poorly paid watchmen sound the alarm soon enough to save a city? Hartford had one huge advantage. In 1800, the legislature passed a bill outlawing the construction of wooden buildings in the city; everything had to be built of stone or brick. Add slate roofs to the preferred building materials list and the chances of an all-consuming conflagration were vastly diminished.[68]

CAPT. CHARLES NOTT

Meanwhile, prostitution and the nascent Hartford police were almost complete strangers. In October 1860, Walter Chamberlin's first quarterly report read as a monotonous collection of arrests: drunkenness, 343; breach of the peace, 80; assault, 55; stolen property (including horses), 21; and keepers of houses of ill fame, 1. The report includes one statistic germane to our discussion of prostitution. In the final paragraph, the account states flatly that, at the time, Hartford had ten houses of ill repute.[69]

At the very same time, religious and civic-minded citizens across America were taking the law into their own hands. In Cleveland, men called "regulators" visited houses of ill fame, breaking all the furniture and daubing it with coal tar. At a riot in St. Louis, "between 20 and 30 houses of ill fame were entirely cleared out, and the furniture was burned in the streets." A year later in Terre Haute, Indiana, a mob destroyed eight houses of ill repute. This is only a tiny sample of the great divide in opinions on prostitution during the Gilded Age.[70]

Despite the weightiness of the subject, funny things did happen. In early 1862, seven police officers descended on a house of ill fame on Mercer Street in New York and arrested the madame and five of her girls (the prostitutes were all under sixteen). The old man playing the piano threw himself on his knees and wailed, "Officer, for God's sake, spare me the disgrace of arrest. I am a member of an uptown church, and get a salary as an organist." The police were so amused by the decrepit pianist that they left the old guy alone.[71]

In a Connecticut case, "Nelly Adams (an assumed name) was arrested in Hartford for being a common prostitute. On her promise to go to her home in North Adams, Massachusetts, she was let off. Nelly was a rather good-looking girl and was infatuated with the son of a well-known citizen. Upon her arrest she sent for the son, but the messenger mistakenly arrived with the father. The ugly scene that ensued must be left to the reader's imagination."[72]

Lastly, from Washington, "A drunken man was taken from a house of ill repute to a lock-up, and upon him was found a bankroll of $3,000 and a paper showing that he was a judge of the U.S. court in a western state. The awed policemen took him home."[73]

When Jennie McQueeney's family relocated to Providence, this stubborn, eighteen-year-old beauty fell under the influence of Bridget Creed, another Irish immigrant from Providence who lived in Hartford at the time. In 1861, this connection between Providence and Hartford wasn't considered extraordinary or even peculiar. After two New England railroads merged to form the Hartford, Providence, and Fishkill Railroad—with the connection to Providence completed in 1854—an enormous amount of passenger and freight business jostled between these two small cities.[74] While central Connecticut became famous for rifles, revolvers, leather industrial belting, silk manufacture, thread production, hardware and precision tools, the environs of Providence had a rich manufacturing history too. Providence's cotton and woolen textile production became the largest in the nation. Brown and Sharpe became the country's largest producer of machine tools and the Corliss Steam Engine Company towered as the granddaddy of all engine manufacturers.

Bridget Creed had adopted the name Angelina—which later morphed into Angeline—making it fairly obvious that she began her working life as a prostitute. She worked in a roadhouse in Providence owned by an entrepreneur, William L. "Billy" Prentice. Billy's wife, Delila, had been married before and had a five-year-old girl, Ann. Billy Prentice operated like most men in the prostitution business; driven by money, often they got derailed by beautiful and treacherous women. For these men, temptation was their handmaiden, and drama and chaos followed them everywhere.[75]

By 1861, Billy and Delila were divorced, and Angeline and Billy were married. Born in Connecticut, Prentice probably thought Angeline was a Rhode Island native since she claimed that all her life. Angeline's father, Peter Creed, and her mother, Bridget Creed, were hardworking, illiterate Irish immigrants, but lived quietly and within the law. Angeline was the outlier. Though not much of a fib during the Gilded Age, Angeline lied about her roots and birth date as circumstances dictated. When Angeline married thirty-eight-year-old Billy Prentice, she was twenty-four despite her claims to twenty-one. Her last husband, the National League baseball player Joe Start, thought Angeline was only six years older than him, while eight years represented the truth![76]

Billy Prentice may have been in a dirty racket, but he took the business seriously. As such, he scouted constantly for the opportunity to open another bawdy house. He wanted a place for Angeline to run while he tended the roadhouse in Providence. The house he chose sat on a lonely stretch of the New Britain road just outside of Hartford. The location seemed perfect—far enough from Hartford's incorporated limits for the police to dismiss it and yet easily accessible to patrons. By keeping low profiles and arranging their affairs just so, neither Billy nor Angeline Prentice ever suffered a prostitution arrest. In business matters, they were extremely careful.

By Angeline's own testimony (four decades later), during the time she ran this roadhouse on the New Britain road, Jennie McQueeney—now using the name Jennie Taylor—worked as a prostitute and learned the trade. By Angeline's account, Jennie took well to the business and became on the whole very astute at the management side of the brothel business.[77]

Angeline and Jennie both started out as prostitutes, and curiously, in an age of large families and no birth control, neither of the two women ever birthed a single child. This could be the result of congenital defects, but it is far more likely that poorly performed abortions, or disease, damaged their reproductive systems. (One simple fact: each successive bout of Pelvic Inflammatory Disease—often brought on by gonorrhea—increased the chances of infertility.) With promiscuous young women, pregnancy was a foregone conclusion in the 1800s and abortions of all types were common. There were doctors who performed abortions in their offices (after hours). Or, if a woman had enough money, she could get an abortion in a hospital under a medical *nom mal approprié*. Moreover, some women chose self-abortion, though every bit as dangerous as it sounds. In July 1881, a St. Louis resident, Mrs. Kate McClure—a woman who had performed five self-abortions—bled to death. On the autopsy report, the medical examiner noted that "splinters" were found." (Most women preferred crochet hooks, but in a pinch they weren't fussy.)[78]

Despite a dubious history, Jennie McQueeney always showed gratitude to Angeline Prentice for giving her a start in the business. Later in life, when the two women traveled together, Jennie McQueeney (Hollister) always paid Angeline's way. Jennie also gave Angeline clothes. (They were the same petite size.) This closeness between a madame and one of her former prostitutes, beggars belief. Then again, one must consider that the demimonde overflowed with lepers. Perhaps one simple friendship, no matter what the circumstances, offered a small comfort that the average person could never understand.[79]

When it comes to recording the lives of the half-world, the word *demimonde* has been with us since the close of the eighteenth century. In New York's salacious Shaw-Carstang case, it developed ever so slowly that the St. Louis spinster, Miss Effie Carstang, wasn't a respectable member of society, but a soiled dove of the demimonde. At the last moment, Henry Shaw—Miss Carstang's wealthy, octogenarian lover—called off the wedding and the couple endured a lengthy legal battle instead of a week of unabashed carnal frenzy. In the first trial, the jury sided with the jilted maiden and awarded her $100,000. But in the second go-round, a different jury found for the skinflint bachelor, Henry Shaw. During the reprise, the world enjoyed a kiss-by-hug chronicle of Miss Carstang's lusty past. Sadly, the jury had to decide whether or not Miss Effie Carstang belonged among the respectable people or down in the demimonde.

Ah, there's that lovely French word again. *The Herald,* one of New York's sleaziest penny dailies, was kind enough to elaborate. "Demimonde is a French term for a class of women very well known abroad and not altogether unknown in certain circles in the United States. The best definition of the demimonde woman extant is given in *Le Demi-Monde,* the play of M. Dumas *fils,* by the famous comparison of the peaches: the fruit as it is exposed to view in the basket looks all alike, but here and there you find a specimen with a spurious spot under the skin—not a large spot, but still a spot. The unsound peaches represent the demimonde women, who are clever, handsome, well-bred, cultivated, agreeable, and so on—but they have the taint."[80]

"The demimonde woman has no affections—she has only appetites; she has no heart—only a sort of air pump; her rule of life is founded upon interest tables. The question of money is the only vital matter with her. She is a gambler, and her game varies according to the circumstances and the surroundings of her victim. . . .We must do the common street woman the justice to say that she is not acknowledged by the demimonde. That interesting class regards the *lorette* with a degree of holy terror, compared to which the virtuous indignation of ancient maidens and venerable dowagers is extremely mild. No, the demimonde woman may be found oftentimes at the tables or in the *salons* of very nice people; not infrequently, she has a pew in a fashionable church and attends to her religious duties with rigid regularity. . . ."[81]

In the milieu of Gilded Age prostitution, the young girls, their boyfriends, and countless hangers-on made up the half-world. Sometimes a woman of the demimonde was said to be a *demimondaine*. Enjoying the fast life gave these young voluptuaries all the reason for living that their twisted souls needed. One day, they were working as clerks in a state or government office building, and the next, they were part of the demimonde. *Laissez le bon temps roullez!*

Even in the demimonde, there existed an established order. A Hartford man visiting New York in the mid-1880s saw a lovely young woman, walking with her maid. The woman wore a muted cotton suit with lovely gloves and boots. She wore her hair in a severely pulled back style, leading the man to think of her as prudish. When he mentioned the young woman to friend, he was stunned to find out that she was a queen of the demimonde. Apparently "it was the new order of things in the half-world, that the flaunting, loud style was left to those of the lower degree . . . the correct thing was to 'assume a virtue if you have it not' as the style most attractive."[82]

In the years just following the Civil War, Jennie McQueeney had done her time as a prostitute and itched to open her own house. She had become friendly with one of Hartford's native sons, Tom Hollister, who rented 165 State Street—the "old Bange mansion"—built in the early 1820s. While the building was no longer a virgin, it still maintained a proud façade, embellished with seven distinctive white pilasters. Beginning with Tom Hollister, a number of different proprietors ran bagnios on the upper floors. (Landlords often rented the first floor to shopkeepers or storeowners, while they let the upper floors to madames and proprietors of bordellos.)

Originally from Amsterdam, Frederick Bange was one of Hartford's most successful West Indies traders in the first few decades of the nineteenth century. Like every other man in the West Indies trade, Bange shipped lumber, produce, and livestock to the islands and brought back sugar, molasses, rum, salt and other tropical cargoes. Bange became a partner in the firm of Wolcott, Kilbourn & Bange of 22 Ferry Street, but left Hartford around 1827 and died in New York four years later.

Tom Hollister ran a quiet, but very profitable house. On the south side of State Street, from the Old State House to the Connecticut River, practically every other building did business as a house of ill fame. State Street—and all the streets leading off of it—comprised Hartford's tenderloin. In and among these pleasure palaces, there were some places the police never raided—or so it seemed. Tom Hollister's house figured high on that list. The Hartford police's "hands off" policy was partly enlightened self-interest inasmuch as the city didn't want streetwalkers— and the police didn't want to deal with them. Keeping prostitution indoors and out of sight pleased the city fathers enormously.

165 State Street, Hartford

In truth, Tom Hollister's special treatment derived from another source. Hollister had astonishing pull because his father had been a New York City policeman. So said, Hollister received the treatment reserved for a member of the family, as opposed to that of men like Joe Weeks, Woodruff Cadwell, or Dorrance Cadwell—all notorious proprietors of houses of ill repute. Tom Hollister made the proper payments and gave generous gifts to all the officers at Christmastime. In short, he acted like a gentleman and was treated like one.

Another iniquity loomed. While saloon owners had to pay $450 for their annual license, proprietors of bawdy houses didn't pay a thing. The city couldn't charge the proprietors of brothels a licensing fee because their businesses were illegal. Naturally, this inflamed the saloonkeepers—and may have accounted for a few backroom operations that otherwise might never have come into existence. In a couple of American cities, the common councils tried to skirt this dilemma by registering the prostitutes (and collecting fees). However, this created a messy system where the prostitutes developed a sense of entitlement and the initiatives eventually collapsed. Hartford, like the overwhelming majority of cities in the country, didn't even attempt to register prostitutes, but used raids to gather "taxes" or "licensing fees." Tom Hollister had good business sense and understood the nuances of the system completely. By paying for the privilege ahead of time, he managed to avoid any arrests for prostitution or keeping a house of ill repute during more than thirty years in the business.[83]

Meanwhile, Billy Prentice, died suddenly in 1873. Not given to excess sentimentality, Angeline quickly set her sights on the professional baseball player, Joe Start. In the early going, Angie exhausted her huge collection of wiles, but still couldn't get Joe Start to the altar. He simply didn't want to get married. As one of the biggest stars of baseball's early years, Joe Start has always been considered the premier first baseman of the nineteenth century. This allowed him to bounce from team to team, postponing his retirement seemingly forever. Joe Start began his baseball career in 1871 with the New York Mutuals. When the National League was formed in 1876, Joe Start played only one year for the "New York Mutuals of the National League." He played with the Hartford Dark Blues for the 1877 season and then joined the Chicago White Stockings in 1878. After a single year in Chicago, he played seven seasons for the Providence Grays and managed one final year with the Washington Senators in 1886. At the close of his career, he was a forty-three-year-old man who had been playing a little boy's game since his days in short pants.[84]

Joe Start probably had some misgivings about Angeline's past, but Angie came across as an "effervescent little woman."[85] Angie could scheme with the best of them, but everyone always loved her in the end. Though contemporary accounts say that they married in 1885—Joe Start's last season with the Providence Greys—the evidence is murky. In the 1900 census records, the Starts said they had been married for fifteen years, leading people to believe they tied the knot in 1885. That said, there is no 1885 marriage certificate for them anywhere. Deepening the mystery, there is an April 25, 1893 marriage license on file in Jersey City, New Jersey, recording the coupling of Joseph Start, born in 1845, and Angeline Creed, born in 1839. It is worthy of note that these are not common names and the birth dates on the New Jersey document are the ones the couple always used. Moreover, the birth dates maintain the six years age difference that Angeline preferred over the truth.

One suspects that the mysterious 1885 marriage never took place and Angeline finally won over her man in 1893—as they say, in one of Joe's weaker moments. Despite all the drama, the marriage proved a good one. The Starts ran the Hilltop Hotel until the early 1920s and were together for fifty-eight years.[86] When they sold the Hilltop Hotel, the new owners quickly changed the sign to Lakewood Inn. The Starts moved into Providence, first renting an apartment on Tucker Avenue, then another one on Haskins Street. Bridget "Angeline" Creed Prentice Start died on February 27, 1927. Her death certificate says eighty-eight, but she had already hit ninety. Joe Start died a month later, on March 27, 1927. He was eighty-two.

It would be unfair not to recognize that Bridget Creed chose one of the toughest businesses on earth, but still managed to survive. History is replete with the stories of beautiful young girls who chose life in the demimonde because it offered them excitement and more money than they could make in any other industry. For a woman to work in the prostitution business, and make it to the age of ninety, must be deemed something of a miracle.

In early 1867, Tom Hollister began to invest his ill-gotten gains in real estate. His first piece of property rested at the foot of Kilbourn Street near the river. In several different purchases, he picked up 41 and 43 Kilbourn Street plus some adjoining property. The only places closer to the Connecticut River were shacks rented to the black families of town. Since the spring freshet usually flooded everything up to Front Street, real estate on Kilbourn Street attracted few takers. During the good months, the properties on Kilbourn Street were rented to marginal citizens who could barely hold a job. But Tom Hollister may have had some inside information. He may have heard about the new Fenwick Hall beach community at Old Saybrook and the Connecticut Valley Railroad, whose tracks would run along the river beginning in 1871. The two projects would complement one another and the Valley road would need the land at the foot of Kilbourn Street. That said, with Tom Hollister's contacts in the police department, a tip seems likely.[87]

In 1867, Jennie McQueeney began renting a house from Tom Hollister at 43 Kilbourn Street. Once upon a time, Kilbourn Street sat in the thriving business center of the city. In and among the ship's chandleries and other maritime businesses, sailors, fishermen, ferrymen, raftsmen, and bargemen crowded Kilbourn, Ferry, Charles, and Commerce Streets from early morning until late at night. However, that was a half century ago. Now, individuals and families, who could barely meet society's minimum requirements, rented places on these streets. Owing to the abysmal location, Jennie McQueeney hoped the police would choose to ignore her. She undoubtedly felt that since Tom Hollister owned the property, she might be able to ride his coattails with the authorities. But at twenty-five-years-old, Jennie Taylor still had a lot to learn about the police department and city government in general.[88]

On Wednesday night, May 13, 1868, the police raided a number of houses of ill fame on Kilbourn Street. They arrested Jennie Taylor for keeping a house of ill repute at 43 Kilbourn Street. Since the average madame at this time was over thirty and had eight years in the business, for Jennie Taylor to start her own house at twenty-six, with only four or five years experience, was astounding. Jennie had undoubtedly learned plenty under the tutelage of Angeline Prentice, but now she would learn even more through the school of hard knocks. In police court, Judge Monroe Merrill gave her a fine of $20 plus court costs. William Case, Jennie's runner, was fined $40 plus court costs for frequenting a house of ill fame.[89] By 1868, the fines in police court for prostitution matters varied from paltry to crippling.

Another madame caught in this raid, Mary Ann "Polly Ann" Atherton, kept a house of ill repute—the "Bluebird"—at 32 Ferry Street. The judge—at the urging of her attorney—adjourned her case until the following Monday, undoubtedly to give Mary Ann's attorney time to jawbone the prosecuting attorney into a deal. Mary Ann Atherton, considered the most notorious madame in town, muddied up the police blotter badly—and for forty years![90]

Oddly enough, about a year before the Hartford police arrested Mary Ann Atherton in 1868, an out-of-town newspaper, *The Marshall City Republican,* of Plymouth, Indiana, writing an article about Mary Ann, claimed that "The oldest and most notorious keeper of houses of ill fame in Hartford, Connecticut has professed religion and now is a regular at church and an ardent Christian; and, as a consequence, one of the lowest sinks of iniquity . . . has been broken up." This lovely story must have stiffened the spines of all the God-fearing people of Plymouth, Indiana, but it bears no resemblance to Mary Ann Atherton's appalling police record or her future plans as a madame in Hartford.[91]

In 1870, Jennie McQueeney came up with a different plan. The arrest for keeping a house of ill repute clearly bothered her, so she incorporated some fancy footwork into her business model. She rented a house at 21 Sheldon Street, another of Hartford's "old yellow blocks," sporting a lousy reputation. Sheldon Street, part of the Third Ward, sat just south of the infamous Fifth Ward—alternatively called "The Ward" and "Pigville"— where she had been working. A couple of doors away, at 11 Sheldon Street, lived a pistolmaker, Joseph Bullock, with his wife, Mary, and his two-year-old son, John. Even as Jennie Taylor decorated 21 Sheldon Street, she realized that confusion could work to her advantage. If she called herself Josephine Bullock—"Jo" Bullock, for short—the police might raid the wrong house and leave the area scratching their heads. (Newspaper compositors sometimes set her name as "Joe;" other times, they went with "Jo.")[92]

So now Jennie McQueeney—as Jo Bullock—had a new bawdy house on Sheldon Street—very close to Main Street—and, in theory, a new lease on life. As a twenty-eight-year old madame, she wasn't much older than the girls who worked for her. The oldest, Janice Wheeler, pretended to be a twenty-four-year-old drape-maker from Massachusetts. The youngest was eighteen-year-old Estella Smith, a milliner from Massachusetts, and two years older was Minnie White, a milliner from New York. All the girls could read and write, and Minnie White's parents were the only ones who were foreign born. When Hartford native, Dr. William W. Sanger, gathered the data for his groundbreaking study of the oldest profession in 1855, he found that 61 percent of the 2,000 prostitutes studied were foreign born. About six decades later, when George J. Kneeland repeated the study in 1912, he found that only 28 percent of the prostitutes were foreign born. Therefore, at the tail-end of the Gilded Age, it was perfectly in line with these numbers that Hartford prostitutes . . . "were typically young, native-born, white women from working- or lower-class backgrounds."[93]

Though nothing tells the whole story, we must go further here. A number of studies of young prostitutes have shown that 26 percent were feeble-minded. Working from the opposite direction, only 16 percent of participants were shown to be normal, both mentally and physically. In the main, of all the prostitutes that had been studied at institutions up to the First World War, 33 percent appeared to be below par mentally.[94]

Unfortunately, Jo Bullock's exquisite planning did little more than waste time. One of the little covenants associated with the police allowing the brothels to operate openly was the understanding that the keepers of the houses would be scrutinized endlessly. Regardless of understandings and unwritten laws, on August 25, 1870, Grand Juror Thomas McManus issued a complaint against four proprietors of houses of ill fame. Jo Bullock was not exactly rising in her chosen field, as her three co-defendants were considered very low-class operators indeed—Joe Weeks, Clarinda Crowell and Kate Lamphere. Clarinda Crowell and Kate Lamphere, though not nearly as bad as Joe Weeks, were embarrassments to the other madames.[95] They both worked out of State Street "joints" and both had been in trouble with the law before, principally for violations of the liquor laws.[96]

Luckily, all parties involved caught a break because Attorney Samuel Jones appeared out of nowhere. Jones was a high-priced criminal attorney who appeared regularly in cases involving prostitution—perhaps because he thought it lunacy to blame only the women. Jones asked the court, "Why are these girls here? Who has gotten them into lives of shame? There are merchants, merchants' clerks, and men holding respectable positions in the community who, in a measure at least, give support to these places. It is not the unfortunate women themselves that are alone to blame; men have a responsibility in this matter. And if the court is to expand the law, let the frequenters of these houses understand the punishment they may receive as well as the girls visited."

To which Grand Juror Thomas McManus replied, "Let brother Jones and myself be included with the rest" (laughter). Attorney Samuel Jones could be an aggressive advocate, but he also had a good sense of humor.[97]

Jo Bullock wasn't the only person having trouble. The Hartford police had their own problems. On May 30, 1871, the police commissioners voted to suspend Chief of Police Walter Chamberlin, without pay, for writing scandalous and indecent letters, for publishing a libel, and for conduct unbecoming the chief of police. Captain Charles Nott took over Chamberlin's duties temporarily.[98]

The allegations against Chief Chamberlin were nonsense. Chamberlin knew his correspondent was a prostitute, so naturally he wanted everything in writing. In the letters, he simply tried to arrange with this woman from New Britain a convenient time for her to reclaim a gold watch that she had left at the police station in a complicated collateral arrangement for a friend. One newspaper jokingly wrote later that Chamberlin "made indecent proposals to an indecent woman."[99] Chamberlin, a Democrat, should have been among friends, because the police board was top-heavy with Democrats, including Mayor Charles R. Chapman—one of the most partisan mayors ever elected to the top job in Hartford. Unfortunately, even Chamberlin's fellow Democrats on the board felt that the chief deserved suspension, pending some sort of investigation.[100]

While the police board dawdled in dealing with Chief Chamberlin's suspension—and how the whole matter would be resolved—on September 1, 1872, they were forced to suspend Captain Nott, a Republican. Now Lt. Packard, a Democrat, was running the police department![101]

CHIEF CALEB PACKARD

Captain Charles Nott's problems were potentially more serious than those of Chief Walter Chamberlin. Attorney Henry Selling, acting for a

Market Street madame, Hannah Coogan, leveled the charges against Captain Nott. Henry Selling's complaint respectfully submitted—

> That Charles D. Nott, captain of police and acting chief of police, has in the execution of his office been guilty of improper, immoral, illegal, and tyrannical conduct in that Nott did, for purposes of personal revenge, on or about the fifth day of June 1871, enter into a conspiracy . . . to charge Mrs. Hannah Coogan of the crime of keeping a house of ill fame, of which offense Coogan is innocent . . . and for that purpose did pressure [Elias Kohn] . . . to commit the crime of fornication with a woman whose name is unknown to your petitioner, upon the premises occupied by Coogan.

The charges were spurious. Even Hannah Coogan's attorney later admitted that he had been hoodwinked and didn't know that his client was a madame. Be that as it may, the complaint called for Captain Nott's suspension until a hearing could be held.

Cutting to the chase, the police board realized that they couldn't rehire Captain Charles Nott without first reinstating Chief of Police Walter Chamberlin. It was such a mess that one commissioner said mirthlessly that the board had created a jug with two handles—both on the same side! Having heard all opinions, the board was so flummoxed that it began to daydream about resignations. They would be voluntary—as far as the public was concerned—but at least Chamberlin and Nott would be ancient history. Along with them, any "scandalous and indecent" letters would disappear along with the unfounded charges that Captain Nott tried to frame a madame.

On November 20, 1871, the police commissioners accepted the resignations of both Chief Walter P. Chamberlin and Captain Charles D. Nott, all in the name of reorganizing the police force. The Democrats on the commission tendered one name to head the new department—a Democrat, Lieutenant Caleb L. Packard. A quick vote showed unanimity for Packard. A short time later, Mayor Washburne R. Andrus of Oakland, California became the new chief. Strangely, after Democratic Mayor Joseph Sprague got one year under his belt, in April 1875, he lobbied for, and then reinstated, Ex-Chief Walter P. Chamberlin. Sitting Chief Caleb L. Packard was forced to resign—without cause. In the never-ending political shenanigans of city government, Chief Chamberlin was eventually accused of taking a bribe from a gambler—falsely it turned out—and he had to resign effective January 1, 1882.[102]

Speaking of police irregularities . . . . The larger-than-life poster child for police corruption in the Gilded Age has always been New York City Policeman Alexander "Clubber" Williams, who was as colorful as he was controversial. Born in Nova Scotia in 1839, he emigrated at a young age and apprenticed as a ship's carpenter at William Webb's shipyard on the East River. Together with Donald MacKay of East Boston, Webb and MacKay were the finest shipbuilders in the United States. But Alexander Williams wanted excitement. In 1866, he joined the NYPD and did two years in Brooklyn before transferring to Broadway, an area infested with thugs and toughs of every description. William quickly became known as a vicious street fighter and earned the nickname "Clubber Williams." [103]

Clubber Williams advanced quickly, and in 1872, was promoted to captain of the East 35th Street Station. In no time, he broke up the Gas House Gang and was transferred again, to the West 13th Street Station, a precinct house in the middle of the city's nightclubs, gambling joints, and houses of ill repute. Williams was a master at selling police protection and quipped to a friend, "I've had chuck for a long time, and now I'm going to eat tenderloin." This remark is said to be the genesis of the term "tenderloin district."[104] (Note: Maps of San Francisco and other notorious cities, before 1872, do not include the word "tenderloin.")

Clubber Williams stayed in the tenderloin for two years before his methods were called into question. Despite being brought up on charges eighteen times, Williams was always acquitted by the Board of Police Commissioners. Clubber Williams remained in charge of the district until his promotion to inspector in August 1887. Williams was such a keg of dynamite that even after he was badly discredited and embarrassed by the Lexow Committee in the mid-1890s, New York City's three-man Police Commission, headed by Theodore Roosevelt, decided that it would be best for everyone if Williams retired with a yearly pension of $1,750. (The average annual wage in 1895 was $438.)[105]

If Clubber Williams represented a policeman gone bad, Hartford-born Joe Weeks single-handedly gave prostitution a bad name. Weeks's father, a respected Hartford grocer, had four sons, three of whom took their places in society without difficulty. But Joe was a bad seed. From the time he reached manhood, Joe Weeks differed markedly from his brothers. In an incredibly short career of sixteen years, Joe Weeks partnered in more than a half-dozen houses of ill fame, found his way into police court four times for prostitution or liquor violations, made his way behind bars twice for beating his wife and once for refusing to pay his city taxes. The very first time he appeared in police court, Judge Samuel Jones said "he had always supposed the defendant had kept a house of questionable reputation and that he was one of the most noted keepers of houses of prostitution in the city." Judge Jones worked hard to control his temper when he dealt with Joe Weeks.[106] (Note: Judge Samuel Jones was the same attorney who defended madames in police court in the 1870s.)

Joe Weeks so completely destroyed his good name, he had to relocate to New Haven where he spent the last twenty years of his life. When he died, Rev. Henry Kelsey gave him a mass of Christian burial at the Fourth Congregational Church on Main Street, including a lovely burial at the Old North Cemetery. This would have appealed to Joe Weeks enormously, since he once kept a house of ill repute on Main Street directly opposite the Fourth Congregational Church. One assumes that his descendants visit his grave as often as they can!

When the police raided houses of ill fame, chiefly those of unsavory characters, usually revenues were the driver. Moreover, it was money that should have been proffered at the beginning of the year. Joe Weeks's arrest for not paying his taxes makes it clear that he was simply a money-grubbing proprietor of brothels and a poor businessman.

During the course of Jo Bullock's run-in with the police in August 1870, it quickly became clear that she was not under arrest. Beyond that, she had the good luck to get an associate judge and a prince of a man to hear her case. "Genial George" Sumner studied law with David Calhoun of Manchester. As the Civil War concluded, Sumner landed a position with the law firm of Waldo, Hubbard & Hyde in Hartford. Two years later, the people of his native Bolton elected him to the state House of Representatives. Not long afterward, he settled in Hartford and became an alderman in 1868. Rising like the star that he was, Sumner then served as city attorney and did a hitch as associate judge of the city court. In 1873-74, he acted as chairman of the Democratic State Central Committee.[107]

What Jo Bullock didn't know at the time of her police court hearing was that Judge Sumner and Ella Gallup of Plainfield were scheduled to marry in October—two months hence. In any event, Sumner put Jo Bullock and her three co-defendants under $100 peace bonds. Sumner claimed that the only purpose of the hearing was to let the frequenters of these houses know they were under the surveillance of the police, who intended to see that the peace bonds were kept.

Sure enough, in October, Judge Sumner married Ella Gallup and they had two children—William Gallup and Julia Gallup. Neither of the children reached the age of two and Sumner's wife, Ella, died in March 1875, leaving him alone in the world. (At the Wadsworth Atheneum, the Ella Gallup Sumner and Mary Catlin Sumner Collections Fund was founded and named for the wives of George Sumner and his younger brother, Frank.)[108]

"GENIAL GEORGE" SUMNER

Tested as few men are, Judge Sumner soldiered on. In 1878, he beat Morgan Bulkeley in the city's mayoral race. In his inimitable way, Sumner appointed the best men he could find—irrespective of party—for the positions in his administration. Judge Sumner held a number of different positions in state government, even serving as Lt. Governor of Connecticut from 1883 to 1885 under the divisive Gov. Thomas Waller. (Democrats called Waller "Connecticut's Little-Giant," while Republicans—like Gen.

Joe Hawley—referred to him as "this cheap man.") Judge Sumner never remarried and died of heart trouble at sixty-five.[109]

Jo Bullock's latest brush with the law—albeit without adding another arrest to her record—bothered her terribly. Still her options were few. In a businesslike manner, she made the appropriate payments and kept as low a profile as possible. Although Jo Bullock's interest in prostitution derived from basic needs, there exists a mountain of historical background that would have interested her. To begin, fornication [carnal copulation] was never an offense under American common law. The Massachusetts Puritans, however, made fornication a statutory offense in 1692, two years before the law against adultery. The fornication statute was reenacted by the Massachusetts legislature in 1785.[110] Meanwhile open and gross lewdness was an offense of American common law [open and gross lewdness meant two unmarried people living together]. American common law forbade keeping a bawdy house. Massachusetts' colonial legislature made this a statutory offense in 1790 and the General Assembly followed suit in 1793.[111]

In 1796, Connecticut's general statutes said that "if any man shall commit fornication with a single woman . . . each of them shall pay a fine of six dollars . . . or be corporally punished by whipping, not exceeding ten stripes each. . . . "At the time, Connecticut was no haven for adulterers either . . ."Whosoever shall commit adultery with a married woman . . . both of them shall be . . . punished by whipping on the naked body . . . or burned on the forehead with the letter "A."[112]

Connecticut's first legal crack at houses of ill fame came with an 1845 law stating, "Every person who shall keep a house of ill fame . . . for the purpose of prostitution . . . shall be punished by imprisonment in the common jail, for a term not exceeding six months, or by a fine not exceeding one hundred dollars." Legislators made a distinction between houses of ill fame and disorderly houses. (A prostitute could scream loud enough to wake the neighbors, but as long as she wasn't engaged in sex, the dwelling was only a disorderly house. The keeper of a house of ill fame could get six months in jail, while the person with a disorderly house got only three months. Both were subject to one hundred dollar fines."[113]

As usual, the law proved some very creaky machinery. Oftentimes the judges of the police court had a hard time figuring out the crime, the level of culpability, the history of the accused, and, of course, a reasonable punishment. Since the complete list of variables made the head spin, justice varied wildly and the arrested parties were completely flummoxed.

Jo Bullock probably thought her house at 21 Sheldon Street was a double for Ada Leffingwell's enormously successful place at 5 Arch Street. Both houses were very close to Main Street—in the best neighborhood in the city. This latest brush with the law—even at the gentle hands of Judge Sumner—caused her to rethink the whole matter. However, before she did anything, she talked to Tom Hollister—the Hartford-born businessman with the kind of police protection money couldn't buy.

Chapter 3

A Different Tack

After two run-ins with the police in as many years, Jennie spent her days in a dither. Like so many other women of her time, she had a grammar school education and no marketable skills. She couldn't afford to quit, but she couldn't afford to get arrested or detained again either. There was a point where the police would give up on a house and "break it up." She couldn't afford to let that happen.

So Jennie concocted a plan. To begin, she approached Tom Hollister about buying one of his houses on Kilbourn Street. Most operators in the prostitution business only leased their houses so that they could disappear in the event of real trouble. By owning her house, Jennie would have an easier time convincing a judge that the girls living with her were friends and not prostitutes. The second prong of this attack followed along the same tack. By owning a place in the worst part of the city, the police would be more inclined to leave her alone—she continued to believe.

Tom Hollister clearly had a soft spot in his heart for Jo Bullock because he sold her 43 Kilbourn Street. By April 18, 1871, the date of the title transfer, Milton Clyde of Springfield had already begun work on the Valley Railroad. (Since the tracks hugged the Connecticut River all the way to Old Saybrook, Clyde bought a cabin cruiser and ran the whole job from fifty feet offshore.) The reason that the Kilbourn properties were of interest was that the Valley Railroad needed the land by the river in Hartford. Naturally, those who owned property in the area would be handsomely rewarded. In May of 1873, Tom Hollister and Jo Bullock sold their Kilbourn Street property to the Valley Railroad for a nice profit.[114] (Though at this stage of her life Jennie called herself Jo Bullock, when she bought and sold property she still reverted to Jane McQueeney.)

It's clear by the way these documents were handled that Tom Hollister and Jo Bullock were working together now. She began to spend more and more time helping Tom Hollister run his State Street house and through the 1870s they set the stage for a life together.[115]

For Jo Bullock, it seemed like a smart move. Tom Hollister's business skills were better than hers and previously he depended on other women to act as madames at his house. Jo could be the new madame at the State Street place and things would continue smoothly. Incidentally, great instability characterized the tenderloin districts across America. Partnerships were formed and then collapsed; inmates left for better pay or a nicer madame; police court judges offered young prostitutes a choice between jail or a one-way ticket out of town; inmates got sick, or simply decided to quit the life. The players moved about constantly.

At the time, there were three inmates at Tom Hollister's house. From Vermont, there was a twenty-four-year-old dressmaker, Jenny Ford; another dressmaker, twenty-two-year-old Nettie Livingston, hailed from New York; and the nineteen-year-old Texan, Carrie Anesworth, pretended to be a milliner. Dressmaker and milliner were two of the most popular fantasy careers of young prostitutes. Another favorite—more popular in the Midwest—was clerk in a dry goods store. In Rhode Island, girls claimed that they "worked in a cotton mill." But in Hartford, they preferred "worked in a silk mill," as the Cheney Brothers hired thousands of young silk workers for their huge plants on Main Street—in the huge brownstone that later became Brown, Thompson's—and then later Market Streets. Hands down though, dressmaker proved the most popular fantasy career.[116]

One of Dr. William Sanger's questions to his 2,000 patients concerned their trades before they entered prostitution. Almost half (933) were servants—though the girls who chose prostitution in the central Connecticut area clearly saw their choice as preferable to cleaning houses and entered prostitution before they would have begun work as domestic servants or housekeepers. According to Dr. Sanger's data, another 499 lived with their parents; 121 were dressmakers; and, 105 were tailoresses.[117]

Far more interesting in Dr. Sanger's study was the average weekly pay of women and young girls before they became prostitutes. A shocking 26 percent were making only $1 a week; 44 percent were making $2 a week or less; and, of all the 2000 women in the study, 55 percent made $3 a week or less. (The average weekly wage for a man in 1855 was about $7.)

Roughly one-half of the women had Protestant backgrounds, while another half were reared as Roman Catholics. The parentage of Sanger's patients told an interesting tale. All of the women's fathers were uneducated workingmen—farmers, laborers, carpenters, blacksmiths and so forth, while 94 percent of their mothers had no income outside the home. As one ponders these statistics, it becomes obvious that society had no work for young girls in the Gilded Age. If a young woman didn't marry, she could work in a mill, a manufactory, or as a clerk in a store, but beyond these simple outlets, there were few choices.

In Howard Woolston's 1921 text *Prostitution in the United States,* his sample group of 1,000 prostitutes showed that if young girls entered the available trades, they could expect to earn $14.48 a week, while the inmates in the bordellos made $45.44 a week—more than three times as much. This windfall didn't ensure happiness or a good life, but for those without education or prospects of any kind, it surely must have looked attractive.[118]

In 1878, the social evil formed such a confused muddle across the United Sates that in Cincinnati, a wholesale raid of all the houses of ill fame ended in lunacy. Word quickly got to Police Superintendent George Ziegler that "the order was only intended to apply to Monte men, loafers, and prostitutes . . . not to 'respectable houses of ill fame.' At 2:30 p.m., the station houses were told to cease raiding and release all the prostitutes on their own recognizance. . . . When the few prostitutes—arrested before the order was quashed—were paraded into court the following morning, Judge Wilson discharged them all on the grounds that none of them were arrested on warrants, as required by law. Then the judge strongly impressed upon the officers the importance of warrants in matters of this nature."[119]

In her move to State Street, Jo Bullock accepted a few tradeoffs. Thanks to Tom Hollister's police connections, there remained very little chance of trouble with the police, but if something went wrong Jo Bullock would have to take the arrest. She might even be forced to spend a night in jail. Tom Hollister would do whatever he could to get her out on bail—or whatever else his lawyers could arrange—but Jo would have to accept the indignity. Besides the police connection, one last safeguard remained. Tom Hollister's house on State Street catered to men of the highest rank and station. Judges, lawyers, legislators, businessmen, elected and appointed officials, and a host of other men of status sought out Tom Hollister's luxurious house. These men, of course, did not want their favorite sporting house raided or compromised in any way. And lest we forget, some of these men called the tune for the mayor and members of the common council as well. In effect, this added another layer of protection.

Jo Bullock and Tom Hollister dated through the mid-1870s, and on January 5, 1878, they married. As the license states, Tom Hollister, a forty-seven-year-old bachelor, married thirty-four-year-old Jane McQueeney, also single. Owing to the brutally cold New England weather in January, Rev. Samuel A. Davis married the couple in the rectory of the Universalist Church on Main Street. The Hollisters were members of the Universalist Church despite their lack of regular participation. Owing to the Hollisters' business—and complete lack of penitence or intent to reform—attendance at weekly services would have caused too much hostility among other congregants. Logically, Jennie and Tom Hollister did not attend services very often.[120]

Rev. Davis was ordained in 1834 and partook of the pioneer work of Universalism in Pennsylvania and Ohio. He traveled continuously, preached constantly, and helped nurture the growth of the Universalist Church.[121]

Besides his duties as a cleric, Rev. Davis was anti-slavery from his earliest days and his home in Ohio acted as a stop on the Underground Railroad. As such, he helped fleeing slaves safely negotiate the territory between the Ohio River and Canada. Rev. Davis was also active in temperance work. In 1862, Rev. Davis and his wife, Charlotte, relocated to Hartford. Mr. Davis served as state missionary of the Connecticut Universalist Convention for over twenty years.[122]

One of the members of Rev. Davis's Church of the Redeemer was the builder Hiram Bissell who, for seventeen years, fought the earliest battles of the Hartford Water Works. Bissell also built Christ the Redeemer Church so that his fellow parishioners could leave Central Row in Statehouse Square and enjoy larger quarters on Main Street. (When the Hollisters moved to Wells Street in 1883, they had a magnificent view of the Soldiers and Sailor Memorial Arch in Bushnell Park, another of Hiram Bissell's building projects.)[123]

When Rev. Samuel Davis married Jennie and Tom Hollister, he was sixty-eight and still active in the ministry. Davis retired in 1892, but was still far too busy to stop for death, so it kindly stopped for him on March 17, 1897. He was eighty-seven.[124]

Jennie and Tom Hollister were given their license by City Clerk John E. Higgins, who originally came from New London. He moved to Hartford after landing a job as a mechanic at Colt's Patent Fire-Arms. A veteran of three years' service in the Civil War, Higgins became Hartford's city clerk and registrar in 1874. His job was an elective one, but Higgins proved so competent and well-liked that on Election Day his name appeared on both the Democratic and Republican ballots. [125]

When Jo Bullock officially became Mrs. Thomas Adams Hollister, owing to the nature of their work, nothing about their marriage found its way into the city's newspapers. This was to be expected inasmuch as the city pretended that the demimonde didn't exist. Many years later, when Tom Hollister died, the *Courant* added tastelessly in his obituary, "in 1878, he married 'a well-known woman,' Jane McQueeney." During the Gilded Age, this was code for prostitute.[126]

This points up a sad fact of Jennie and Tom Hollister's lives. They might have earned a comfortable existence and even managed a modicum of admiration or respect among certain folks in Hartford, but they lived outside the law. The everyday pleasures of ordinary people were denied them. The Hollisters didn't often go to church and rarely attended baptisms, weddings, or funerals. What they knew of city government and politics they read in the newspapers or wrested from their educated and highly placed patrons. Beyond the company of one another, their lives were characterized by a lingering emptiness. This fact, of course, was disguised by their gorgeous home, lavish clothing, dazzling jewelry, and the fine horses and elegant carriages they maintained.

The prostitution business followed the same rules as any other business in that a proprietor catered endlessly to the regular patrons, clients, customers or whatever the end-users were called. During the 1870's, the Hollisters watched as Hartford's legislators outmaneuvered their counterparts in New Haven to become the sole capitol of the state.

Connecticut's experience with capitols was tortuous. After October 1636, the state legislature met at Hartford until 1700. In October 1701, the legislators met for the first time in New Haven. From 1713 forward, the May session played out in Hartford and the October session in New Haven. During the Revolutionary war—after October 1776—the legislature stopped meeting in New Haven. With the Constitution of 1818, the October session ended and the May session alternated in a completely random fashion between Hartford and New Haven. There were times when the legislature met at Hartford three years in a row and then only went to New Haven for a single year before returning to Hartford. There simply was no logic to it at all.

After the War of the Rebellion, establishing one capitol in Connecticut became a cause célèbre. The committee responsible for the final decision chose Hartford, and in 1875, the state legislature met at New Haven for the last time. Chaos still reigned though. Even as the new capitol rose on the old Trinity College site overlooking Bushnell Park, the legislature met at

Middletown in 1878. One year later, when everything except the dome was completed, the legislature began meeting at the new capitol. The old Statehouse became City Hall, with Mayor Morgan G. Bulkeley—the state's all-time most accomplished vote-buyer—assuming the role as the first mayor to take the oath of office in those dignified chambers. Mayor Morgan G. Bulkeley took over the governor's office in the southeast corner of the first floor.

Looking at this strictly from a business standpoint, the cross-town move of the members of the General Assembly put too much real estate between the Hollisters and their best customers. From 165 State Street, the Statehouse could be hit with a stone, but the new capitol building was almost a mile away. Whether or not to remedy the state's shortsightedness was a vexing question for the Hollisters. They could remain on State Street or find something closer to the new capitol building. Both options had pluses and minuses.

On the plus side, there were three bordellos on State Street that were considered untouchable and they all sat on the first block east of Statehouse square. The first was Frank Russell's saloon at 107 State Street. As one writer noted, "Who does not know this house? Many, and hilarious, have been the hack parties that some night hawk . . . has piloted to this house in return for a consideration from the proprietor."[127] The Bange mansion at 165 State Street had the Hollister name written all over it. By settling up with the police in a timely fashion and doling out Christmas presents like Santa Claus, the Hollisters amassed the most fabulous clientele in town. Lastly, Carolyn Webster's lavish sporting house rested invitingly at 181 State Street. When a certain director general of Connecticut died, one of Carolyn's housekeepers murmured sadly, "In his death, the house lost its best customer."[128] All three of these proprietors understood the game intimately and made the necessary payments without any prodding.

The location of these houses offered them a certain amount of protection too. The American Hotel sat on the east side of Statehouse Square and faced west. No surprise, the manager of the American Hotel knew how to supply needy guests with prostitutes and did it with all the élan of someone in the assignation business. Behind the American Hotel sprawled the trolley garage and livery stables of the Wethersfield and Hartford Horse Railroad Company. East of this point sat the three untouchable brothels, plus two others, on the south side of State Street, leading down to Front Street. This area was considered the heart of the tenderloin. By and large, the captains of industry, legislative nobility, and randy tourists did not want to throw fortune to the wind by traveling too far down State Street in the dark of night. Therefore, this first block of brothels—between the horse railroad garage and Front Street—were the houses that had the best chance of attracting wealthy, highbrow patrons.

On the negative side, thanks to the really depraved houses on the lower end of State Street, the tenderloin got seedier every year, irrespective of the location of any particular house. If the proper piece of real estate could be found—in a location that would offer the Hollisters some exclusivity—wouldn't it be smart to leave State Street?

As the old Statehouse underwent the necessary remodeling to become Hartford's new City Hall, the Hollisters finally decided to move closer to the new capitol building. The new legislative chambers sat atop a lovely hill overlooking Bushnell Park. Though some streets were clearly off limits, something in the vicinity of Bushnell Park would be ideal. However, for Jennie and Tom Hollister, the right piece of real estate wasn't on the market. They had no choice but to wait.

As early as 1836, a beautiful forty-acre park in the center of downtown Hartford became the obsession of Rev. Horace Bushnell. As pastor of the Third Congregational Church on Main Street (corner of Morgan Street), Bushnell was a force to be reckoned with when it came to the intricacies of city planning. Bushnell became a lawyer before attending Divinity School, so he wasn't a dilettante. Also, though he waged a lifelong battle with tuberculosis, he projected the image of a man of indefatigable energy. When the idea of a central park for Hartford sprouted in Bushnell's mind, the area he liked best was a squalid low spot in the landscape, crowded with mills, slaughterhouses, dye works, tenements, and garbage dumps. These eyesores sat on the banks of the Park (Little) River, a smelly stream that delivered a witch's brew of nauseating waste to the Connecticut River. Truth told, the whole mess resembled a snapshot of Hades.[129]

Compounding the issue, before Union Station became the rail hub of the city (on Union Place) a single spur of tracks ran easterly through this low spot to Hartford's railroad depot at the bottom of Mulberry Street. This small station was a block from Main Street, at the bottom of a lane filled with junk shops, tenements, and saloon-brothels. Mulberry Street seemed a complete inappropriate name, but other streets failed to meet their potential too. By 1879, hard work and solid planning turned this revolting wasteland into a verdant Eden showcasing magnificent foliage, interwoven with miles of well-groomed bridle paths, and surrounded by a much-improved Park River—with vertical stone-flagged embankments. Finally, a towering brownstone arch, memorializing the soldiers and sailors who served in the Civil War was completed in 1886.[130]

It took Jennie and Tom Hollister three years to find the right property, but eventually they struck gold. Cyprian Nichols had bought the land—on what was once Maiden Lane—from Nathaniel Patten for $500 in 1806. (By

1825, it became Wells Street, after John Wells who manufactured wooden printing presses on this lane.) During that period, the west side of this narrow street had houses and mills that drew water power from the Park (Little) River. Cyprian Nichols's candle-making and soap-boiling business was in a small building opposite his home and a little to the south—closer to Daniels' Mills. A good guess is that Nichols drew power from the Daniels' Mills dam on the Park River. (The buildings on the west side of the street were razed when Bushnell Park came to completion after the War of the Rebellion.)

Practically every city in America had a soap-grease man, whose horse and wagon trundled up and down the narrow, dirt lanes as he yelled "Soap-grease! Soap-grease!" Cyprian Nichols was a soap-grease man. That said, Cyprian Nichols could trace his roots back to the founders of the city. Beyond that, he was a justice of the peace, an estate administrator, a grocer, a real estate speculator, and a director of the Phoenix Bank. Though Nichols may have had helpers driving wagons from house to house, he kept a small shop in Statehouse Square—"20 rods west of Messrs. Hudson & Goodwin's Printing Office [66 State Street]." Later he rented a shop on Main Street—"First door south of the brick Meeting House [corner of Central Row]." Nichols sold candles and soap, and he was constantly purchasing "for cash, tallow, ashes, grease, damaged butter, or lard." He made "mould and dipped candles, yellow bar soap, white soap for woolen manufacturers, shaving soap, and soft soap."[131]

Lemuel Humphrey learned the business from Cyprian Nichols and a few years later the men formed a partnership—Nichols & Humphrey. In 1822, Cyprian Nichols sold his home on the east side of Maiden Lane, with a "dwelling house and other buildings thereon standing," to Lemuel Humphrey for $3,000. Nichols & Humphrey continued to thrive, shipping large quantities of soap and candles to New York and Richmond, Virginia, where they had networks of agents to sell their products. When Cyprian Nichols died in 1853, Humphrey teamed up with the Seyms brothers to form Humphrey, Seyms & Co. A decade later, Lemuel Humphrey retired to his new home and gardens at 61 Lafayette Street and rented the Wells Street property. While settling his father's estate in April 1882, Henry Humphrey, Lemuel's only son and a businessman from Philadelphia, sold the property for $7,000 to George Richardson, an agent from Boston.[132]

Two months later, on June 2, 1882, Jennie and Tom Hollister bought 76 Wells Street from George Richardson for $7,000. (Richardson's commission obviously was paid out of closing.) Since they had to invest so much money in improvements—including a huge new addition on the back of the main house and steam heat throughout—the Hollisters only put down $500 and arranged a $6,500 mortgage with Society for Savings. Old city maps show the Hollisters' finished home as markedly different from Lemuel Humphrey's dwelling house. The old building was almost completely demolished in order to build a house specifically designed as a house of ill fame. The old foundation could be used to support the new structure, but little else had any value.

The finished product at 76 Wells Street was a 6,000 square foot, seventeen-room, white clapboard home with a mansard roof of deep gray Pennsylvania slate. Atop the building sat towering red brick chimneys— almost phallic in nature—and the whole incomparable pile of finery and fashion sat embarrassingly close to the new state capitol. Architects categorized the Hollisters' new place as Second French Empire. No matter, the average person just stared at it in awe. This jewel—directly across Wells Street from where the old rail depot once sat—rested on land close to everything, isolated to just the right degree, and with coveted views of

Bushnell Park. In time, 76 Wells Street became the best-kept secret in Hartford, as men of rank and privilege, men of the highest station in life, ventured there for some sport.[133]

Jennie Hollister acted as madame, though sometimes old patrons still referred to her as Jo Bullock. As one reporter noted more than a decade later, "Jo Bullock is past the beautiful period of her life, but is still considered to be a good-looking woman."[134]

Tom Hollister was a huge asset to the business because he was "well known to almost every senator and representative that ever visited Hartford."[135] The brilliant white clapboard house was cavernous—close to 6,000 square feet on three floors—and had a long, white wooden porch on the south side, with a matching trellised entryway at the front door. The third-floor gabled windows that gracefully leaned out from the mansard roof were white and the windows of the first and second floors were trimmed with red shutters. A black wrought-iron fence encircled the 20,000-square-foot property, which boasted 200-year-old trees, earthbound phyla, and every kind of hedge plant and flowering shrub that New England could support.

In front of the house—on the other side of Wells Street—flowed the Park River, on the eastern edge of the park. After the eye takes in the long expanse of Bushnell Park, it lifts skyward to capture the towering majesty of the lovely new State Capitol building—granite spires, curious gargoyles, white flagpoles everywhere, and a shimmering gold dome as big as the Ritz! In short, the Hollisters' house of ill repute on Wells Street had a location nonpareil.

It staggers the imagination to think that the Hollisters spent such a huge sum of money on the most beautiful bordello in Connecticut—but a place that could be shut down at any time by the police. Jennie and Tom

JENNIE HOLLISTER'S PLACE - 76 WELLS STREET, HARTFORD

Hollister must have had unassailable feelings that Hartford's bishops would allow prostitution to continue unabated. This one fact fleshes out the Gilded Age in a way that future generations might never completely understand. In any event, thanks to Jennie and Tom Hollisters' attention to detail and a steady flow of high-testosterone aristocratic patrons, they were able to burn the mortgage in 1885.[136]

By 1886, Jennie and Tom Hollister had been in their new quarters at 76 Wells Street for four years and were doing extremely well. Probably with some nudging from Jennie, Tom Hollister bought an old farmhouse on the New Britain road near Cedar Mountain. It wasn't much to look at, but was located in the southwestern part of the city, far enough from the downtown tenderloin that a couple might be able to make a decent living and stay out of trouble.

Angeline and Joe Start rebuilt this old place into the Cedar Mountain House, a restaurant-saloon-brothel, and soon enough were doing a comfortable business. When Jennie and Tom Hollister bought this old farmhouse to get Angeline and Joe Start on their feet in Hartford in the 1880s, they had a double agenda. On the one hand, Jennie was paying back Angeline for the older woman's help when Jennie was only eighteen and just getting into the business. Beyond that, Jennie was also bringing her best friend to Hartford, where the two could see each other regularly and perhaps even travel some. No matter how successful a couple might be, the prostitution business could be lonely. Having a close business pal nearby might even be seen as an act of self-preservation.

Tom Hollister leased this place to the Starts. As the Cedar Mountain House, it was a comfortable step above the old farmhouse that it had been, and Angeline and Joe Start delighted in their new business in Hartford. Unfortunately, about 7:15 on Saturday night, November 27, 1886, the

Start's roadhouse caught fire. Apparently, the light of what was a considerable fire quickly lit up the southwestern part of the city, but the alarm wasn't called in until 7:35 from a call box on the corner of Retreat Avenue and Washington Street. The fire broke out while Joe Start and some friends were at supper and it got out of control quickly. When fire-fighting units arrived at the blaze, the men splashed the contents of an old cistern on the fire, but with negligible results. The building was a total loss. The damage estimate of the Cedar Mountain House fire came to $3,000.[137]

The Starts never rebuilt the Cedar Mountain House, perhaps because the authorities now knew the true nature of the place. The Starts moved back to Warwick, Rhode Island. About eight months before his death in 1894, Tom Hollister sold this property to Ludwig Forrester.

Angeline Start always claimed that Jennie "stayed with them [Angeline and Billy Prentice] in their place on the New Britain road" when Jennie Hollister was first starting in the business. Some might suspect that this property on the New Britain road was in some way connected to the earlier roadhouse where Angie and Jennie worked in the early 1860s, but the two places were in no way linked. Upon Angeline and Joe Start's return to Rhode Island, they ran the Hillside Hotel—with a backroom operation—in Warwick for decades.[138]

Though Wells Street seemed déclassé when the city's soap-grease men lived and worked in the area, Bushnell Park's improvements turned the whole area around. The nexus of Wells and Mulberry became a German neighborhood and was delightfully Teutonic in character and custom. As early as 1859, Andrew Heublein, born in Prussia, conducted his restaurant-saloon-hotel at Mulberry and Wells Streets, facing Bushnell Park. When the new Heublein Hotel rose in 1891—at the corner of Wells and Gold Streets—it sat just a few doors to the north of Jennie and Tom Hollister's place. Andrew Heublein's old venue at the corner of Mulberry and Wells Street became part of the new hotel, making it the only structure on the whole block between Gold and Mulberry Streets. The Heublein Hotel even had a carriageway directly into the heart of the building, delivering patrons to a huge indoor atrium on the first floor. The Heublein Hotel—due to the extraordinary good taste of Andrew Heublein and his sons, Gilbert and Lewis—stood as the most fashionable hostelry in Hartford. Guests, of course, loved the hotel's fabulous view of Bushnell Park, and the Heublein family loved to boast that the hotel "had a window and an oriental carpet in each room."[139]

Closer to Main Street—at 27 Mulberry—Henry Ernst's continental café earned a reputation for its sauerbraten and imported delicacies. George Pfeiffer's German steamship agency, with the big North German Lloyd sign hanging outside, operated at 31 Mulberry Street. George Pfeiffer also sold German books and periodicals, and ran a rooming house for his fellow countrymen who were in the process of settling in America. His employment agency helped newly-arriving Germans find jobs quickly. In the rear of Pfeiffer's place was the office and press of the weekly *Hartforder Herold*, established in 1883 and distributed as far as New Britain, Bristol, Rockville and Meriden. Later, the Schuetzen Haus, another oasis, blossomed forth at the southeast corner of Mulberry and Wells Streets. Even the Irish cop on the beat spoke fluent German.[140]

While Jennie and Tom Hollister remodeled 76 Wells Street to meet their unusual needs, other madames and proprietors of bawdy houses were becoming permanent fixtures in the demimonde. When Tom Hollister moved from State Street in 1883, first Lizzie Cadwell, then "Billy West" and "Grace Howard," and lastly, Billy West and his wife, Cora—tried to match the Hollisters' remarkable success. Easier said than done. None of them had the special protection from the police that Jennie and Tom Hollister nurtured, and none of them had the good looks and poise of Jennie Hollister. Police and court reporters went so far as to call her "the stately Jennie Hollister" as she mulled around the station house after a *faux*-raid for a liquor violation in 1895. (The judge fined her $10.)[141]

Another important point is that the demimonde of Hartford functioned as a divided club. The wild, young girls—who loved life in the fast lane—made up the core and gloried in the knowledge that they didn't have to slave away as mill workers or dressmakers. They lived for the parties and friendships, completely oblivious to the future—or even if they had one. Apart from this group of fast fillies were madames who had been in the business long enough to know about its highs and lows. Jennie Hollister reigned at the very top of this collection of madames. Whenever there was trouble, Jennie posted bonds for other madames and their inmates as needed.

Ada Leffingwell wasn't a central figure in the demimonde because she was a meretricious strumpet without youth, beauty, grace or style. Despite these crushing handicaps, her sporting house on Arch Street did well financially.

Adella "Ada" E. Leffingwell was born in Farmington, Connecticut to Oscar and Elizabeth Curtis, but the date remains a mystery. (In the middle of 1900, Ada claimed to be forty, but that hardly seems possible. Fifty might be closer to the mark.) "Broken-nosed Ada" emerged as the chubby proprietress of a well-known resort at 5 Arch Street, one door from Main. Besides being physically unattractive, Ada had a voice that irritated even as it offended. Her cleft-palate-style speech impediment grated so much that people said "she was a much better companion when she remained silent."[142]

5 Arch Street
Hartford

Ada's place presented nicely as a three-story brick structure, with white marble lintels above the windows and a front door that stood right on the sidewalk. Located in the most respectable portion of the city, guests at 5 Arch Street came and went freely. In 1891, Ada leased the house, and then bought it from the estate of Mary Warner in 1893 for $3,250. Ada had seen generations grow old, but like the brook, her business went on forever. Ada didn't have the pull of the Hollisters, and she had been raided once in the summer of 1892. So said, the police usually left her alone.[143]

Ada pulled stunts constantly in an attempt to increase her take. She used to give each of her four girls a little, personal strongbox to keep in their rooms. As inmates first met patrons downstairs, Ada gave the girls brass tokens. The girls, of course, dropped these brass tokens in their strongboxes. There would be an exchange on payday, but by that time, Ada had used her duplicate key to remove some of the tokens from the different strongboxes. The girls confronted Ada, who smoothed their feathers by explaining how lucky they were to be living in a house where they were loved and well treated. Ada mollified the girls nicely and then cheated them again the following week![144]

Another of Ada's gimmicks lowered the grocery bills. Ada told her girls they were gaining weight and this fact upset her terribly. Naturally, Ada's altruistic and overarching concern was the girls' health. A sample of Ada's new diet follows: For breakfast, oatmeal, milk, and coffee; for dinner, barley soup, codfish, hash and apple pie; for supper, bread, butter, a doughnut and tea. The girls could not survive on this fare and threatened to strike. Ada relented, but the food never got much better. During weeks when the girls were good, they got their meals regularly, but were hungry all the time anyway.[145]

Happily for Ada, her inmates were young women who always behaved themselves in public. This behavior, combined with Ada's orderly manner in the operation of 5 Arch Street, kept the police at bay. For law enforcement, it was simple: Pay your fees, keep an orderly house, and we'll look the other way.[146]

Still, Ada loved to levy fines on her girls. If they stayed out late and were not in promptly in accordance with the hours laid down in this palatial establishment, they were fined $2.50. Besides the fine, the demimonde whispered in mock horror that the girls were sent to bed like little children without their supper! If they failed to return for the entire night, owing to something like a carriage ride with a friend, they were fined $5. For minor offenses, they were fined anywhere from $ .10 to $1. The girls complained, but Ada appeased the girls by pointing out what a happy home they had found with her.[147]

More than anything, Ada dreamed of herself as a class act. Poor, fat Ada envied Jennie Hollister for this very trait. Ada's place was sumptuous on the inside and she maintained a respectable client list, but she never attained the lofty spot in the business that Jennie Hollister enjoyed. Ada wanted her girls to be classy and she thought she could lead by example.

One story illustrates this point nicely. A local hackman assumed that he could wait in Ada's front parlor until his fare decided to leave. However, just as he plopped into an overstuffed chair, Miss Ada disabused him of his assumptions and escorted him to the "bicycle room"—a small storage room for trunks, boxes, luggage, and, of course, bicycles. With practiced haughtiness, Miss Ada drooled out, "You'll have to wait here, hackman. I can't have you in the parlor with the gentlemen and ladies."

If Jennie Hollister's digs at 76 Wells Street glistened as the very model of a well-run sporting house—and Ada Leffingwell's house of ill fame at 5 Arch Street sat either half-way up or half-way down the brothel ladder, depending on your point of view—then Mary Ann Atherton's River House at the foot of Ferry Street was a cesspool.

River House - 76 Ferry Street, Hartford
The "great red hotel on the river"
with warehouses showing in back.

Mary Ann Atherton—a.k.a. Polly Ann Atherton—wasn't a figure in the demimonde either. She never really had a chance to be one of those pretty young things in the diamonds and fancy clothes, because Mary Ann lived on the wrong side of town and ran bawdy houses where bedbugs refused to visit and her patrons were on twenty-four-hour passes from hell.

Mary Ann Wright was born in England in 1836. Old documents make it clear that Mary Ann never even knew where her parents were born, suggesting a badly broken family. Eighteen years later, Mary Ann crossed the North Atlantic to New York with her two sisters and they settled first in New York and then Hartford. At nineteen, Mary Ann met Newton Chamberlain Atherton, a thirty-seven-year-old, illiterate blacksmith. Newton Atherton's first wife, Harriet Hall of Hartford, gave him a daughter, Amy, but then died suddenly after fifteen years of marriage. In 1855, Newton C. Atherton married Mary Ann Wright. The couple settled at 47 Kilbourn Street and quickly had two boys, John and Joseph, neither of whom lived more than a few months. In March 1862, they had another boy, Edward, who, as an adult, went by the name E. Newton Atherton. Sadly, Mary Ann's husband, Newton C. Atherton, died in 1863 at the age of forty-eight. Judging by the flimsy evidence extant, Newton Atherton's life was volatile. For instance, his blacksmithing business operated from seven different locations in fifteen years, and when he wed Mary Ann Wright, he married a woman eighteen years his junior.[148]

From 1863 forward, Mary Ann Atherton had a difficult time making ends meet. She had no skills worth mentioning and a young boy to rear. The death of her husband not only left her penniless, but also living in the worst part of town.

Before 1810, when Hartford got its first wooden covered bridge to East Hartford, Ferry Street figured as the most active area in town. The wharfs of the wealthiest merchants in town splayed like fingers out into the Connecticut River, a waterway with square rigged West India brigs, offloading rum and molasses. Coastal schooners, sloops, and fishing craft crowded the docks of the city from the wooden bridge to Dutch Point on the south. Because Hartford was the head of navigation on the river, it enjoyed more business than the size of the city warranted. The city also enjoyed a big salt provision export trade with the West Indies—salt beef, pork, and fish in barrels. These shipments went either directly to the West Indies or were shipped to commission houses in New York.

The riverfront brimmed with cement and building supplies, piles of grain and lumber, and plenty of horses and oxen earmarked for the American South. Kilbourn, Front, Market, Ferry, and Charles Streets were filled with men who sounded like they were from Barbados, but cursed in a Yankee dialect when demanding dock space. Ship chandlers' were plentiful, and cordage, spars, and other nautical items were in heavy demand.

An old building at 25 Kilbourn Street housed the customs office. Bartlett's tavern did a big business at 11 Ferry Street, while the Ferry Street Hotel at 32 Ferry Street, run by Calvin Sears, later became the first brothel of Mary Ann Atherton. At 28 Ferry Street, the Fifth Ward Hotel did a good trade, and the River Hotel on Charles Street welcomed rivermen and bargemen. On Charles Street, the Steamboat Hotel operated just south of the covered bridge. The Tremont House at 88 Front Street (later a saloon-brothel), like its competitors, did a robust maritime business.[149]

As the wooden covered bridge shifted the business center of the city, Ferry Street declined steadily. When part of the covered bridge washed away in early 1818, the owners refused to rebuild until the state legislature forced the ferry to cease operations. The General Assembly discontinued the ferry company's charter, which touched off a decade of legal battles. In the end, the ferry was doomed—along with the neighborhood. Historians universally hold that no improvements were made on any streets near the waterfront since the completion of the wooden bridge in 1810. More and more, the area served coal companies, lumberyards, warehouses, flophouses, flag taverns, bawdy houses, and a few grocery stores. For a century, the whole district felt like the day after the circus left town.

One of the few businesses that flourished in such a dissolute part of town was prostitution. Just by living in the area, Mary Ann Atherton must surely have learned the rudiments of the trade. Unfortunately, she wasn't an apt pupil. Mary Ann rented "a miserable old hovel" at 32 Ferry Street called the Bluebird, and she brought in some girls, spreading the word as best she could.[150]

Mary Ann Atherton's first arrest for keeping a house of ill repute occurred in November 1863, probably only a few months after her husband's death. Twenty-month-old Edward probably wasn't even walking yet and his mother had an appointment with Judge John Peters at the police court. Peters placed her under a $30 bond "to establish her character for six months." The three prostitutes in her house were allowed to pay only court costs on their promises to leave town immediately. Judge Peters was obviously of the Judge Bulkeley school. A dozen years had passed since Judge Bulkeley reigned over the police court, but prostitutes and madames were still treated with extraordinary judicial restraint. The police and the courts availed themselves of every opportunity to discourage entrepreneurs from getting into the prostitution business.

Mary Ann Atherton thought that she could set up a nice, quiet little business on Ferry Street without making any payments to the police. Since the payment of fines was considered by everyone to be simply a licensing fee—or payments made in lieu of licensing—proprietors of houses of ill repute had to make payments if they expected the police to look the other way.

Regardless of what the court decided about Mary Ann Atherton's character—or what she thought of the city's quaint little payment system—she didn't change a thing. As night follows day, the police arrested her again eight weeks later. This time, the judge fined her $20 and costs, plus a sentence of thirty days in jail.

Apparently, a chastened Mary Ann Atherton finally came to grips with the city's "licensing system" and made her payments like everyone else. After she saw the light, Mary Ann Atherton—who ran the River House almost to the end of her life in 1901—was only arrested once more for keeping a house of ill fame; that came in 1899 when the city had already made the irreversible decision to close the brothels—as the new Hartford Bridge opened for business. Like many other madames, the police sometimes arrested Mary Ann for selling liquor without a license, but it was thirty-five years between her arrests for prostitution. Mary Ann Atherton stayed in the business so long that, in the 1890s, newspapers around the state referred to her as "decrepit."[151]

For her second husband, Mary Ann Atherton chose James Wilson, an illiterate machinist originally from Massachusetts. Recognizing the kind of money that could be made in prostitution, Mary Ann (Atherton) Wilson had no trouble talking James Wilson into building the River House.

At the foot of Ferry Street sat a small grocery store run by "Old Uncle Billy Brown," who lived in the nearby Fourth Ward with his Irish immigrant wife, May, a woman twenty years his junior. Uncle Billy's grocery store made very little money and suddenly burned to the ground in 1870. The first man to sense an opportunity was George Robinson, a forty-year-old English plumber who partnered in Robinson & Nevers on Asylum Street. Robinson sensed that the property could continue making money as a grocery store. Clever with a dollar, Robinson probably knew in advance his return on investment, regardless of the future.

Robinson bought the property and began the restoration process when James Wilson approached him. Wilson was a few years younger than Robinson and the two got on well. Somehow Wilson convinced Robinson to sell the fire-damaged structure so that it could be rebuilt as a four-story hotel on the river. Considering the neighborhood, Robinson probably thought Wilson had gone round the bend, but sold him the property anyway.

By 1871, James Wilson completed the River House Hotel, a four-story, red-brick colossus with expansive porches on the second and third floors. Atop the third floor porch stood a simple asphalt roof. Adding a little panache, a large cupola towered over the whole structure. Owing to the inevitability of the spring freshet, sailboats, rowboats, shells, gigs, and canoes were stored on the first floor. The second floor had a kitchen, sitting rooms and parlors, while guest bedrooms filled the top two floors. Near the River House grew a monstrous sycamore tree, the biggest curiosity of the whole neighborhood. The tree "was probably the oldest tree in Hartford" . . . measuring "twenty-four feet in circumference at the base, and . . . believed to be 300 years old."[152]

By 1880, James Wilson and Mary Ann Atherton were no longer married. Mary Ann drank too much and wasn't a stable helpmate. At some point after 1880, James Wilson gave the River House to Mary Ann Atherton and moved to New York, where he opened a dime museum, an entertainment oddity that flourished in large numbers from about 1840 to 1910.

When the new Hartford Bridge came to fruition at the beginning of the twentieth century, all of the old brothels, flophouses, and saloons along the waterfront disappeared. Along with them went the sailors, drifters, and toughs, who populated the area. Arguably, the largest of these icons of vice was the River House. The Connecticut River Bridge and Highway Commission bought the River House from Mary Ann Atherton's son, Edward, in 1904, and tore the building down in late 1907.[153]

During the Gilded Age, almost every city in the United States had a tenderloin where sex was sold from hotels, tenements, houses of assignation, restaurants, saloons, and cigar stores—almost every place of business imaginable. In 1896, Hartford Mayor Miles Preston said "This city has thirty houses of ill fame—if not more." Even such a sweeping comment did not include all of these disparate outlets. In short, the problem wasn't the thirty houses of ill fame, it was the many other places where sex could be bought and young girls' lives destroyed. More pointedly, no one really understood how big the problem had become.[154]

The houses of ill fame were the pillars of the sex industry. The other outlets were far more difficult to categorize. During the peak of the saloon era—from the War of the Rebellion to about 1900—the number of saloons in the U.S. tripled.[155] In Hartford's river wards—the Fifth and Sixth—the two biggest businesses during these years were grocery stores and saloons. These saloons were the social clubs for day laborers and workingmen. Immigrant entrepreneurs were rare, but immigrants ran many of these saloons. Front Street, alone, had 12-18 percent of all the saloons in the city. (Main Street was the only avenue where there were more.)[156]

According to John J. McCook, a Trinity College professor of the time, the houses of ill repute were not typically immigrant-run businesses. On the other hand, Irish saloonkeepers ran four out of five soliciting places, and seven out of eleven gambling houses. It could be fairly stated that Frank Russell's saloon on State Street and Joe Cronin's place on Front

Street were the forerunners of the saloon-brothel business in Hartford. The number of saloons with backroom operations increased year by year until there were probably twenty or more. These businesses, along with the houses of ill fame, were finally closed in 1911.[157]

Chapter 4

The Demimonde

Once Jennie and Tom Hollister teamed up at the Bange mansion on State Street, business activity edged up nicely. One big difference between the Hollisters and other proprietors was the way they treated their inmates. Unlike Ada Leffingwell and her crowd, they didn't try to make money on the room and board expenses of their girls. Nor did they try to cheat them by playing games with the inmates' brass tokens. By catering to the highest clientele in the city, Jennie and Tom made enough money so that everyone was compensated fairly. Not to make the Hollisters sound like saints among sinners, but they were at great variance when measured against many of the other madames. In the heart of the tenderloin, this was particularly the case with the proprietors of the dives down by the Connecticut River. The houses near the top of State Street were lavish by design and had a better clientele. Not surprisingly, the houses were operated in a more orderly fashion. The farther a patron went down State Street, the wilder—and more dangerous—were the houses of sin.

From Front Street down to Commerce Street—with street numbers between 209 and 257—the houses of ill repute were considered notorious—even depraved. From Commerce Street to the Connecticut River—with street numbers between 259 and 287—the bagnios were life threatening. Knife fights were common, with unidentified bodies later found floating in downriver towns. The saloon-brothels situated on State, Front and Commerce Streets fell roughly into the same category in terms of depravity. Saloons with backroom operations were spread far and wide in the city by the turn of the twentieth century. On Temple Street alone, William C. Dwight, W. W. Hunter, Hibbert "Hub" Smith, and Mrs. Rudolph Davis were the most noted Temple Street barroom-backroom proprietors. By 1900, probably close to fifty hotels, rooming houses, saloons, restaurants, massage parlors, and cigar stores offered prostitution services to guests, customers, or clients.

In the houses of ill fame, conditions inside these dens varied markedly. At the top end of Sate Street, the appointments were lavish and bad behavior almost non-existent. But on the lower part of the tenderloin, very little effort was expended making the "joints" sumptuous or even comfortable. Without belaboring the point, Jennie and Tom Hollister's place was very classy compared to the competition and it was the public behavior of the madames that set the pace. When Jennie Hollister went out to an appointment or to do some shopping, she dressed in a refined manner, but very understated. Other madames flaunted their position in the demimonde and gathered as much attention as they could as they sashayed about the city. These women couldn't help themselves, but the police frowned on this type of behavior. Leading impressionable young girls to think that prostitution was a soft path to a lucrative existence wasn't anyone's idea of how to run an orderly house.

This point can be illustrated by two madames who were the antithesis of one another—Jennie Hollister and "Diamond Lucy" Chapman. As we have seen, Jennie Hollister learned the hard way how to get along in Hartford's tenderloin. She finally acquiesced to "paying her registration fees," and by personal experience and training, Jennie had learned to keep a low profile. Meanwhile, Diamond Lucy Chapman couldn't help but put on an elaborate show as she walked about town. She hid her age well and resembled an eye-catching butterfly—perhaps a painted lady or a great spangled fritillary. Diamond Lucy loved every minute of her walking tours of the city, as young boys—and even not so young boys—followed her around. What woman wouldn't love this?

Lucy bathed in the attention, but her lack of self-restraint was precisely why the police—and maybe some other madames—sought to remove her from the scene. Diamond Lucy's place on State Street got raided more than average, and as she tried to resolve an early arrest in 1878, Judge Arthur Eggleston even suggested—in a fatherly way—that Lucy get out of the business. But Lucy wasn't about to give up the adulation and she rejected Judge Eggleston's kindly advice, soldiering on with her sporting house.

Diamond Lucy Chapman strutted around Hartford for only ten years—from about 1877 to 1887—not as just another pretty madame, but as the "Queen of Bohemia." During this small window of opportunity, Lucy became one of the best-known and most popular women of the Capitol City's half-world.[158]

When she first opened her house of ill fame on State Street, she was forty-seven, but looked more than a decade younger. She fascinated men. Lucy had luxurious clothing and sparkling diamonds that were as big as dwarf potatoes. One particular pear-shaped diamond pendant mesmerized those who adored great baubles. In her day, Lucy probably had the largest collection of stones owned by any Hartford woman—of the half- or the whole-world.[159]

As the Queen of Bohemia, Lucy glided through life. The courtiers who worshiped at her shrine were only too willing to meet her every demand and she swayed life in the half-world for years. Some of the city's most prominent men once considered themselves lucky to be counted among Diamond Lucy's friends. Judges, jurors, lawyers, and businessmen in fair numbers were once on her visiting list. As young bucks, they were proud of the association. But time marched on. If asked about Lucy later in life, these same men would feign ignorance.

As Lucy's old admirers took their places in society, they married women from the finest backgrounds, raised large families, and bought houses "on the Hill." Their friends and families would shudder to learn of the days when a certain pillar of the community followed Diamond Lucy around like a little puppy.

Age caught up with Lucy, and others with youth—and the same deceptive beauty that Diamond Lucy brought to town—gathered up all the concupiscent imaginations of towheaded young boys and pimply-faced young men alike. Lucy stepped aside without remorse. Didn't she have those days all to herself not so long ago? Spiritualism offered Lucy a new avenue of escape. She moved to Boston for a short time and held Bohemian séances. Unfortunately, the Boston police—many of them Irish Catholics—didn't go in much for spirits and séances, and eyed Lucy as suspicious. One step ahead of serious jail time, Lucy returned to Hartford. Late in the 1880s—for reasons no historian has seen fit to record—Diamond Lucy relocated to New Haven.

Diamond Lucy Chapman was born Lucy Ann Rich on March 2, 1830 on a sixty-five-acre farm in Ware, Massachusetts (twenty miles northeast of Springfield). Her father, Jonathan C. Rich, and her mother, Lucy Hardy

Rich, were both reared in Ware and married in May, 1825, when they were in their late teens.

The farm was small. Jonathan Rich, in his early forties, kept one horse, seven cows, two bulls, and a pair of oxen. Each year he managed to raise fifty bushels of Indian corn and twelve bushels of oats. The total value of the farm barely amounted to $1,250 and, as can be imagined, the family barely got by.

Lucy Ann's mother birthed three children—Jonathan C., Jr. in 1826; Otis in 1828; and Lucy Ann, the youngest, in 1830. For some reason, Lucy Ann was born eight miles to the southwest in Palmer, Massachusetts. (The family could have been visiting friends. Alternatively, there might have been a problem with Lucy Ann's birth and her parents sought the help of a midwife or doctor in Palmer.) The youngest child in a family is often a handful—spoiled, wild, willful and manipulative—and that seems true in the case of Lucy Ann Rich. As we shall see, there were times in her later life when she just refused to go along when it would have served her purposes best; she could be pigheaded in matters of little importance.

When Lucy was eighteen she fell in love with Perry Cheever, a laborer from Princeton, Massachusetts (twelve miles to the northeast). The couple married on January 5, 1850, when the groom was twenty-one and the bride only nineteen.

In heartrending fashion, sometime between the wedding and August 14, 1850, Lucy Ann (Rich) Cheever found herself confined to the State Lunatic Hospital at Worcester. Her new husband, Perry Cheever—also at the hospital—acted as Lucy Ann's attendant. The hospital records have long since disappeared, but many physical and mental diseases surface in early adulthood. In view of her later life, schizophrenia seems unlikely, while some form of depressive or bipolar disorder fits the bill nicely. Incidents in Lucy Ann's future behavior buttress this speculation.

Lucy Ann must have responded well to treatment, because she gave birth to her first child, Daniel W., in May 1851. From that date to 1869, Perry and Lucy Ann Cheever had six more children. Perry supported the family as a farmer in Ware, Massachusetts. There are no known signals of trouble, but in 1871, when Lucy Ann was forty-one, the marriage cratered. Much later, a newspaper reporter wrote, "She had diamonds and fine clothes, but in an evil moment, she did something wrong, and she never had the courage to face her people, and asked for one more chance. . . ."[160] Perhaps in a weak moment, Lucy took this reporter into her confidence? We'll never know.

Lucy Ann and Perry Cheever divorced in the early 1870s, and in 1879, Perry married a woman nineteen years his junior, Martha Gates of Barnard, Vermont. Between 1880 and 1889, Martha Cheever had six children. About the time that Martha Cheever birthed the couple's last child, Perry Cheever turned sixty. He died nine years later.

One supposes that the divorce left Lucy with a financial settlement; and soon thereafter the legend of Diamond Lucy Chapman sprung full-blown from the brow of Minerva. By the mid-1870s, when Lucy Chapman opened her first brothel, she was forty-five, but had aged very agreeably indeed. In some ways Lucy seemed like the woman who time forgot, as she aged but barely showed it. In 1904, when Lucy Ann died at seventy-four, a reporter ventured, "Her age has been variously estimated at from forty-five to nearly sixty years."[161]

Lucy hadn't been in business long before trouble visited. Early on a Saturday evening in February 1878, a fight broke out between two brothers at her house. James Crosby got the worst of it, taking a vicious pummeling from his brother Edward Crosby. Chief of Police Walter Chamberlin interviewed the two men and told them to be in police court Monday morning. One of Lucy's inmates, Belle Sherman, launched a complaint against Edward Crosby in an unsuccessful attempt to trim the case to a small-time dust up. In court, Lucy's lawyer made a strong effort to quash the matter but to no avail. The judge saw the fight as something of such a "disgraceful character" that the law had to run its course.[162]

On Saturday night, March 23, 1878, Edward Crosby returned to Lucy's place looking for more trouble. Crosby broke down the front door and threatened everyone inside. Lucy stood in front of her house screaming until Officer Keegan—more than a block away—heard the racket and responded.

Later at the station house, Lt. Cornelius Ryan, remembering the earlier fight at Lucy's house, sent some officers to arrest everyone at the place. Four female inmates and two men were brought to the station house. Along with Lucy Chapman, they all spent the night in lock-up. Oddly, in all the commotion Edward Crosby disappeared. As there wasn't any special complaint against him, the instigator of all the trouble escaped arrest entirely. On Monday, the judge released everyone on a promise to appear in police court on Wednesday, when the matter could be adjudicated.[163]

One small item must be remembered. On State Street, in the heart of the red light district, the bawdy houses were exceedingly competitive. Since Lucy Chapman was attractive enough to eventually become the "Queen of Bohemia," it's most likely that another madame devised this little scheme to create a lasting rift between Lucy and the police. The Crosby brothers made an enormous amount of trouble in Lucy's house from February to March 1878, but neither of them had trouble with the police before or after that time. Though the matter gave off a foul smell, the proprietors or madames behind the trouble kept their mouths shut.

Three months later, a complaint lodged by seventy-six-year-old David Day of Canaan sparked another raid at Lucy's house. David Day claimed that his overcoat and some money were stolen while on a recent romp at Lucy's place. The newspaper reporters renamed David Day, the "Spirit of '76," and wondered in print how he could represent American manhood so nobly and then lose track of his overcoat and money! In any event, Lucy and two inmates were arrested and taken to the station house.

In police court, Attorney Samuel F. Jones—mentioned earlier—represented Lucy on a charge of keeping a house of ill fame. Jones was a Hartford criminal attorney of the first water. In his prime, Jones's name regularly accompanied the most important criminal cases in a fifty-mile radius of Hartford. When he passed away in October 1891, Attorney George Sill eulogized Samuel Jones, "He never attempted to mislead the court or defeat his adversaries by stratagem or ambuscade. He fought his battles in the open field. He was not cast down by defeat or elated by victory. The former he bore with equanimity; the latter with modesty. . . ."[164] It's anyone's guess how Lucy managed to retain such a prominent attorney, but ultimately Samuel Jones straightened out Lucy's legal problems and kept her in business.

Apparently, the aggrieved sport, David Day, came to Hartford looking for work, but mysteriously turned up in Lucy Chapman's house. After losing his coat and money—or thinking that he had—Day returned in March to search the place again. He became an incredible pest when he returned on Friday and Saturday, June 21 and 22, to search even more. Lucy denied that the old guy ever had a coat when he visited her house in January 1878. David Day sounded honest, and even claimed that he had seen several girls in the place. Lucy denied this charge fiercely, saying that since Judge Arthur Eggleston suggested in March that she give up the business, she had no girls in the house. . . . Lucy said that she saw Day and he saw her, but the only other person in the house was a sick girl upstairs.

The judge fined Lucy $50 and costs, plus a four-month jail sentence. No sooner were these words out of the judge's mouth than Samuel Jones announced he would tender an appeal. The prosecuting attorney, Joseph Barbour then sought to reword the indictment from "keeping a house of ill fame," to "reputed to be a house of ill fame." Jones objected to changing the charge after the court proceedings were completed, but Judge Eggleston disagreed, saying that the law allowed it. A couple of Lucy's (past) inmates, appearing as witnesses, were released. The judge forced one of the girls to leave town at the earliest opportunity.[165]

These incidents represent Lucy Chapman's early days in Hartford, and by the existing record, she seems to have gotten things under control without any unnecessary folderol. Lucy, with the help of Samuel F. Jones, managed to run her State Street place for about a decade and then relocated to New Haven.

When Lucy Chapman arrived in the Elm City, the police were in full combat mode against the houses of ill fame. During the Gilded Age, these crackdowns were predictable and they all ran out of steam—just as this one did. About 1890, the Federation of Churches, the Law and Order League of New Haven, and the *Bridgeport Sunday Herald* began attacking the New Haven police for sleeping on the job. Well and good, but these assaults on vice were ill timed. By 1897, sinks of iniquity could be found everywhere. The bagnios were so numerous that respectable neighborhoods from downtown to the harbor were hard to find. Worse still, the proprietors had little fear of the police.

On Worcester Street—near Union Street—sat the London House, featuring the most elaborate furnishings and appointments. The London House had the reputation as the finest sporting house in New Haven. Madame Hattie Goodman wasn't only the queen of the London House, but rumored to be one of the wealthiest women in the state. Men of the highest caliber visited Hattie's place. A reporter asked a conservatively dressed businessman about the London House, and he replied, "It is a respectable place and run in a very clean manner; it is better to let a place of this kind run than some of the others."[166]

Diamond Lucy Chapman found a new home at 10 Prindle Street in New Haven's most deplorable neighborhood. Lucy kept three inmates in her house, and the six or seven disorderly houses on Prindle Street were all run in the same manner. The lower floor served as a waiting room and the upper rooms acted as sleeping apartments.

Soon enough, the reporters from the *Herald* focused on Lucy Chapman's place at 10 Prindle Street. Lucy had set up business with a sometime boyfriend, Johnny Fellows, in 1889. Prindle Street ran off of Fair Street and it was tucked nicely out of the way, even though it was less than a ten-minute walk from the center of the city. Local reporters insisted that Lucy Chapman's house had a reputation as one of the lowest resorts in New Haven.

As public opprobrium built, the raids began. When the trouble began, the madames of New Haven considered the matter a one-time, money-raising effort. Moreover, the men and women who ran the houses of ill fame had been unmolested for so long that they had come to believe that their businesses were in perfect accord with the law and spirit of the times. After one such raid, Judge Julius Cable of the police court fined Lucy $30 plus costs. The fine was paid immediately and Lucy went right back to work.[167]

Lucy Chapman's partner, Johnny Fellows, struck everyone as a strange character. He sported a diamond stud, valued at $600, and a diamond ring worth $300. His entire collection added up to $2000. People thought Fellows independently well off. In truth, he got a monthly stipend from his wealthy father. By 1892, Lucy and Johnny had purchased 16 Prindle Street and continued the same circus. The property remained in Lucy's name to protect Fellows's interest from his wife's legal assaults.[168]

In 1892, the police bore down. Thanks to these efforts, the respectable residents near Fair, Worcester, and Prindle Streets, heaped praise on Captain James Brewer and his police force. To the decent neighbors, the purification of Prindle Street represented the event of the decade. Old-timers were overjoyed as the street was renewed. They rubbed their eyes in surprise and sung to high heaven.

CAPTAIN JAMES BREWER

Facing Prindle Street, but situated on Worcester Street, a Catholic school educated youngsters for decades without any peace at all. Right around the corner sat the old Fair Street Public School, another longtime sufferer. The bizarre atmosphere and depraved characters of Prindle Street annoyed the young students of both schools, but their teachers saw no recourse until Captain Brewer set to work.

When the police had finally broken out all of the Prindle Street houses, one resident gushed, "Today is the first time that the shades in the windows of the Catholic school have been raised. . . . It was an awful evil which the children from both schools were forced to witness [because they were] so close to it."[169]

In 1900, Lucy lived with Johnny Fellows and a collection of inmates on New Haven Avenue in Derby. Lucy's bizarre life wound down slowly, with little to show for the effort but a worn-out body and broken heart. Completely out of ideas, Lucy Chapman was taken to the poorhouse in Bridgeport on Saturday, February 14, 1903.

A reporter noted, "Lucy led a happy life until the spirits got the best of her and she developed into one of those gay young girls who sought 'pleasure at the very mouth of the canon of destruction.' Anyone could have told her that Johnny Fellows wasn't worth the effort, but Lucy loved him with all her heart. As he was forced from city to town, she followed him faithfully. Men once fought to stand in Lucy's shadow. Now she gave Johnny Fellows all that a woman could give but he cast her off. Even so, Lucy just smiled and said, 'A short life and a merry one.'"[170]

Lucy Ann Rich Cheever Chapman's body was discovered in a cheap hotel on Bank Street in Bridgeport on September 25, 1904. Toward the end, even Lucy's diamonds were gone. No relatives claimed the body, so some former associates met at Kelley's Saloon and raised a few dollars to give Lucy a decent burial at Park Cemetery in Bridgeport.[171]

As early as the 1860s, the fair, pure, generous, cultured young women of the world were changing—and it wasn't necessarily a welcome change.

After the American Civil War, while the great bulk of the population sat comatose with grief, those fine, delicate, young girls from the finest homes began marching in a different direction. For English-speaking people, the London newspapers identified it first.

"At one time 'a fine young girl,' meant the ideal of womanhood—a girl with a pure and dignified nature, who would make her husband's house—a home. Her delicacy derived from being treated like a hothouse flower. She would be an attentive mother, industrious housekeeper, and judicious mistress. American men were mesmerized by the languid grace, subtle fire, childlike affection, and vivacious sparkle of the trim and sprightly Gilded Age women."[172]

But the pendulum halted—pregnant with the potential for reversal— and the new woman emerged. "She dyed her hair and painted her cheeks. She dreamed of a life of fun and luxury. She sacrificed decency because she had become too fast to cope with the old morals. The young voluptuary dressed to please herself, and no garment made a big enough statement for her. If a sensible fashion lifted the gown out of the mud, she raises hers to the knee. She used Rowland's Macassar Oil, frizzing her hair like a savage. The fact that her sticky, oily hair left a nasty stain on seatbacks and cushions was of no consequence to her."[173]

"Along with purity of taste, she has lost the far more precious purity of perception. What the demimonde does in its desperate grasp for attention, she also does in imitation. But when she lowers her dress below her shoulder blades, other mothers shelter their daughters. She cannot be made to see that no good girl can afford to appear bad."[174]

"This imitation of the demimonde in dress leads to degradation. It leads to crude slang and bold talk. Moreover, it leads to the love of pleasure and indifference to duty; to the desire for money before love or happiness. Queens of the demimonde seem gorgeously attired and sumptuously appointed, and our young ingénue knows them to be flattered and feted by men of every station. She is hungry for what the women of the demimonde have—but she counts no costs. She sees the gilding, but not the base metal at the core."[175]

"It is this envy of pleasure and indifference to the sins of the demimonde that does the damage. She brushes too closely to them. Her psyche is damaged in ways unknowable. Ultimately, she pays too high a price for the association. Whatever serious thoughts she might give to marriage, she hasn't a clue that, if children come, they would find only the cold welcome of a stepmother. If her husband should awaken to the fact that he has married someone who will spend his money on herself, and shelter her indiscretions behind his good name, he will be the wiser, but too late."[176]

Yes, the demimonde did not operate in isolation. As Jennie Hollister grew up on Market Street, she saw the women of the demimonde walking in the tenderloin—the precursors of Diamond Lucy Chapman—drawing a crowd as they walked fetchingly along. As a schoolgirl, Jennie Hollister slipped involuntarily into the mold of the nice young woman, but she was easily led astray. While other girls had a strong hand on the tiller at home, Jennie Hollister's parents had their own problems and Jennie had no governor on her imagination, yearnings, and actions. She was free to chart her own course. Like so many hundreds of thousands of young girls of the Gilded Age, Jennie chose poorly, but stuck with her choice bravely nonetheless.

Just as the women of the European demimonde embraced tattooing with abandon, so did their American counterparts. In Philadelphia, a physician fresh out of medical school commented on tattoos as an unreliable means of identification when he noted, "The leg mark [presumably a small lady bug, or some such] . . . would be a poor means of identification in this country, for I know of a number of young ladies in this city who have their limbs decorated in a similar manner. . . . Two young wives, whom I attended recently, had crosses tattooed on their limbs, and one young woman I know, had the initials of her favorite suitor pierced in the skin just above the ankle. . . . Among the favorites are serpents with their tails in their mouths, forming a ring, which are tattooed just above the knee."[177]

Among the demimonde, this physician had seen "any number of cases." He stated that most of the female tattooing was performed at the home of the patron . . . and . . . he was of the opinion that the tattooing would spread like wildfire . . . ."[178]

The Philadelphia reporter went to the heart of the city's red light district—6th and Callowhill Streets—to find out more. He visited the house of a tattoo artist and found a chatterbox, attired in plain silk . . . with her fingers stained in India ink.[179]

"I have to maintain much secrecy . . . for many of my patrons belong to the best families. . . . To some it's painful; others not. I have known some to faint while undergoing the tattooing; still others will laugh and joke throughout the entire operation, evincing no unpleasantness whatsoever. . . My best customers are members of the demimonde. . . . Lately they have become almost crazy over it. Still, I have quite a practice among respectable women . . . ."

"Speaking of the demimonde recalls a little incident . . . . Last week I was called upon by one of them to tattoo the name of a well-known politician on her limb, which I did. The next day another woman of the same class called for the same purpose. I remarked to her the coincidence.

Turning around in the chair, she said, 'If any other woman bears his name, tattoo it on the bottom of my foot, so that I may express my contempt for him . . . .' My prices range from $5 to $25, and for more elaborate designs, $50. Most of my customers, however, are of the $5 class, for which some will tattoo crosses, monograms, or circles."[180]

In Hartford, the wild young girls of the demimonde dressed in the most colorful patterns and allowed their behavior to skirt the outer limits of decency. Meanwhile, Jennie Hollister rested at the other end of the spectrum. Her clothing was of the highest fashion—and conservative. Her jewelry matched her clothing perfectly. Jennie did not flaunt herself. She was a stately woman who did not live like a part of the demimonde; neither did she attend their parties. Jennie's clientele came from the upper echelons of society and the business community. If Jennie Hollister must be considered a part of the demimonde, her lofty perch was out of reach for the half-world's rank and file.

A glaring example of the demimonde's disparate worlds springs from a simple night on the town. Much like the *Mardi Gras* in New Orleans, or *Carnival* in Madrid, the annual outing for the members of the demimonde in Hartford over time became the annual Masquerade Ball and Carnival of the Young German-American Association in the Auditorium Building.

Built in 1860, this brick building with brownstone trim rested at 174-188 Asylum Street—just west of the Allyn House (hotel). The first floor featured Emerson Shoes, Oliver Typewriter, O'Brien's Saloon, Fuller's Trunks, and Boston Candy Company. Mundane office space took up the second floor, mostly leased to Robert Weller, the designer and engraver. The Auditorium consumed the whole third floor. The 87- by 100-foot hall rented out for every kind of political rally, concert, dance, and ball. On this night, it was the German-Americans and—though clearly not designed this way at the outset—the demimonde.

This ball took place in the wonderful time between the Franco-Prussian War (1870-71) and World War I (1914-1918), when German-Americans could proudly display their talented singing groups, show off their gorgeous young *frauleins*, boast shamelessly about their ancestry, and drink steins of first-class German beer all night. Of course, this didn't last, as Americans were forced to kill German boys in France during the First World War. This killing lasted until Supreme War Lord Kaiser Wilhelm II capitulated and finally abdicated in disgrace at the end of the conflict.[181]

The wild young girls and boys of the demimonde had no annual ball of their own. However, since the Germans sold tickets indiscriminately—the half-world simply waltzed in and stole the show. There were plenty of townspeople there—especially young girls—but it quickly became the half-world's marquee night as feral young creatures from the brothels tried to outdo one another in their peculiar displays of raw flesh.[182]

The German-Americans—embarrassingly short on taste—went for broke on the decorations. Filling the empty space above the masked dancers and half-clad women were red, yellow, and green Japanese lanterns, silk bunting, and American and German flags in abundance. At floor level, the crowd thrilled to the whirling excitement of brightly-colored costumes, black masks, and the reckless abandon of the fleshpots of another orb.

The affair began with music from the Pope Manufacturing Band. There were two tableaux—the introduction of the Prince and Princess, followed by the Cradle of Liberty, a small patriotic display just to get things started. The real excitement was the kaleidoscope of beer mugs and half-naked females sailing through the air.[183]

When the *jeunesse dorée* of the demimonde were involved, the balls escalated into untamed affairs. People marveled at the extreme youth of the girls. They were anywhere from thirteen to seventeen, and sitting on the laps of men old enough to be their fathers—the everlasting push of December bucks toward May fawns.

But these girls were daring young things who used the arsenic-based Fowler's Solution "to beautify their forms and create clear complexions. Knowing that the solution was poisonous in careless overdoses . . . they had knowledge of the antidote." Fowler's Solution gave the girls' cheeks a wonderful pink glow as it burst the delicate capillaries of the facial tissue. Add some hydrogen peroxide to the hair, and the result fairly screamed "prostitute!"[184]

While on the subject, *Darby's Prophylactic Fluid,* a very popular disinfectant among prostitutes, figured prominently among the cosmetics of young girls of the demimonde. John Darby—a Williams College graduate—taught botany, mathematics, and chemistry. In 1855, Darby began producing *Darby's Prophylactic Fluid,* a simple vegetable product that gained widespread use throughout the country as evidenced by empty *Darby's* bottles found in a long-lost red light district near Los Angeles's Union Depot. Darby helped found East Auburn Male College in 1856, the forerunner of Auburn University.

There's a twenty-first century belief that the makers of snake oil elixirs were all con men. However, John Darby's story does not follow that line. Patent medicines were compounds sold as medical cures—that sadly didn't work. In the final analysis, the words "patent medicine" meant nothing because these worthless compounds could be trademarked, but not patented. A patent would require proof that the miracle drug in question actually worked—and such proof was not forthcoming. One group of patent medicines—salves that allegedly contained snake oil—made pariahs of snake oil salesmen everywhere.

So said, snake oil and patent medicines were not really the concern this evening of the young voluptuaries throwing themselves into the air and across the dance floor of the Auditorium. After midnight, the young girls who did not have on short dresses bunched up their garments to achieve the same effect. The footgear, socks, and underwear (or lack thereof) thrust upon the unsuspecting party-goers was enough to make the drunken throng of spectators shout and scream with approval, surprise, embarrassment, and unleashed animal spirits.

These parties were supposed to be mixed ale affairs, with a little Rhine wine tossed in to make the Germans happy, but beer and whiskey were the real anchors of the evening, supercharging the high times of the revelers.

At the bar, people stood twelve deep waiting for drinks. When served, the drinks disappeared so fast it might be asked why the revelers bothered to get out of line. One of the great puzzlements of the evening lay with the free flow of intoxicants long after all the saloons in town were forced to close at midnight. This trick was the result of a human chain of watchers from the front of the hall to the street. As midnight approached, these watchers snapped to attention.

As expected, a policeman—on his regular patrol—rounded the corner at midnight. The moment he got within a block, word passed along the line and the sale of all intoxicants stopped. When the policeman arrived, soft drinks flowed down the gullets of the alcohol-laden dancers and their partners. The officer inspected the hall carefully, but found nothing and left.

Liquor sales lasted until four in the morning. Of course, the authorities were acting illogically. If they forced a saloonkeeper to pay $450 for a liquor license, they should protect him. But the police couldn't be bothered.

At this annual masquerade ball, there was always a great many girls who were just venturing astray—just starting down the path of dissolution. Some of them were the ones in short dresses and some wore longer gowns. This first masquerade ball launched the party circuit for 1899, and it was well attended. The light and airy entertainment in the early part of the evening passed off nicely, as did the dancing. The respectable *fraus* and *frauleins* were there en masse and having a good time. The costumes were beyond festive and the trim young girls of the demimonde enjoyed the ball enormously. These libertines never dressed down. As far as these nymphets were concerned, these balls existed for them alone. It was their brief, fleeting chance to make a statement.

At this juncture, the bewitching hour descended over the hall, and the respectable German fathers took their daughters home, leaving the ball to the revelers. Saturnalia took wing. Dozens of the best-known girls of the half-world were present. Girls of all classes were there—all sizes, shapes, and conditions. Their vertiginous dancing—the absolute height of the party—got underway bathed in uninhibited depravity and *verboten* antics. The tricks of these girls could not be described in print. And the girls were all churning cauldrons of sin and wickedness. They exposed all sort of arms, legs, chemises, corsets, and underwear at the same time, so that a lightning-fast pair of eyes saw almost nothing. Each girl joined in the *zeitgeist* of the moment, but insisted that her well-turned lower limbs were the only ones that mattered. The thrustful competition showed through wide, white smiles.

After the common council meeting ended at City Hall, nearly the whole board of aldermen attended the masquerade ball. To the great disgust of the girls, the alderman did not offer to buy drinks. Usually the girls could sweet talk these men into financing some of the fun. One of the biggest hits of the evening was a cakewalk done by three State Street prostitutes. These girls had the grace and agility to go into Burlesque—if they could handle the pay cut!

One young girl, sampling the path of wickedness, disappeared from the hall in a heartbeat. A commotion at the door brought all eyes to a black-bearded man followed closely by his tearful wife. Noticing their daughter across the room—and almost before the girl knew what was happening—they marched her out of the hall.

Almost simultaneously, a loud slap rippled through the hall, as a woman in a short dress disciplined a well-known man about town because he got a little too frisky. The woman tried to separate herself from this sport, but because she was sitting on his lap, their limbs were too intertwined for the desired relief.

There were two mysterious dancers, closely masked, who created a great deal of interest. One girl dressed in black and the other in blue. They performed in perfect unison and then disappeared quickly. Later, word got around that the girls lived "on the Hill." These two were a little more adventurous than most society girls.

At three minutes to five in the morning, the last couple left the hall. For one fleeting evening, one tiny shard of time, the reckless, futureless prostitutes of the half-world enjoyed a morsel of unbridled joy. Maybe they even managed to capture a few moments of oblivion—which is what they really wanted. Their nubile young bodies took a terrible beating in the tenderloin, just so they could drink and dance with friends for a few hours here and there. Sadly, this was all that the empty promises of prostitution could deliver.

The demimonde would attend other parties throughout the year, but this night at the Auditorium kept them going—plenty of intoxicants, laughter, joking, dancing, screaming, yelling, with and without boyfriends. The vast majority of these girls reached a fork in the road years before, and chose the path that would deliver the most fun from every precious moment. Lucy Chapman had a husband and seven children, but she still turned to prostitution. Why? Because she couldn't be the Queen of Bohemia on a tiny, backbreaking farm in the middle of Massachusetts. She traded it all for a few glorious moments on the sidewalks of Hartford, lighting up the days with her theatrical dresses, outrageous boas, flowering hats, and sparkling diamonds. As Lucy loved to say, "A short life and a merry one."

Chapter 5

Tom Hollister's Passing

Life at 76 Wells Street seemed idyllic—considering the location and the views—but the workload was crushing. True, there were women hired to cook, clean, and manage the house, but large and small maintenance chores fell to the only man in the place—Tom Hollister. Besides feeding and watering the horses, he maintained the carriages, buggies, and sleighs. If there were household repairs, he had them all to himself. In the wintertime, the coal-fired, steam heating plant in the basement required stoking and banking throughout the day and night. In the bad months, the walks and drive needed cleaning; in the good months, the lawn and gardens required tending.

After the Hollisters finished the remodeling, Lemuel Humphrey's old house was composed of two thirty- by thirty-two-foot rectangles, one behind the other—and offset by six feet. This lovely house of ill repute had steam heat and gaslights in sconces placed on the walls where they would do the most good.

Guests could access the house through the front door—not an inconvenience because there were no neighbors nearby. The building on the north faced Mulberry Street and the home on the south was about a hundred feet from the Hollisters' place. Nevertheless, if a patron sought extra privacy, he could walk the length of the vine-covered side porch and enter through the back section of the house. Either way, he eventually found his way to the front foyer where Jennie Hollister greeted her guests.

The front foyer was an eight- by fourteen-foot space intruded on only by the last few steps of a mahogany-trimmed staircase. On each side of the foyer were huge oak pocket doors that opened to an eleven- by fourteen-foot library on the north, and an eleven- by seventeen-foot parlor on the south. Guests who relished a quiet evening could wait in the library. Those who viewed their sporting evening as an opportunity to enjoy a glass of champagne with the girls—or trade stories with fellow travelers—used the larger parlor on the south side. Near the center of the front part of the house, the stairs climbed alongside the south wall of the foyer. Up against the north wall of the foyer sat a small desk where Jennie kept track of appointments and other matters. A telephone sat on the desk, something new to Hartford in late 1878, and originally embraced only by physicians and druggists. By January of the following year, the humorist Mark Twain installed a telephone at his home on Farmington Avenue. Twain was usually mesmerized by new inventions, but didn't like the telephone much and mischievously characterized the switchboard operators at the Capital Drug Store on Main Street as "call girls." As a final touch, the Hollisters had a beautiful chandelier hanging from the ten-foot plaster ceiling—a source that sent sparkling rays of light in a million different directions.[185]

For entertainment, the south parlor offered a pianoforte with a talented musician hired for the evening. Sometimes, a phonograph delighted guests in the early years on Wells Street; a gramophone followed later. The Hollisters and their guests used these devices as they became available.

Alternatively, a guest could walk east through the dining room to another lounge area in the new addition. (None of the girls' bedrooms or baths rested over the rooms of the main house or this added lounge area.)

The oak hardwood floors throughout were almost completely covered with beautiful carpets and druggets of every description. Luxurious furniture, paintings, and large mirrors—with ornate gilded frames—added a level of warmth and charm that guests appreciated. The girls' rooms upstairs had brass bedsteads, ornate bureaus, and lavish shades on the windows. Two of the girls at the Hollisters' place also had talking parrots that they spent hours training. (More on the talking parrots later.)[186]

All of this made 76 Wells Street the only New York-style parlor house in Hartford. It featured as the dream property of every other madame in the city. In terms of charm, lavish furnishings and ornamentation, Ada Leffingwell offered the only bagnio in town that even came close to the Hollisters' place. (In a real parlor house, the madame lived elsewhere, but beyond this little modification, Jennie Hollister's place closely resembled the parlor houses of larger cities.) By fashioning 76 Wells Street as a New York parlor house, the place represented an untouchable monopoly in Hartford. This allowed the Hollisters to charge exorbitant prices, which their wealthy customers were more than willing to pay.

Behind the main staircase was an eight- by twenty-foot kitchen where the cook made meals for the Hollisters and the girls. In the last section of the old house—along the north wall—extended a pantry plus bathrooms for ladies and gentlemen.[187]

As far as the Hollisters' business, throughout the country there existed a wide variety of houses of pleasure, from the marquee parlor houses of

New York to houses of assignation (even in tenements) to cheap hotels; and, from saloons to cigar stores.

Parlor houses, at least in theory, were used strictly for prostitution. So said, the inmates still lived on the premises. The truly spectacular parlor houses did not exist outside the largest and wealthiest cities. That said, vice investigations conducted between 1910 and 1916 found almost 2,200 parlor houses in almost thirty American cities. Eight of the largest cities— New York, Chicago, Philadelphia, St. Louis, Boston, Cleveland, Baltimore, and Pittsburgh—had more than 100 each.[188]

Much like the inmates of the parlor houses in New York, the girls at 76 Wells Street seldom left unless they needed dresses, jewelry, cosmetics, or toilet articles. An exception cropped up when one of the girls went for a ride in the country or to some public place of amusement with a friend or paramour. On these little excursions, the girls were dressed, gloved, and booted in such a way as to completely hide their occupations. Often, a gentleman mistook a girl from one of the most prominent houses of ill fame for a member of one of the best families in town. It took a practiced eye to make the distinction.[189]

Keeping in mind that the inmates were treated as family while they worked as independent contractors, it should come as no surprise that girls had to pay about $12 a week for room and board, plus a little extra for hairdressing help and any other toiletries and sundries they wanted. Too, they had to pay for all their own clothes, hats, gloves, shoes, and boots.

Breakfast was usually about ten in the morning; dinner—the big meal of the day—was served in the late afternoon; and, supper presented as a catch-as-catch-can-affair, depending entirely upon the demands of the clients throughout the evening.

The young prostitutes were active for about ten hours a day, running from four in the afternoon until approximately two the following morning. Some girls were more popular than others and had little free time in this ten-hour window. Jennie and Tom Hollister's presence usually ensured that bad language didn't slip into the conversation and common decency prevailed. Profanity obviously existed, as men told stories and passed along the jokes of the day, but it was kept to a minimum. All in all, the colorful language remained at a level found in a first-class hotel.

At 76 Wells Street, no bar could be seen. Champagne and other intoxicants were dispensed from a locked closet near the south parlor. Jennie Hollister's mother and father both drank too much—and since Jennie had to rear her sister, Katie, because of her mother's decline into alcoholism—Jennie never lost sight of the ugly side of alcohol. Champagne was a complimentary beverage at the Hollisters' place—a sparkling wine that kept everyone under control. In an unfortunate liquor raid in May of 1895, the police only found a few bottles of vintage champagne in Jennie Hollister's liquor closet. The police undoubted tipped off Jennie in advance and she left the liquor closet full of exactly what she wanted the police to find. From a public relations standpoint, how much would it benefit Jennie Hollister if the readers of the *Courant* and the *Times* discovered that the only thing served at 76 Wells Street was vintage champagne?

At Ada Leffingwell's place—or for that matter any of the houses that encouraged spur of the moment hack parties—the use of hard liquor was common. Ada kept plenty on hand too. Though some of the parlor houses of New York sold guests champagne at $3 a bottle, a wide variety of beverages existed over the whole spectrum of brothels. Again, intoxication had to be avoided because inebriated men caused problems—damaging the furniture, mirrors and paintings—and perhaps even the reputation of the house. Tom Hollister might even be forced to ask a guest to leave, a complete disaster for everyone. Lastly, alcohol can impede performance, perhaps causing an older patron to lose the use of his muffin-topper. *C'est la catastrophe assurée!*

While working, the young prostitutes were expected to dress impeccably in the most exciting fashions of the day and wear their hair in the most flattering styles. The inmates knew instinctively that they had to offer the very best appearance by the judicious use of creams, jells, lotions, pills, and every other advantageous medicine that a druggist could offer. Not surprisingly—since their income derived from their skill with these deceptive medicines—prostitutes of all ages were chemists at heart. If there were any sort of new complexion-enhancing cream on the market, prostitutes were the first to know about it. Also, the madame of the house helped in any way possible to make the girls more fetching and entertaining. The girls were expected to offer intriguing companionship as well; the better the companionship they offered, the higher the rates and tips.

According to census records, "The investigations of minimum wage commissions in various states . . . showed that in the low-paid trades, the average girl received from $5 to $7 a week." This amount does not differ greatly from the average for all women workers in the United States, as given by the U.S. Census of 1900. Howard Woolston wrote in 1921, "It has been shown conclusively that an independent working woman in cities of the North and the East required . . . from $8 to $10, to maintain herself in reasonable health and comfort. The earnings of girls who turned to prostitution must therefore be considered in light of these findings. . . . A

Chicago Vice Report of 1911 gives $70 a week as the average profit for inmates of a representative $1 house."[190]

In 1900, houses were $0.50, $1, $2, $3, and $5. The New York-style parlor houses, of course, got the $5 fee. Considering that the Hollisters had a monopoly on the Manhattan parlor house operation in Hartford, it is fair to assume that an evening at 76 Wells Street fell into the $5 range; the Hollisters could easily have charged more—and maybe did.

With the girls working for the Hollisters, elegance and refinement were achieved nicely. They earned a good week's pay, but room, board, hairdressing costs, toiletries, perfumes, and other cosmetic articles—not to mention dresses, hats, gloves, shoes and other finery—cut into their profits. Everything considered, the inmates paid quite a price to work at such a rarified level in the business.

On the other side of the ledger, the madame and the young prostitutes customarily split the money 50/50. Throughout most of the Gilded Age, madames used brass tokens in the houses. The inmates received a brass token on their way upstairs with a guest. The brass tokens were saved until payday, when they were exchanged for money and then the finances settled. In some houses, the money was exchanged and split every day. That said, the brass token system was replaced in 1910 with punch cards. Just like a railroad conductor, the madame punched a hole in a card—with the inmate's name on it—each time she escorted a guest upstairs. In a 1912 raid, the New York police located the punch cards for January 9th at a notorious W. 28th Street $1 house and found 30 punches on one girl's card.[191]

Young prostitutes had to make peace with the fact that they had to shell out enormous sums of money weekly to earn the plush living they did. Unfortunately, few prostitutes knew anything about saving for a rainy day, or how they would feed themselves after their youth and good looks had abandoned them. It goes without saying that the four girls at 76 Wells Street did not always get along. Women everywhere seem to harbor a certain amount of envy and jealousy, but when one of their own got sick or fell on hard times, there always existed a warm-hearted compassion among the other prostitutes. Bewildering as sounds, just as the prostitutes kicked in the money to buy Diamond Lucy Chapman a decent plot at Park Cemetery in Bridgeport, the women of the demimonde could always be counted on for their big hearts and open purses when one of their own needed them.[192]

Unfortunately for the girls, Jennie and Tom Hollister designed the Wells Street property almost exclusively to entertain wealthy men and there were few amusements for those who lived at the house. On their own time, the girls were often as lazy as cats. Like prostitutes everywhere, they were not interested in sewing or fancy needlework. They might have read one of Jennie Hollister's books, but beyond that, there wasn't much for them. They were particular enamored of leaving the place for a carriage drive or a tryst with a new swain. Without question, Jennie and Tom Hollister took them shopping and driving as if they were members of the family, but this wasn't a weekly responsibility of a proprietor or madame.[193]

Favorites inevitably emerged among the girls, and those who didn't measure up got special help or were forced to cut their careers short. In all businesses, there are average workers and rainmakers. A girl who learned the courtesan business well—and developed the powers to attract and intrigue men—had considerably more value than a girl who hadn't yet developed the subtleties of the trade. Once upon a time, women knew how to gently touch a man's arm when talking to him, or perhaps when pointing out something of interest to him—such a small thing, yet enormously endearing. Still, this little device of the courtesan seems to have been completely lost over time. The favorites in any given house landed more favors and found it easier to get loans for clothes and cosmetics.

While the madames might wish that the inmates could turn off their hearts while they worked, that wasn't realistic. Typically, each girl eventually fell for a certain man. Although incredibly rare, some of the girls had husbands; others had paramours; maybe one of the girls had paired with a sport, gambler, or playboy of the upper classes. Sooner or later, every madame went 'round the bend with a young inmate who fell hopelessly in love with a client. Eventually, the poor girl chased the man all over the country. The deluded inmate dropped everything in an effort to catch up with her paramour, only to discover that she meant nothing to him at all.

Many madames wouldn't permit the inmates to have lovers who live in, or who visit with any regularity. It was just bad business. If a man were allowed to move into the house, the girl would quickly lose interest in the business and pay increasing attention to him. It's the way of the human heart. The prostitution business presented many ironies, but this one was foremost—girls were trained to feign affection, but if they ever truly developed any, their short careers were probably over.

In the simplest terms, Jennie met men as they arrived, while Tom Hollister acted as conversationalist and bartender. Together, they made every effort to make the guests comfortable while the men waited in the parlors. There has always existed an artificial intimacy that a good madame must learn and Jennie Hollister had to use this device to greet guests, make them comfortable, and collect fees upfront without angering the clientele. Guests had to feel welcome while they spent time meeting the girls and making their choice for the evening. Regular patrons, of course, knew the girl they wanted ahead of time.

Jennie also had to manage the girls, helping them with personal problems as well as medical issues. Usually, a madame could handle four girls. If more girls were required, a second madame, or madame's helper, was hired. Since there were four girls working at 76 Wells Street when Jennie Hollister died, we can assume Jennie knew the business quite well and chose to run the place without help.

Generally speaking, the girls had a certain amount of choice in sex matters. It's an emotional business and different girls had different comfort levels. The girls, of course, had sanitary requirements after each session, so they needed time to use the bathroom facilities and recreate that fresh-as-a-daisy look.

Laundry at 76 Wells Street included the personal needs of eight people, plus bedding and towels for four to six bedrooms and baths. The sheets and towels in the girls' bedrooms and baths had to be changed many times a night. Besides the laundry from the second floor, there were kitchen and table items that needed washing and perhaps ironing. Fortunately, there were plenty of Irish laundresses in the river wards, as well as Chinese laundrymen—like the Wah brothers on Main Street or the Chungs on Shelton Street. As long as the laundry could be done cheaply, it would be a waste of time for a madame to attempt such a massive job.

Tom Hollister's health began to fail when he was only sixty-two years old. He had heart trouble, problems with his kidneys, and dropsy (swelling of soft tissues due to accumulation of excess water). He had been ill since the end of 1892 and had not left his bedroom during the five months preceding his death. Though Tom Hollister was the ninth of eleven children, by 1894, he had only two sisters left to think about—Adeline

"Addie" Louisa Hollister of Hartford and Annie Elizabeth Reed of New Haven. His older sister, Annie, had just lost her husband, Edward Reed, in March of 1892, and he seemed such a dynamic man that his loss would be felt for a long time.[194]

Edward Reed was born in Lancaster County, Pennsylvania, in 1821. Beginning his working life in a foundry, Reed switched to railroads in 1843. Five years later, he joined the New Haven, Hartford, and Springfield road, and the Reeds moved to Hartford.

A decade later, when Hartford built its water works, Edward Reed served as one of the five original water commissioners. He knew so much about steam power that he turned out to be an enormous help on the project. The pump house for the water works housed an Elisha Root-designed steam engine to pump Connecticut River water to a reservoir atop Lord's Hill (on Garden Street near Myrtle). As sometimes happened in city projects, the denizens who knew the least about steam engines fell in love with the Cornish engine—an engine designed to pump enormous amounts of water out of the copper mines in Cornwall, England. Though reliable, each cycle of the Cornish engine brought a colossal piston down with such a bone-jarring thud that it would have shaken the pump house apart in just a few years. Thanks to the efforts of Edward Reed and Elisha Root, the public at last got enough information to make the right decision and avoid a terrible mistake.

In 1872, when a number of roads were consolidated, Edward Reed was promoted to superintendent and moved to New Haven. Two years later, he became a vice president. Reed voted Democratic, but the Republican-leaning *Courant* wrote at his passing, "He was a locomotive engineer and could run an engine, and a machinist and could make one, and a civil engineer and could build a bridge or lay out a curve. He was a large man, with good nature marked unmistakably on his face, and he had very many friends in this city, where he lived so long. His wife and both his daughters were with him at his death."[195]

Tom Hollister's sister, Addie, presented a little more delicate matter. She had never married and still lived in the family homestead at 72 Hudson Street. Tom had to make sure that she remained financially comfortable.

His biggest concern, of course, was his wife Jennie. Her health varied. She had good days, but she had bad days too, and running the operation on Wells Street in his absence would be tough on her. The maid, Jessie Lansing, would stay on, as would Annie Wilson, the cook and housekeeper, but life would still be tough for Jennie.

The *Courant* managed a nice obituary for Tom Hollister, even mentioning, "In his younger days, he possessed a good baritone voice and sang at several concerts." In the Gilded Age, a massive double standard existed along gender lines. Tom Hollister could be memorialized as a man "well known about town and to many people throughout the state, while his wife Jennie—in the same obituary—was referred to as "a well-known woman." For Editor-in-Chief Charles Hopkins Clark to allow the use of this code-phrase for prostitute right after Jennie Hollister lost her husband seems beneath contempt, but Clark was known for his tedious rectitude and pompous personality. Be that as it may, the *Courant's* tribute to Tom Hollister sounded much like that offered for Connecticut's immensely popular Democratic Governor Thomas Seymour who died in 1868—"Probably no one man has more friends in the state."[196]

After Tom Hollister's interment at Cedar Hill, Jennie's health began to decline and Angeline Start became a frequent visitor at 76 Wells Street. Angeline liked to think that she offered an enormous amount of advice and counsel during Jennie's last few years, but the evidence suggests otherwise. Jennie gave Tom Hollister's horses, harnesses, and other equipment from the barn to Angeline and Joe Start. She also gave clothing to Angeline regularly and always paid Angie's way when the two of them traveled together. As far as advice and counsel, one reporter laughed and wrote, "Jennie Hollister was not the kind of woman who needed a great deal of advice or counsel."[197]

At 9:00 a.m. on December 27, 1894, Thomas Adams Hollister died of interstitial nephritis (ureamia), a condition in which the kidneys lose their ability to pass urea. Bodily waste (urea) then finds its way into the bloodstream. Tom Hollister suffered greatly from headaches, swelling, and nausea. The funeral began at 2 p.m. on Monday, December 31, 1894 in the big front parlor at 76 Wells Street, and Tom Hollister was buried at Cedar Hill Cemetery later the same day. (In the 1800s, as long as gravediggers could turn the earth with a shovel, gravesite services continued along customary lines. Only when frost made the ground impregnable were caskets stored in crypts until spring.)[198]

Tom Hollister's last will and testament had been drawn up on February 1, 1891. For a man who owned quite a bit of property, the will wasn't complicated. His older sister, Annie Reed, received $500. Since her husband proved so provident in all things, Tom could rest assured that Annie would be fine. Obviously, if she ever needed help, he would be there—or so he thought.

In an effort to set Addie up for the length of her natural life, Tom gave her $2,600 and took back a mortgage for $1,400 on 72 Hudson Street. Better for him to hold the mortgage—which he could simply forgive if necessary—than to have it in the hands of bankers. Lastly, Tom gave the remainder of his estate, both real and personal, to his wife Jennie Hollister, his administrator.

The appraisal of Tom Hollister's estate showed the follow:

½ interest in 76 Wells Street	$4,500
2 horses	$150
wagons, sleighs, and barn app.	$165
cash in banks . . .	$1,247
. . .	$1,078
. . .	$2,244
1st mortgage, 72 Hudson St.	$1,400
farm (New Britain Ave.)	$1,012
1 diamond stud	$100
1 diamond ring	$100
1 gold watch	$85

=============

$12,083

Tom Hollister's physician, Dr. Nathan Mayer, was a Bavarian immigrant. Nathan's father, Rabbi Isaac Mayer—who lost his land during the German revolutions of 1848—served in Cincinnati and Rochester before settling in Hartford in 1859. Isaac Mayer became the first rabbi of Congregation Beth Israel in Hartford on April 1, 1856. Rabbi Mayer, a scholarly man, taught Hebrew and published one of the first Hebrew grammars in the United States in 1854, translated *Sirach* (Ecclesiasticus) into German, and wrote a textbook *The Source of Salvation* for Hebrew schools in 1874.

Dr. Nathan Mayer was born on December 25, 1838, emigrated with his father in 1849, and graduated from the Cincinnati Medical School in 1859. He then returned to Europe for a two-and-a-half-year study-residence at

Munich, Vienna, and Paris. In January of 1862, the twenty-four-year-old physician once again sailed for America and began his medical career as a field surgeon in the Union Army. In March 1862, he was commissioned assistant surgeon of the 11th Regiment Infantry Connecticut Volunteers, stationed in North Carolina. Later, he was promoted to surgeon with the 16th Regiment Infantry Connecticut Volunteers, replacing Abner S. Warner of Wethersfield, who had resigned. The 16th Connecticut wasn't well trained and at the last minute was tossed into the fighting at Antietam—the bloodiest one-day battle of the War of the Rebellion. The regiment suffered 52 percent casualties at Antietam, but fought two-and-a-half months later at Fredericksburg, where they struggled through another bloodbath. Dr. Nathan Mayer was appointed surgeon of the 16th Connecticut on December 24, 1862, and Dr. Warner—who had mustered in on August 24, 1862—resigned on January 9, 1863.[199]

Dr. Mayer was initially entrusted with thirty typhoid patients. He housed them in tents and crude log barracks left behind by the Confederates. Additionally, he trained all of the male nurses, stole a cow for milk, bought some beer to "stimulate his patients—Munich-style," and even oversaw the operation of the kitchen in his spare time.

All the while, Dr. Mayer was responsible for twenty-five smallpox patients who were squirreled away in the woods a half-mile from the typhoid unit. When the soldiers had recovered or been moved to the new hospital at Newbern, North Carolina, he burned everything and returned to his unit. When the 16th Connecticut was captured by the Confederates at Plymouth, North Carolina near the end of the war, Dr. Mayer landed in Libby Prison. He remained there a month, at which time he joined in an exchange of non-combatants. Not long after, he became a brigadier general and served as medical officer for the Union soldiers at Newbern. Dr. Mayer mustered out in 1865 and returned to Hartford.

In civilian life, Dr. Mayer became one of the finest physicians in central Connecticut, running his medical practice from an office on Main Street while living on Pearl Street. As surgeon general of Connecticut under Gov. Marshall Jewell, Dr. Mayer wrote an 1873 report on the state's prisons and jails. Like his father, Dr. Mayer was a scholar, known as a writer, poet, and music critic for *The Hartford Times* over a span of forty years. As a founding member of St. Francis Hospital in 1897, Dr. Mayer enjoyed an estimable position in the medical field. In early May 1912, he entered Hartford Hospital with weakness of the heart and a general breakdown of his system. Two months hence, in the late afternoon of July 10, 1912, he breathed his last.[200]

Tom Hollister's passing was discreetly noted in the local papers, but newspapers like the *Bridgeport Sunday Herald* found it cause for lusty satire and comic bacchanal. Bridgeport has always been a blue collar manufacturing city—and the home of legendary hucksters like P.T. Barnum—but the Park City trailed Hartford in residents. In 1900, the population figures for Hartford and Bridgeport were roughly 80,000 and 70,000, respectively. Also, during the Gilded Age, the per capita income in the Charter Oak City was the highest in the country, while Bridgeport lagged considerably. Additionally, since Hartford was the Capitol City of the state, it would always outshine a smaller manufacturing city. Bridgeport had a chip on its shoulder and always ached to humiliate the Capitol City in print. With this in mind, Tom Hollister's obituary in the *Sunday Herald* served Bridgeport's needs well—

> The funeral of the late Tom Hollister took place from the family's residence, No. 76 Wells Street, this afternoon at 2 p.m. and was largely attended by the friends and relatives of the dead philanthropist. The

services were conducted by Rev. E. S. Westcott, a lifelong friend of the deceased. A quartet of female voices, Misses Eva, Fanny, Cora, and Hazel, all of whom have for some time been members of the household of Col. and Mrs. Hollister, furnished the music. The selections were Watts' charming hymn *Her Golden Hair Was Hanging Down Her Back*; Cardinal Newman's *I'm A Little Too Young To Know,* and Tennyson's *O, The Midway.* [The first two stanzas of the Watt piece tell the whole story.]

> There was once a country maiden came to London for a trip
> And her golden hair was hanging down her back
> She was weary of the country so she gave her folks the slip
> And her golden hair was hanging down her back.
>
> It was once a vivid auburn but her rivals called it red
> So she thought she could be happier with another shade instead
> And she stole the washing soda and applied it to her head
> And her golden hair came streaming down her back.

The honorary bearers were men of various secret disorders in this city. Among the floral arrangements was a wreath of immortelles inscribed: "To My Old Landlord From A Reclaimed Woman;" a bank of flowers inscribed: "From Hazel;" a broken column from the *Courant* staff; and "a white dove carrying in its beak a card upon which was written: 'I will see you later—Tate.'"

A large assemblage from all walks of life attended the funeral. It has been ordered that the court go into mourning for three months.[201]

Rev. E. S. Westcott was Attorney Edwin S. Westcott, an ornery, erratic lawyer from Glastonbury. About six months after Tom Hollister's death, Attorney John Hooker asked Westcott to collect $200 from a client, yet

Hooker never saw the money. Westcott claimed that the money was needed for "medical purposes," and then ignored the matter. In turn, John Hooker launched a complaint with the Hartford bar. On May 28, 1895, Judge John M. Thayer disbarred Edwin Westcott "for conduct unbecoming a member of the bar." Westcott's life collapsed thereafter. His wife, Olive, sued him for divorce in 1900, claiming that he had deserted her on April 23, 1897. The last anyone heard of Edwin Westcott, he resided in Scranton, Pennsylvania, while working feverishly on a new patent medicine.[202]

The song *And Her Golden Hair Was Hanging Down Her Back* was an 1894 popular song released on Berliner Records by Dan W. Quinn. Monroe H. Rosenfeld wrote the song—with music by Felix McGlennon. The satirists at the *Bridgeport Sunday Herald* attributed the "hymn" to Isaac Watts, the eighteenth century English hymnwriter, in an effort to heighten the humor and avoid any copyright problems, since the newly released song came out very close to the time that they composed this parody of Tom Hollister's obituary.

The "I will see you later . . . Tate" reference traces to Nahum Tate's 1681 rewrite of Shakespeare's *King Lear* entitled *The History of King Lear.* Tate's version is similar to Shakespeare's, but features a happy ending.

Tom Hollister probably knew that his fifty-eight-year-old sister, Addie, was seeing a gentleman, because only five months after his passing, on June 5, 1895, she married Omri R. Brewer, a seventy-one-year-old farmer from East Hartford. Addie Hollister was a noted cook and baked all the pies for the café at Brown, Thompson & Co. on Main Street. The wedding took place at Addie Hollister's homestead on Hudson Street and the bride and groom planned to live on the Brewer farm in East Hartford. In preparation for married life, Omri Brewer had extensive renovations done to his home on the corner of Main and Willow Streets.[203]

Sadly, the marriage of Omri Brewer and Addie Hollister wasn't necessarily what Addie needed. She died only three years after her wedding and was buried at Cedar Hill with her parents, Joseph and Louisa, as well as her brother, Tom, and his wife, Jennie Hollister. Omri Brewer is not buried with Addie.[204]

Chapter 6

To Every Season

Jennie and Tom Hollister made an unbeatable business couple because they complemented each other so well. Tom Hollister was such a likeable person that meeting and entertaining politicians and businessmen from all over Connecticut turned into the easiest part of his job. He seemed at peace with his choices in life and was considered a boon companion. Meanwhile, Jennie Hollister had become the perfect hostess. An evening at 76 Wells Street—in the days before mass entertainment—tempted more than its fair share of men.

Not to argue that houses of ill fame competed directly with other types of evening entertainment, but it should still be considered that options existed. There were opera houses, theaters, and concert venues all around town. Gone were the days at mid-century when the incomparable Jennie Lind—the Swedish Nightingale—had to perform at the Fourth Congregational Church on Main Street and bill her concerts as religious recitals.

The Robert's Opera House on Main Street had been taken over by Jacobs & Proctor in 1886. Jacobs & Proctor's Opera House began their run by completely renovating the theater. They even installed a telephone so that patrons could reserve tickets without leaving home. Jacobs and Proctor's offered everything from grand opera to traveling indoor circuses. (Vaudeville didn't hit Hartford until 1910.) Despite the best of intentions, and a laudable pile of improvements to the theater, the partnership of Jacobs and Proctor only lasted a couple of years, after which Frederick Proctor worked alone until 1896. After that, the Hartford Opera Company leased the building. Competitors included Allyn's Opera House on Asylum Street, numerous variety shows at Germania Hall, and the Horse Guard Armory on Main Street. The biggest auditorium in the city, Foot Guard Hall, was located on High Street and hosted the Governor's Ball among other extravaganzas. Additionally, there were a dozen billiards halls and several bowling alleys. Though P. T. Barnum died in 1891, his circus—and its descendant, Barnum & London Ten United Monster Shows—still toured the eastern United States, usually hitting Hartford in early June. (It would take a very poor businessman indeed to close a show that made a profit of $10,800 in just two days!)[205]

The early 1890s offered more amusements than had been seen before. Even the Panic of 1893 did not alter the great shift in American life. The Republican President Benjamin Harrison had three favorite hobbies: billiards, driving, and shooting. So said, in 1889, Connecticut Senator Joe Hawley went duck hunting with President Harrison and four other men in Cypress Swamp on a James River estate belonging to the president's Virginia relatives. During that outing, President Harrison—an arrantly bad shot—mistook a farmer's hog for a coon and dispatched the fat "porker" with great panache.[206]

The demimonde grew in the Capitol City each year, right up to the turn of the century. There wasn't anything to alter the girls' wicked ways, especially those who were just starting down the path of ruination. The Hollisters had become the oldest members of the Capitol City's prostitution business. For this reason alone, they were completely separated from the unbridled younger members of the half-world. In 1890, Tom Hollister celebrated his sixtieth birthday, while Jennie turned forty-eight. At the same time that the flighty young girls in the tenderloin worried only about the next party, the older proprietors and madames were drawing up wills—Tom Hollister's will was penned in 1891 and Jennie's in 1893. Still, new characters heard the *Lorelei's lieder* of the wide open city on the Connecticut River and steered a course toward the Capitol City's tenderloin district.

Billy West was arguably the biggest sport that ever lived in Hartford. When it came to fast girls, horse races, or prizefights—not necessarily in that order—Billy could never get enough. His exploits were a constant topic of conversation in the half-world and he ran one of the best houses of ill repute—Jennie and Tom Hollister's former house, the old Bange mansion on State Street.

Billy's real name was Ernest H. Stetson and he came into the world on January 21, 1862, in the small farming town of Ashfield, Massachusetts—twelve miles southwest of Greenfield. His father, James M. Stetson, worked as a farmer and stableman, and married Janey Bard at Halifax, Vermont, in 1858. Ernest Stetson's grandfather, Merritt Stetson, owned a stagecoach company and his son, James M. (Ernest's father), drove stages until he turned to farming when he was twenty-three.[207]

On April 6, 1864, James M. Stetson joined Company H of the Massachusetts 57th Regiment, organizing at Worcester and Readville. A month later, James M. Stetson and the 57th Regiment stumbled into the Battle of the Wilderness, torturously played out from May 5-7. James Stetson suffered serious wounds in battle, and on May 30, 1864, in a dreary hospital tent in rural Virginia, he died of his wounds. Stetson served for only fifty-five days. During the War of the Rebellion, many soldiers were given a $15 Springfield muzzleloader, taught to march in formation and were dead two months later.[208]

When James M. Stetson died, his son, Ernest, was only two. The boy, of course, never knew his father, and when Ernest was only seven, his mother, Janey, married a Vermonter ten years her senior, George D. Belcher. Janey's new husband worked as a machinist. George and Janey Belcher—along with Ernest Stetson—settled in Chicopee, Massachusetts. Ernest remained an only child until he turned nineteen. In 1881, Janey Belcher produced another boy, Fred Belcher. Stepfather and stepson continued to get along well. Ernest learned the machinist trade from George Belcher, but the younger man wasn't happy turning and filing machine parts in a noisy, smelly manufactory. He longed for something better. Beyond his restlessness in machine work, Ernest had an unquenchable thirst for life. He dressed in loud clothes and his friends were the riffraff of the half-world. He loved fast women, houses of ill fame, the National Trotting Circuit, and bare knuckles prize fighting. In short, he chased action with abandon all his life.[209]

While still living in Chicopee, Ernest became involved with an eighteen-year-old girl who was wilder than an acre of snakes. She used the name "Cora Bordeaux" and claimed Windsor, Connecticut, as her birthplace. Regardless of her real birth name or where she grew up, on October 18, 1884, Ernest Stetson and Cora Bordeaux were married in Chicopee. A married man now, Ernest Stetson decided he needed a better job, so he finagled work as a contractor at the Warwick Cycle Mfg. Company of Springfield, Massachusetts. George T. Warwick founded the company in 1888 to build bicycles, but failed in 1890. Local capitalists reorganized the firm and bicycles were built until 1899 when automobiles were added to the mix. The company became the Warwick Cycle & Automobile Co. Unfortunately, the business folded in 1905, about a decade before the Pope-Hartford Automobile Company closed its doors in Connecticut. The Midwest became the center of the nascent automobile business and none of the New England auto companies were able to meet the brutal competition.

While at Warwick Cycle Mfg., Ernest Stetson learned from a co-worker that the really fast money was in vice—above all, houses of ill fame. Not much later, thirty-one-year-old Ernest Stetson left Warwick Cycle of Springfield in favor of Hartford, Connecticut and started using the name Billy West. Instead of taking his new wife, Cora, to Connecticut—in his Lotharian way—he brought along another member of the fast set, Grace Howard.[210]

Grace Howard was an attractive, fun-loving woman with a Rubenesque figure, who had been out behind the barn a few times. There was nothing wraithlike about Grace Howard, but she fascinated men. In addition, she had somehow picked up the rudiments of running a house of ill fame. When Grace Howard and Billy West took the train to Hartford in 1893, she was twenty-eight. It's dangerous to attempt to calculate where a young woman descended into the irredeemable abyss, but in Grace Howard's case, it may all be traceable to her father's sudden death—under some truly ugly circumstances.

Grace's real name was Smith. In early 1887, her father, Henry Smith, had been sworn in as a "Special" Deputy Marshall. Along with two friends,

Smith formed a three-man posse for Deputy U.S. Marshall John Phillips, on an ill-fated assignment in Oklahoma. In truth, Henry Smith worked as an Internal Revenue Agent in New York, but since 1872, U.S. Marshals had helped revenue agents—who didn't have arrest powers—in the enforcement of whiskey laws, including those in Indian Territory. Keep in mind that before the days of personal income taxes, the federal government had limited sources of income. Tariffs on imports and taxes on whiskey were two of its biggest revenue streams and agents of the government were obsessed with the collection of whiskey taxes to the point where they would break up stills and chase down a single Indian over a few bottles of firewater. So said, John Phillips—and his three-man posse of Eastern greenhorns—headed for Oklahoma.[211]

The marshals arrested Seaborn Green (Kilajah), an eighteen-year-old Creek Indian who the Feds wanted on a federal whiskey charge. The marshals of the posse established a camp near Hillabee, Indian Territory, while John Phillips rode to Eufaula on business. The three remaining deputies took turns watching Green during the night, but somehow he got hold of the camp hatchet and butchered all three marshals. Adding insult to injury, Green then burned the men's bodies. When Phillips returned, he was aghast, but buried his friends before tracking down Green. Phillips arrested Green on January 28 and brought him to Fort Smith. A jury found Seaborn Green guilty of three counts of murder, and on October 7, 1887, he was hanged near the courthouse at Fort Smith.[212]

Because Grace Howard's father worked as a lawman, just like Tom Hollister's father, the Hartford police gave her special treatment. Sometimes they were forced to include her house in a big raid, but they usually charged her with serving liquor without a license instead of keeping a house of ill repute.[213]

Amusingly, the Chicopee-Springfield sporting crowd seemed hopelessly unimaginative when it came to aliases. Grace Smith probably took the alias Grace Howard because Billy West grew up at 33 Howard Street in Chicopee. Also, Cora Stetson's grandfather, William "Billy" West had a farm in Dalton, Massachusetts. Lastly, when Billy got his first resort on State Street in Hartford, he hired Dottie Emmons as one of his inmates. More than a decade later, Billy took the name William Emmons when he opened a bordello in Norwich, Connecticut.[214]

The plan—if anything Billy West ever put together could be called a plan—was to have his wife, Cora Stetson, join him in Hartford after he secured a lease on a sporting house and got the place up and running. When Billy West and Grace Howard hit Hartford, they pooled their money and bought out the lease of Lizzie Cadwell at 165 State Street—the Bange mansion. Levitt Knoek, a pawnbroker and hardware dealer at 188 State Street, owned the property. This house was the same place Jennie and Tom Hollister ran from about 1870 until they moved to 76 Wells Street in 1883. Perhaps influenced by all the fictitious names of tenderloin characters, Knoek began calling himself "Knock" in his newspaper advertisements. The tenderloin churned with illusion and fantasy, so one could blame a long-established businessman for joining in the nonsense.

Knoek had to remain in the dark regarding Billy and Grace's plans for the property—or at least maintain plausible deniability—because some of the city's religious leaders hounded the police relentlessly about closing the brothels. One of the clerics' favorite dreams was to go after the landlords of Hartford's tenderloin buildings. The clerics felt that if sufficient pressure were put on the landlords, the houses of ill fame would close. Well and good, but by the 1890s State Street sported so many bawdy houses that Knoek would have been surprised if Billy West and Grace

Howard had other plans! So the two Springfield entrepreneurs simply walked in and continued Lizzie Cadwell's business. Billy West and Grace Howard turned the old palace of sin into the city's newest and most palatial den of iniquity.[215]

Before doing anything else, Billy met with Chief of Police George F. Bill and paid the necessary "licensing fees." In the course of business, clients often asked why his place wasn't raided. His answer? "We have never been bothered by the police because we 'fixed' things with the authorities."[216]

Chief of Police George F. Bill

Impatience dogged Billy West. Instead of sitting back and waiting for patrons to appear, he went out to promote his business. West walked up into Statehouse Square and took a position directly in front of the United States Hotel—on the north side of the square—where he chatted up traveling salesmen who frequented the hotel's reading rooms. Slowly, he brought the conversation around to the sporting life. If the salesman showed interest, Billy would direct him to the Bange mansion. Of course, West never had time to go with the man, but promised to catch up with him later.[217]

Eventually, the proprietors of the United States Hotel asked Billy West to move on, and he pulled the same stunt at Prospect Street's Brower House. In the process of drumming up business in front of the Brower House, Billy became good friends with William "Bill" Crowley, one of the partners in the hotel and another disciple of the sporting life. Crowley later sold his interest in the Brower House to his partner Morgan Sherman and opened a hotel in Old Orchard Beach, Maine. Just as always happens when kindred souls meet, Bill Crowley and Billy West became close friends and spent considerable time at the racetrack and at prizefights. Despite this newfound bond, even Crowley had to ask Billy West to hustle up business somewhere else besides the front steps of the Brower House.[218]

WM. "BILL" CROWLEY

As an aside, the Brower House eventually wound up in the hands of the Connecticut River Banking Company. The bank's officers knew that it was a house of ill repute, but decided that they would simply let it run. Unfortunately, a big depositor of the bank created a fuss and the bank had to sell the Brower House. It reopened in 1900 as the Hotel Climax, an all-male rooming house. As could have been predicted, the boarders had more girls in and out of the Hotel Climax than were there when it was the Brower House; the sale accomplished nothing.[219]

The Bange mansion under Billy West featured very young girls and many of these girls were from Springfield. One especially exotic filly almost closed the place in her first week. She was only sixteen and when this fact came to the attention of the Chief of Police George Bill, he told Grace Howard to send the girl packing. At first, Grace did as she was told, but the young girl proved too great an attraction and Grace begged her to return, offering protection from the police in the deal.[220]

With that kind of attention to detail, it wasn't surprising that the Bange mansion enjoyed a new lease on life and prospered mightily during the inappropriately named "Gay 90s." Grace Howard had all the élan of a talented madame, and later claimed that she made Billy West $2,500 in the two years that she ran the place.

Billy West had been enjoying the sporting life for about two years when his wife, Cora Stetson, arrived in Hartford. Of course, now she would use the name Cora West. Since Grace Howard and Billy West were not expecting Cora, trouble erupted immediately. Billy solved this little dilemma by convincing Grace Howard to leave, so that Cora could run the house. Grace assumed that her friendship with Billy would continue, but when she later needed a $50 loan, Billy gave her a huge horselaugh—textbook Billy West.[221]

As a result of their 1884 marriage, Cora last name was technically Stetson, while her husband strutted around Hartford as Billy West. After Cora cemented her position as the madame at 165 State Street, she pressed her advantage by forcing Billy West to marry her again. They became William and Cora West in 1895. However, marriage meant so little to Billy West that the license was practically worthless. Sadly for Cora, Billy West had the attention span of a child. The only ironclad fact that Cora could bet on with any certainty was that Billy would eventually leave her. The characters of the demimonde had no loyalty or commitments—only appetites.

With Cora running the State Street place, the money continued to pour in. It was about this time that Billy West established his reputation as a sport. "He attended all the prize fights, and became chummy with Adolph "Al" Russell, Jim Campbell, "Harry" Rosenthal, "Mo" Harris, Jim Manion and others of the Capitol City sporting crowd. He wore fancy clothes and spent exorbitant sums of money. While sitting ringside at the fights, he became friendly with a couple of New York sports—Herman Rosenthal and "Billiard Ball Jack" Rose, who suffered from *alopecia universalis,* an ailment that caused the complete loss of hair on his body.

Jack Rose became a nationally-known fight promoter and lived in Hartford for a time. Rose partnered with Mo Harris in the Charter Oak Athletic Club (1891), and he was constantly starting "joints" like the Tremont Hotel in Bridgeport, a future gambling Mecca he bought in 1898 with Al Russell. He also had the Jack Rose Social Club on Main Street in Hartford (1902) and the Grand Athletic Union in New York (1908).

Herman Rosenthal had amassed quite a bit of money with New York gambling houses, but he was a world-class complainer. To restore harmony among the New York sports, Jack Rose arranged for four gunmen to silence Rosenthal for good on July 16, 1912, in front of the Hotel Metropole on W. 43rd Street. The four gunmen—Harry "Gyp the Blood" Horowitz, Louis "Lefty Louie" Rosenberg, Frank "Dago Frank" Cirofici, and Jacob "Whitey Lewis" Seidenshner—were executed on April 13, 1914 at Sing Sing, while another behind the scenes puppeteer, New York Police Lt. Charles Becker, sat through a similar fate at Sing Sing on July 30, 1915. Jack Rose was the only one who walked. Though Rose never stopped looking over his shoulder, he died of natural causes in 1947.[222]

The New York gamblers played rough, but Billy West was more of a lover than a fighter. In the spring of 1897, beautiful, petite Gertrude Camp caught Billy's eye. Gertie was one of the hundreds of girls who worked at Plimpton Manufacturing Company on Pearl Street—the source of all U.S Government stamped envelopes after 1874. Plimpton's didn't exactly have a reputation for its outrageously good-looking women, but the company really set a standard when it hired Gertie Camp and her friend Maggie Doyle—two legendary head-turners. Apparently, each of these girls spent the evening hours discovering their special talents, and after confidences were exchanged, they decided to go into business together.[223]

One reporter daydreamed, "Maggie Doyle is a pretty girl, a very pretty girl, one of those plump, squeezable girls that makes one think of love, lusciousness, voluptuousness, and so on. . . ."[224] Unfortunately for the girls' new business, a tall, dark stranger from Springfield caused Maggie to swoon and the lovers relocated to New York's tenderloin district. Some members of the demimonde swore he was a lawyer; a few said he had come into inherited wealth; still others claimed that he descended from a very respectable old Springfield family. The only thing that everyone agreed on was that no one knew his real name—and probably no one ever would.[225]

Of course, all this romance left Gertie Camp high and dry, but Gertie was a beauty and a real charmer. Not long after Maggie left town, Billy West fell hard for Gertie. He set her up in a lavish set of rooms on Church Street and began spending his free time there while Cora kept an eye on the Bange mansion.

In the summer of 1898, Gertie Camp captivated everyone at Charter Oak Park, the horse track in the Elmwood section of West Hartford. (In 1874—a year after Burdette Loomis opened Charter Oak Trotting Park on

New Park Avenue—the train station in southeastern West Hartford took the name Elmwood.) Charter Oak Park had never seen such a beauty. Billy West was floating on air and after the season closed at Charter Oak Park, he and Gertie began to follow the National Circuit Trotting races.

Billy West had plenty of time for Gertie Camp in the summer of 1898, thanks to a visit by Secretary Samuel Thrasher of the Law and Order League of New Haven. This upstart group demanded that all the houses of ill fame in Hartford be closed, which put Chief Bill in a tough spot. Hartford's reputation as a wide open city put enormous pressure on Chief of Police George Bill, and though he received his marching orders from the mayor not Samuel Thrasher, he simply had to do something. So in early May, Chief Bill sent the following notice to all the brothel keepers—

To_____:

Owner, Agent or Lessee of No. _____Street.

You are hereby notified that the above premises are used as a house of ill fame. Under the Statute (Section 1,531) if you permit your premises to be used after notice from an officer of the community, you are liable to a fine not exceeding $500, or imprisonment not more than six months. This notice is given in accordance with the above law and for the purpose of carrying out its provisions.

Respectfully,

GEORGE F. BILL

Chief of Police[226]

According to Chief Bill's order, the houses of ill fame had to close by July 1, 1898, or he would personally drive the proprietors out of town—as the statute provided. Owing to this memorandum, the fast women of Hartford were in a dither. Some were going out to the roadhouses near New Britain and some to a roadhouse on East Windsor Hill; others were preparing to open new houses in the suburbs; still others took up residence with friends. While everyone else scrambled, Billy West closed his place on State Street and took Gertie Camp to the races. As long as the money lasted, a long vacation wasn't a bad idea. But trouble followed Billy West around, probably because he was such an inveterate plunger. At Cleveland, in the middle of August, Billy bet almost everything he had on a horse—and lost. Three weeks later, Billy and Gertie were back in Hartford.[227]

When Billy West and Gertie Camp returned in September 1898, everything had changed. Gertie returned to her lavish digs on Church Street and Billy reopened the Bange mansion—but it wasn't the house of old. Billy West was scrambling. Now he was without the fancy diamonds he used to wear on his fingers and couldn't even afford a good winter coat. Though counterintuitive, all of the houses did not close when Chief Bill issued his threat. Some proprietors defied his order and, in no time at all, the vast majority of them were back in business.

Nevertheless, in the three months that the Bange mansion was closed, State Street had lost its reputation as the heart of the tenderloin. Grace Howard opened a bordello on Trumbull Street with her lover, Harry Arnold. From there, she rented rooms in a building on Upper Main Street—the 500 block—at Needham's Corner, a quarter mile north of Statehouse Square. Later, she leased rooms above *The Hartford Times* on the corner of Main Street and Central Row. Though Ada Leffingwell tried to groom Grace Howard to take over 5 Arch Street, Grace ultimately turned back the clock and took the Bange mansion off Billy West's hands in late 1901.[228]

The Law and Order League of New Haven operated as the most questionable municipal reform group. It first came together in 1884, using the Citizens Law and Order League of Massachusetts as a model. The group never achieved any semblance of professionalism and proved ineffectual under its first president, Mark S. Chapman of Winchester, Connecticut. In 1893, a reorganized Law and Order League arose under Secretary Samuel Thrasher, a grandstanding egomaniac who was determined to clean up the State of Connecticut with "piratical police work."[229]

Thrasher made enemies. Rather than convincing the police of his seriousness in stamping out vice in the state, he quickly got the reputation as a craven grandstander. In New Haven, Police Superintendent James Wrinn prepared to raid three illegal "policy" shops when Thrasher, with his Law and Order League, ran a raid two days in advance of Wrinn's sortie. He did the same thing to the New Haven police in March 1900. Since the policy writers knew every cop in the city, the collecting of evidence proved difficult. Meanwhile, Thrasher collected the evidence quickly because "he hired 'passe' ministers, jailbirds, and students hungry for a few dollars." Quickly then, Thrasher ran his own raid.[230]

CAPT. JAMES WRINN

167

For the longest time, Samuel Thrasher refused to visit Hartford. When pressed, he said privately that it served the League's interest best—financially—to leave immoral Hartford to her fate. But the newspapers came down hard on Thrasher. "There is more wickedness to the square inch in Hartford today than there is in any of the cities which the [League] has visited; still, Hartford is given the go-by in the league's action. . . . The immoral condition is so well-known that people looking for a good time leave Bridgeport, Waterbury, New Haven, Stamford, and other cities, to visit Hartford and have their time out. . . . "[231]

Samuel Thrasher's integrity was on the line and he at length had no choice but to visit the Capitol City. The work of the Law and Order League, coupled with pressure from the muckraking *Bridgeport Sunday Herald*, began taking a toll on Chief of Police George Bill as well as Hartford's Democratic Mayor Miles Preston (1896-1900), not to mention his successor, Republican Mayor Alexander Harbison (1900-1902).

MAYOR ALEXANDER HARBISON

Samuel Thrasher's Law and Order League conducted a series of liquor raids in Hartford. One January, the Law and Order League raided several drugstores on liquor law violations. In February of the following year, they raided fourteen disorderly houses and found wine and beer in ten of them.

168

The owners were arrested for selling liquor without a license and were forced to appear in police court.[232]

This annual visit seemed like the most absurd farce that any city had to endure. The proprietors weren't molested for a whole year, and then the Law and Order League showed up for a little winter housekeeping. Not only did this antagonize the local police, it irked the public because Thrasher's bunch acted like interlopers.[233]

Samuel Thrasher's power grew for a decade, but eventually the public turned against the Law and Order League because it secured evidence against liquor dealers by entrapment, which fair-minded people disdained. Sensing an end to his game, Thrasher pitched the General Assembly on the idea of a state police department, which would replace the Law and Order League. Naturally, Thrasher hoped to land the top job, but he got nothing. The Connecticut State Police Department was organized in 1903, with Superintendent Thomas F. Egan of Southington at the helm and Arthur L. Story of Norwich acting as his assistant.[234]

Hartford's Chief of Police George Bill had adopted a hard line, but ten months after he had given the written orders to close, most of the old houses were back in business and new ones were springing up like weeds—in previously respectable neighborhoods. Beyond that, the number of streetwalkers reached a new peak. It was time for another raid. Chief Bill planned this latest raid meticulously and waited patiently at the station house for the madames and their inmates to arrive. Later, Chief Bill said outright that this new raid resulted because his order to close on July 1, 1898 had been ignored. The proprietors and madames had discounted all risk in the name of profit.

On St. Patrick's Day in 1899—beginning just before midnight and lasting until two in the morning on March 17—the Hartford police staged their biggest raid yet. Over forty women of the half-world crowded into the muster room of the new police station on Market Street. The massive room, with its big white pillars, resembled a stock exchange, with all the houses of ill repute represented. The madames and girls of each house were clustered together in groups around the big room. Like members of different trading firms, the girls from each house banded together.

Reporters detailed the important players. Of course, commanding the most attention stood the stately Jennie Hollister "who has lived unmolested for twenty years." And what raid would be complete without decrepit Mary Ann Atherton of the River House, with almost forty years in the business? Last among the big three was Ada Leffingwell. Poor, fat, broken-nosed Ada, wanted desperately to be a class act, but always came up short. Besides these premier madames, and their girls, were the lesser lights who on this special night, were not ignored. The others—who had built their houses on State, Main, Front, Commerce, Market, Ford, Ann, Grove and Temple Streets into something of substance—were there too. Representatives of all the houses passed by the captain's desk with decorum. The mayhem filled a special notebook of the event, and reporters scribbled excitedly, "The scene was a lively one. Messenger boys were scurrying to and fro, darting in and out of the big doors. Hacks drove up and whipped away. Diamonds flash and silken skirts rubbed together. . . . Here and there, a tear was shed, but for the most part, forced smiles filled the room. . . . Some, in evening dress, were protected by seal skin jackets, while all wore head gear profuse with plumes. . . . Outside the closely curtained room, a large crowd of men, boys, and girls, could be seen at the doors eager to get a glimpse of what was going on inside."[235]

"Jennie Hollister was released upon bonds furnished by Ada Leffingwell and the other girls in the house were released upon bonds furnished by Jennie. Ada was released on bonds furnished by Jennie Hollister and the girls in the house were released on bonds furnished by Ada. (Self-bonding was not allowed.) Mary Ann Atherton and her girls were released on bonds furnished by the bail bondsman Angelo Conti."[236]

The bonds of Billy and Cora West, and Al Russell and his madame, Annie Castaybert, were all posted by Mo Harris, another sport who traveled regularly to New Haven prizefights with Billy West and Al Russell.[237]

Jennie Hollister posted the bonds for Carolyn Webster and Jennie Smith of 181 State Street. The various proprietors were charged with keeping disorderly houses and their bonds were placed at $300 each. The bonds of the frequenters were fixed at $100 each. Judge Bill was kept busy for two hours taking bonds.[238]

According to the chief's well-orchestrated plan, the police made simultaneous raids on all the houses of ill repute just before midnight. Upon appearance in the police court the following day, because of a nasty backlog, Judge Perkins continued the cases until Wednesday, March 22, 1899. All of the proprietors pleaded not guilty. They posted bonds and were released until their appeals could be heard in superior court.[239]

On June 6, 1899, the June term of the superior court began with Judge Alberto T. Roraback on the bench. Nine proprietors charged with keeping houses of ill-fame were in court—Jennie Hollister, Ada Leffingwell, Mary Ann Atherton, Carolyn Webster, Emma Kealey, Lillian Stanley, Anna Castaybert, William West and Eva Beck; another eighteen women were charged as frequenters, and Billy West's wife, Cora, was charged with living in a house of ill fame. Judge Milton Shumway—who made a switch with Judge Roraback at the last minute—heard the cases. As he mulled over an appropriate sentence, Judge Shumway said that he thought a fine of

$100, plus three months in jail, would satisfy the court. The lawyers for the proprietors had their work cut out for them. Nonetheless, by arguing that Judge Bill in the police court had only envisioned a $100 fine, Judge Shumway hesitated. After a little more wrangling, the proprietors each received $100 fines, but no jail time.

Democratic Governor Luzon Morris of New Haven, Connecticut, appointed Judge Milton Shumway of Danielson to the superior court. Morgan Bulkeley denied Luzon Morris his rightful place as governor in 1891, by using a technicality to steal a second term right out from under Morris. Not to be denied, Morris won the office in 1893 and served one term as governor. When Judge Shumway dangled the possibility of jail terms under the noses of the biggest brothel keepers in the city, one might suspect that Morgan Bulkeley had explained his plan to the judge. Though this has a refreshing feel, it is extremely unlikely. The two men probably had no working relationship at all. That said, Judge Shumway's interest in putting the proprietors of Hartford's houses of ill fame in jail suggests that he had strong moral feelings against prostitution, and tried—albeit without sufficient resolve—to shut the bawdy houses down in 1899.

Police court continued in this manner—with no significant number of madames or proprietors receiving any jail time—for another seven years. It appeared that none of the judges in the police court, or in the superior court, wanted to be the first to break with tradition. If the massive shift in vice led to 2,000 streetwalkers in Hartford—and the people of the city lost faith in the change—where would they focus their wrath? Probably on the judge who took the first step!

The Saint Patrick's Day raid of 1899 signaled a massive shift in the way the police handled vice in the city, though few involved would necessarily have come to that conclusion. Mary Ann Atherton, just as a simple example, had been arrested a number of times for keeping houses of ill fame—going all the way back to 1863. Would she think that her days as a madame were over? Probably not. On the flip side, it had been a decade and a half since such a wholesale raid of houses in the city had been made, *and this one included Jennie Hollister!*[240]

Many proprietors and inmates knew no other business or trade and determined to continue as usual. It's only fair to mention that some newspapermen figured out precisely the connection between the new Hartford Bridge and the need to crush the city's tenderloin and scatter the demimonde. Shortly after the Saint Patrick's Day raid of 1899, Hicks Street—on the north side of Bushnell Park—saw its first two bordellos. The residents complained and the bawdy houses closed apace, but the pattern wasn't a surprise to the police or the city's elected officials.

As the effects of the Saint Patrick's Day raid—and others—built up in the early 1900s, the pressure mounted on the tenderloin. Inmates were harder to keep, as they assessed correctly that the city's attitude toward the demimonde had soured. When a city wallowed in vice for a half-century— and earned a reputation as a wide open place—any reduction in the number of bagnios brought difficulties and chaos. Essentially, it converted inmates into streetwalkers—not only in Hartford, but in other cities as well. Prostitutes go where they can make a living.

Waterbury got the worst of it. Even as Hartford tried to coerce change, the Brass City quickly became inundated with *nymph du paves*. The greatest number of displaced inmates from the houses of ill repute in Hartford left for greener pastures, but more went to Waterbury than any other city. Making matters worse, Bridgeport and New Haven coincidentally started cleaning house at the same time and some prostitutes from these two cities relocated to Waterbury too. As if that weren't bad enough, the fierce new competition forced the girls of Waterbury's remote roadhouses to enter the downtown area of the Brass City just to make a living. Waterbury was in trouble.[241]

During the Gilded Age, prostitution was generally regulated as a specific type of vagrancy. When prostitutes were punished as sexual deviants, the statutes used were those against adultery, fornication, or "common nightwalking." Streetwalkers and nightwalkers were simply women who stroll the streets in search of sex-for-money transactions. From 1699, nightwalking was a punishable offense in most of New England, while the various state legislatures did not enact the necessary laws until near the end of the eighteenth century. Oddly enough, in Massachusetts, it was not until 1917 that a prostitute could be arrested and jailed for prostitution."[242]

In all cities, there existed an enormous disparity in the fines levied on madames, inmates, frequenters, runners, cooks, piano players, and other persons associated with houses of ill repute. This shows itself to be especially the case on a coast-to-coast inspection.

As has been already noted, in the early 1850s, judges like Eliphalet Bulkeley often just discharged a young madame. One would almost expect that there was some kind of tit-for-tat in these proceedings except that Judge Bulkeley wasn't the type. It seems unlikely that the Judge would attend The Pearl Street Congregational Church every Sunday and attend the meetings of the Pearl Street Ecclesiastical Society every Tuesday night, only to accept IOUs—of the slap-and-tickle variety—from members of the demimonde.

On average, the cost of a first offense for keeping a bagnio ran between $10 and $20 plus court costs. The second offense was usually double that. Of course, if a madame thought she could run a house without stopping by the station house for a cup of coffee first, her fines could be draconian. Ada Leffingwell found this out in 1892 when she was fined $100 plus costs. Fortunately for all concerned, Ada learned her lesson quickly and prospered in the years ahead. Interestingly enough, when Jennie's father, Timothy McQueeney, was fined $35 plus costs in 1852 for assaulting Hooker Clapp, madames were getting away with $10 fines or nothing at all. This offers a privileged glimpse into how much the denizens of Hartford cared about assault and how little they cared about prostitution.

New Haven could be a tough place to figure out because the authorities sometimes acted like whiny, petulant children when it came to madames despoiling their gorgeous city and they assessed fines accordingly. As the pressure grew to close all the houses of ill fame, judges upped the ante—as they did with "Mother Mary" Moran in 1899—levying against her the highest fine ever—$100 plus costs. In fairness, it should be mentioned that the 1899 encounter was "Mother Mary" Moran's thirteenth pinch for running a house of ill repute! Bridgeport, New London, Norwich, Danbury, Waterbury, and Meriden all fell below these costs in their dealings with the characters of the tenderloin.[243]

In 1872 Dallas, the law was a trifle lenient. "If any person shall keep any brothel house within the limits of this city . . . for the purpose of prostitution . . . every such person so offending, shall . . . be fined in any sum not less than $5 nor more than $100, and may, in addition . . . be imprisoned for not more than 15 days."[244]

Memphis citizens were not exactly tickled when they learned of the game in their city. Much like Saint Paul—though without licensing prostitutes—a monthly fine of $25 was levied on madames, with a $10-$15 kicker for each of their inmates, "who more deserve commiseration than to be plundered.". . . They are . . . extortions, not one jot more justifiable than [bandits] who capture a traveler, demand a ransom . . . of his friends, and, if they refuse, cut off an ear and send it to them.[245]

As late as 1895, some towns were far behind the curve. In Alexandria, Louisiana, it was ordained "that . . . after the promulgation of this ordinance, no house of ill fame shall be conducted in the corporate limits of Alexandria, within 200 feet of a house where parties reside, when such party shall object . . . or they shall be subject to arrest and fined not less than $10 for each . . . day that they shall conduct said house of ill fame, or shall be imprisoned not less than forty-eight hours for each offense."[246]

Sometimes hardheads got exactly what they deserved in court. Adam Metzler, an Indianapolis saloonkeeper who ran a dive at the corner of Missouri and Pearl Streets, was given the limit allowed by the law on three separate charges. "Judge Whallon found him guilty on all charges, fined him $100 and costs and sentenced him to 100 days in the workhouse for keeping a house of ill fame; $100 and costs, and 90 days in the workhouse for selling liquor to minors; and $100 plus costs, and 90 days in the workhouse for allowing minors to loiter in his saloon. . . . Judge Whallon kept his word and gave the keeper of the resort the limits of the law."[247]

The Chinese Exclusion Act, passed by the U.S. Congress in 1882, essentially declared open season on bigotry. This held especially true for San Francisco with its large collection of Chinese aliens. White citizens who frequented white houses of ill fame received a fine of $30, or 30 days in the county hall of detention. Men of Chinese extraction, who frequented Chinese bordellos, were given fines of $300, or 300 days in county detention. These outrageous fines went across the board. Sue Chun, an inmate in a house of ill repute, received a fine of $150, or 150 days in jail. Ah Fook, caught frequenting a Chinese bawdy house, was fined $200, or 200 days in jail. [248]

With Hartford's demimonde scrambling, Billy West showed his survival skills. In the Saint Patrick's Day raid of 1899, West narrowly escaped jail, and he had no intention of hanging around the Capitol City until confined to a cell for three months or more. As luck would have it, he found a fantastic deal in Norwich, Connecticut. At the top of Summit Street—on Hardscrabble Hill to the west of the harbor—sat a tumbledown mansion owned by George and Clara Warren. This house had been in business for decades, and though the Warrens hardly looked like keepers of a house of ill fame, that's exactly what they were. Over the decades, "Uncle George" and "Aunt Clara" managed to run a model sporting house. It was so revered that "it had never been raided. The whole population of that part of town would have risen up against such a sacrilege. Why, the brother of the Mayor of Norwich, and one of its wealthiest men, married a [woman] from that house."[249]

But George Warren's health began to fail. After an operation in Boston, he died. Clara tried to continue, but took sick herself. Then, about 1896, lawmen raided the house, along with six or seven other places, as Norwich's tiny police force flexed its muscles. Only Clara and an attractive young girl were home. They rode to the police station and appeared in court as dignified as a grandmother and granddaughter out of a Norman Rockwell painting. A little over a year later, the city police raided Clara Warren's house on Hardscrabble Hill again, as Norwich fell into the habit of collecting "license fees" once a year. After that, Clara gave up and moved to Boston.[250]

Pretty Jennie Barlow of Bridgeport had the place for a time, but Jennie Barlow courted trouble by hiring girls who were far too sporty for a slow town like Norwich. Enter Billy West.[251]

As stated previously, Billy West changed his name to William Emmons when he decided to resuscitate the old Warren mansion in Norwich. Billy ran the Warren place for almost a decade and then disappeared forever. In 1910, the house atop Hardscrabble Hill was taken over by Fanny Green Feuer, a woman known for her late hours and everlasting stable of lovers. The police raided Fanny Green's bagnio in October 1913, and soon thereafter her husband, the long-suffering David Feuer of Bridgeport, was granted a divorce on the grounds that his wife was guilty of adultery, keeping a disorderly house in Norwich, and harboring females for purposes of prostitution.[252]

Billy West was so typical of the men of the demimonde. As an only child, Billy grew up into an incredibly self-centered adult. As Grace Howard found out the hard way, Billy West had no loyalty at all. He shuffled the women in his life whenever it suited him and floated around Connecticut, making his living by the ruination of young girls. That didn't bother West at all, but he changed his name regularly as if to launder his soul. No doubt, he changed his name for a final time just before he met Saint Peter.

Though Billy West originally ran Jennie and Tom Hollister's old place—a simple brothel noted for its luxurious appointments and prominent client list—big money was always at the heart of Billy's scheming. West probably liked the Warren mansion in Norwich because it almost qualified as a New York-style parlor house and the distinction allowed him to charge exorbitant rates.

When Billy West, Grace Howard, and a few other proprietors of bawdy houses received Chief of Police George Bill's 1898 order to close their houses, Billy closed up the Bange mansion and began to follow the trotters with Gertie Camp. However, Grace Howard had a better idea.

Talking with a reporter, Grace Howard said airily, "I'm going into the country to take a vacation now. Don't you want to come? Just you wait until I get my new place and I'll show Chief Bill. . . . He should go after the young girls, and the sporty 'push,' and the married women that have other women's husbands hanging around . . . . We do an honest business and don't disturb anyone. My house has been quiet. We're a necessity. We're here for the accommodation of unmarried men. It always makes us mad to see a married man with a nice home come here. Of course, we take his money, but we're not here for such as he. . . . We'll be back here in Hartford before long, just the same as ever. If we don't, half of Hartford will be running after us. We are just as much a necessity as the Capitol. . . . I'll bet that Thrasher has been around worse people, but I suppose he has to earn his bread and butter."[253]

With her lover, Harry Arnold, she rented the Hotel de Ryer on the Old Saybrook road in Rocky Hill, Connecticut, a no-license town. The previous owner, Lawrence Ryer, a German brewer, became discouraged after a long series of raids for selling liquor and gave up on the property. The Hotel de Ryer had been closed for two or three years before Grace Howard and Harry Arnold took the keys from Ryer. Not without justification, a townsman suspected Grace and Harry of selling liquor and filed a complaint. The local constable organized a raid, but no intoxicants were found. (Grace buried the liquor in the back yard.) Still and all, the authorities harassed Grace Howard endlessly and the Hotel de Ryer never really had a chance. In less than twelve months, Grace and Harry were back in Hartford.[254]

Billy West was doing fine with the airy, old Warren place on Hardscrabble Hill, but down on Water Street, there were places where no self-respecting sport would venture. This brings up a grim problem of the times—venereal disease. It could be argued that the different diseases were spread evenly among the houses of ill fame throughout the United States, but the $0.50 hellholes catered to a much lower class of client and could be expected to see far more disease than the $5 New York-style parlor houses.

After Dr. William Sanger conducted his study of 2,000 New York prostitutes in 1855, he advocated the regulation of prostitution in order to better prevent the spread of venereal disease. In Sanger's 1855 questionnaire, 821 (41%) of the women were willing to admit to having had a venereal disease. The social stigma undoubtedly forced some of the women to lie, making the true number much higher.[255]

Around 1910, 4.5 percent of all emergency room visits to Hartford Hospital were for venereal disease issues, though studies almost unanimously peg venereal diseases at 10-20 percent of the population during the Gilded Age. (In 2008, the CDC claimed that *at any given time* there were 110 million cases of STIs in the United States. Based on a 2008 U. S. population of 304 million, the number of Americans with a STI *at any given time* was around 36 percent. However, by subtracting children (fourteen and under) the number of adults caring STIs *at any given time* jumps to 45 percent. Taking into account multiple STIs per person, the percentage is obviously lower. A good guess as to the number of adults with a STI *at any given time might* be 40 percent.)[256]

In the last half of the nineteenth century, syphilis and gonorrhea were the two biggest concerns. To begin, even the doctors who went to the very best medical schools were not well trained. It was much easier to get a medical degree than it was to get a medical education. For the bulk of the nineteenth century, doctors weren't even licensed. Though licensing began in the first third of the 1800s, it proved so unpopular with the electorate that it was eliminated all over the United States by 1840. In Connecticut, licensing wasn't restored until 1893.

A physician knew that if he diagnosed a patient with syphilis or gonorrhea, that person would go to another doctor. Even though doctors—by today's standards—were substandard, they weren't stupid. Would it really endear him to a patient if he chased the etiology of the disease? This was especially true if the doctor couldn't do a thing to cure it. By treating only the symptoms, doctors were able to keep their patients, hold families together—an important consideration during the Gilded Age—and keep patients from enormous mental anguish. Often, doctors were caught in an appalling ethical dilemma: A male patient had a venereal disease and still intended to marry and have children. Barring a miracle, he would infect his wife and she would infect the children. There was no easy solution and each doctor handled the problem in his own way.

The makers of Bristol's Sarsaparilla constantly ran ads in the *New York Daily Tribune* for a vegetable medicine that could relieve the symptoms of Dyspepsia, Gangrene, Leprosy, and Secondary Syphilis.[257] From the 1830s to 1900, there were dozens of snake oil medicines, each touting their ability to cure syphilis—Winer's Arcanum Extract, Kidwell's Compound Fluid Extract of Beech Drop or Cancer Root, Samaritan's Root & Herb Juices, Dr. Mott's French Powders, Cuticura's Resolvent, Acker's Blood Elixer, and Africana. One guesses that blacks favored Africana, although the marketing data is no longer extant.[258]

As a result of the U. S. Public Health Service's scandalous "Tuskegee Study of Untreated Syphilis in the Negro Male" some truths about syphilis surfaced. The study ran for forty years, from 1932 until 1972 and involved 600 mostly illiterate black sharecroppers—399 with syphilis, 201 without.[259] By 1972, 28 of the 399 men died of syphilis and another 100 died of complications attributed to the disease. If we make an enormous leap and assume that the results in black and white populations—male and female—would be roughly comparable, we now know that if you were a young person with syphilis in 1932, you had a 68 percent chance of surviving until 1972.

Of course, the outrageousness of the Tuskegee Study was that these men could have been cured with penicillin anytime after 1943. Instead, they were allowed to suffer and die. In 1973, as the result of a class action suit, the study participants and their families received $9 million, but the guilty parties were never prosecuted.

The great breakthrough in the cure of syphilis came in 1909 when German scientist Dr. Paul Ehrlich discovered Salvarsan—an arsenic-based cure for the disease. Ehrlich served as chief of the German Government Institute at Frankfort. Dr. Ehrlich partnered in many scientific breakthroughs and shared in the 1908 Nobel Prize for Medicine. He died in 1915.[260]

Gonorrhea differed greatly from syphilis. It crippled and incapacitated, but rarely caused early death. In 1848, one physician noted in a textbook on venereal diseases, "We do not know of any substance, which, taken into the system, is an antidote to the infection of gonorrheal matter. . . ."

At mid-century, the two most popular "cures" for gonorrhea were *cubebs*, an Indonesian variety of pepper of which the dried, powdered unripe fruit was used, and *balsam of copaiba*, extracted from a South American tree. Though many publications, even into the 1890s, supported these two botanicals, they were worthless. Vaccines against gonorrhea began to appear in the early part of the twentieth century, but with mixed results.[261]

The search for anti-bacterial drugs began in the 1890s and most of the drugs that surfaced were metallic compounds of arsenic, antimony, gold, and mercury. However, it wasn't until 1937 that sulfanilamide surfaced as an effective treatment. One researcher noted, "The advent of sulfanilamide has established . . . that effective chemotherapy of microbial diseases is attainable. Data from the U.S. Army showed that the sulfanilamide drugs had cut hospital stays in half, but lasting results did not materialize and cardiovascular problems made the sulfanilamide drugs problematic.

In 1943, the U.S. military hospitals began testing penicillin. Impurities in the available penicillin dictated small doses. Typically, patients were given 80,000 to 160,000 units of the drug in divided doses in twelve hours, delivering a 96 percent cure rate. A second dose cured the other 4 percent. This, of course, represented the most satisfactory treatment to date. (Penicillin G is natural penicillin, and 1 mg is equal to 1,440-1,680 USP units. Therefore, the 80,000 to 160,000 units mentioned above figures roughly the same as 56 mgs to 96 mgs, though there are many factors—among them purity—that make this calculation uncertain.)

Modern medicine isn't static. From penicillin, the preferred drug became aureomycin in 1949. Then in 1966, tetracycline took center stage. A year later, spectinomycin captured the lion's share of the market. Fortunately, pharmacological research continues, and futurists would not be reckless in suggesting that all sexually transmitted diseases will eventually be eradicated.

As for protection, nothing existed for women in the Gilded Age. Conversely, men had options. Before the twentieth century, men experimented with chemically-treated linen and animal tissue (bladder and intestine). The earliest condoms were found in an excavation in England and dated to 1642. Goodyear manufactured the first rubber (reusable) condom in 1855, probably originating the expression, "A battlement against pleasure; a fishnet against infection." Latex came along in 1920, and the first latex condom came from Young's Rubber Company in the United States. Polyurethane condoms were introduced in 1994 and polyisoprene in 2008.

The Hartford Bridge—glacially slow to achieve erection—indeed acted as the biggest catalyst behind the crackdown on vice in the Capitol City. Nevertheless, changes in the center of Connecticut should not be viewed in isolation.

Consider other cities in the Nutmeg State. New Haven has always been the largest city in the state. During the Gilded Age, the Elm City had 35 percent more people than Hartford. (By 2012, this gap had closed to 5 percent.)[262] Perhaps owing to Yale University and the hegemony of the First Ecclesiastical Society, New Haven—unlike Hartford—never got the reputation as a wide-open city. At different times, there were houses of ill fame on Chapel, Crown, State, Fair, Prindle, Union, Worcester, and Main Streets. When James Bryan ran the Sterling House at 674 Chapel Street, it was a notorious place. The London House on Goodwin Street sunk pretty low, but the shrewd madame, Hattie Goodwin, always made her payments on time and raids at her place were rare. In 1899, the New Haven police salivated at the idea of running Kittie Reilly out of town, and if they could include Agnes Scollard—whose depraved bagnio was at 65 Union Street—so much the better. Unfortunately, both women had staying power.[263]

Prindle Street had become an especially well known fixture of New Haven's tenderloin. By November 1899, Captain James Brewer's "Flying Squadron" had done a fairly meticulous job of reducing the city to only a few dens of iniquity. As noted in print, "The local tenderloin is a disintegrated collection of fragments today. Its former glory is gone. . . .'Mother Mary' Moran, a twenty-year fixture of the demimonde, was visited by . . .[the police] at her residence at 63 Fair Street, resulting in a fine of $100 and costs, the biggest fine New Haven has ever seen." ("Mother Mary" Moran was no financial cretin, as she owned the Tremont Hotel in Bridgeport as well.) Humorously, the New Haven police had a secret respect for "Mother Mary" Moran, for when they brought her in, the officers sang "The Harp That Once Through Tara's Halls" to the melody of "I Dreamt I Dwelt in Marble Halls" from Michael William Balfe's 1844 Opera *The Bohemian Girl.*[264]

Superintendent of Police Eugene Birmingham in Bridgeport seemed different from other police chiefs. He operated as a quietly competent man who refused to have anything to do with politics, which says a lot in a city like Bridgeport. Nevertheless, the people of Bridgeport loved and respected Chief Birmingham and he did his job exactly as his personal code dictated. As a result, by the turn of the twentieth century, the Park City had only five or six houses of ill fame. Chief among them were the Piedmont House on Tulip Street, the Golden Valley Hotel on Water Street, and the Tremont House on Middle Street.

Moreover, in East Bridgeport, there were a few brothels—mostly frequented by blacks—on Pierpont Street, near the corner of Pembroke. All of these disappeared early in the twentieth century.

Danbury's tenacious Captain Edward Ginty had eliminated every last house of ill fame by 1894. This despite Ginty's belief that prostitution was a necessary evil and that the houses of ill repute should be licensed by the city and confined to a red light district. As seriously as Ginty took his job, there were still a dozen women keeping furnished rooms as places of assignation.

Waterbury and Meriden were a lot like Danbury in that there were no houses of ill fame within city limits. Waterbury had a half dozen roadhouses operating just outside of town, but authorities were loath to work outside their jurisdiction.

New London had several houses operating in the town's eighty-year-old red light district—Bradley, Potter, Bank, and Water Streets. For all of its long history in prostitution, New London learned very little. Bradley Street remained as vile as ever and always witnessed some of the ugliest business in the state. In the first decade of the twentieth century, the local police arrested Rena Smith (a.k.a. Rene Thornton), a madame at 93 Bradley Street, for detaining fifteen-year-old Viola Peters. Almost concurrently, the police arrested Addie Burns, a madame at 41 Bradley Street, for raping fifteen-year-old Mary Burns (no relation).

Norwich had half a dozen houses near the waterfront around Water, River, and Ferry Streets. Of course, George and Clara Warren's old mansion on Hardscrabble Hill always figured in the mix. Norwich seemed like such a quiet town, but the city fathers met fire with fire. As long as the businesses ran in an orderly manner, they didn't interfere much.[265]

One ironic feature of the old red light districts was that they were usually located within shouting distance of the main police station. The police wanted to watch them carefully and react quickly when trouble broke out. Also, since these houses were raided for revenue on a regular basis, it made sense to keep them close by.

Chapter 7

Two Random Events

In 1895, two seemingly unrelated events converged to trumpet huge changes for Hartford. The first was the organization of the Hartford Yacht Club; the second was a fire, on the night of May 17, 1895, that destroyed the Morgan Street covered bridge over the Connecticut River. There were 20,000 people watching while the bridge delivered a red-white-orange, fiery extravaganza—as one by one the individual spans gave up all utility and promise, and collapsed into the river. In the end, the only vestiges of the bridge, that had served the Nutmeg State for eighty-five years, were the six stone piers sitting in the river. A fair guess is that not a single spectator realized the full import of the fire.[266]

Consider for a moment the progress of the city. Hartford had telephones, electric lights, and there were sewing machines in all the finest homes. The new electric trolleys had replaced all the old horse-drawn cars, with the exception of a single line on Blue Hills Avenue. (The Blue Hills driver, Patrick Hagarty, drank a bit, and executives at the Hartford Street Railway Company decided to let him retire in 1896 before they electrified the Blue Hills branch of the system.) In 1895, the busiest street in the city, State Street, was paved with asphalt; Main Street received a coating of asphalt the following year. Speaking of electricity, all the major streets of the city had electric streetlights and battery powered automobiles had just burst on the scene.

In America, all cities of size had a water works in place, which meant toilets in homes and fire hydrants on street corners. The great conflagrations of the 1860s and 1870s were over and simple household sanitation had never been better. Thanks to cleaner water, common waterborne diseases like typhus and cholera had become rare. It truly was the dawn of a new age.

The city now had a high school, and its sons went to Yale, Trinity, or Wesleyan, depending on their religious persuasions. Right after mid-century, the city was a manufacturing colossus, but now banks and insurance companies were foremost in the pantheon of financially successful enterprises. By 1890, Hartford Fire, Aetna Fire, Phoenix, Connecticut Fire, National Fire, Orient Insurance, Hartford County Mutual Fire, and State Mutual Fire competed for business. In a period of just thirteen months—from October 1873 to November 1874—Aetna, Hartford and Phoenix were called upon to contribute to policyholders in Chicago and Boston more than $9 million, or 200 percent of their aggregate capital. This highlights an important point: Hartford did not become the insurance capitol because it had the most or the biggest companies, but because these firms paid their claims.[267]

Besides fire insurance companies, Hartford had nine life insurance companies adding nicely to the city's strong financial base. Additionally, the city had seventeen national and state banks with total deposits of more than $15 million. In short, wealth infused the Capitol City, which was poised for a powerful burst of growth fueled by its financial and manufacturing sectors. But had Hartford gotten past the growing pains that all successful cities must endure? Or was the Charter Oak City's coming-of-age chapter yet unwritten?[268]

Hartford had made huge strides in some areas, but hadn't paid attention to problems in others. In 1860, there were only ten houses of ill fame—and the idea of a whole demimonde subculture didn't seem possible. By 1900, there were thirty brothels and a demimonde spreading steadily across the city, influencing in a profound way, the young people. In a half century, vice had risen much faster than the population and taken on the inertia of a Cunard liner. How would Hartford continue its tremendous lunge forward when vice was growing so rapidly?

On April 23, 1895, a group of boating enthusiasts assembled at the State Street blacksmith shop of Joel Alexander to form a yacht club. Thirty men joined together that night, and with a crude constitution, they adopted the name Hartford Yacht Club. In the weeks and months that followed, they elected officers and began the search for a permanent clubhouse.

For their Commodore, they chose William Watrous, the president of William Rogers Manufacturing Company on Market Street. William Miner, the proprietor of the American Hotel, was chosen Vice-Commodore, while Ernest Way, a retired merchant, was appointed Rear-Commodore. Worthy candidates were also chosen for Fleet Captain, Secretary, Treasurer, and Fleet Surgeon. Two of the six directors worth mentioning were Charles Northam, the wealthy wholesale grain dealer and cofounder of Smith, Northam and Company, and John H. Hall, Vice-President of Colt Patent Fire-Arms. The group included clerks, blacksmiths, and successful businessmen across the spectrum. For many of them, the only thing they had in common was a love of boats.[269]

They attracted fifty members the first year, including young men from wealthy Republican families on the west side of town. The members immediately began planning regattas and even Middletown and Old Saybrook stations of the Hartford Yacht Club. Thinking small wasn't their game!

Despite all the fun, the location appeared to be one of the biggest drawbacks of the Hartford Yacht Club. In order to get to the river, the members had to walk down State Street—right through the heart of the tenderloin. While the tenderloin did not necessarily intimidate the members, the whole East Side was a rough place. Every other building on the south side of State Street was a bordello, and the inmates, as a group, bored easily. For lack of better entertainment options, the girls hung out the windows of the different houses and kibitzed with one another—perhaps the way different species of birds chatter to one another in the wilderness.

The old yellow block at the corner of State and Commerce Streets comprised the greatest collection of fallen women; and, they were of many ethnicities—French, Italian, German, and Irish. On the warmest nights, the doorsteps and windowsills were full of half-clothed prostitutes. It became common to hear one's name called out when passing the window-sitting inmates, who spoke with a lilt that betokened acquaintance. Somehow or other, the girls found out the first names of the yacht club members. The prostitutes then teased the young men. A young prostitute might spot a banker's son and say, "Same time Saturday night, Freddie?" Of course, if Freddie had his girlfriend with him, there might be some explaining to do![270]

Let's not kid ourselves, this was happening all over the country. In Sacramento, California, police arrested three madames—Genie, Julia, and Leone—for violating the ordinance prohibiting the occupants of houses of ill fame from posing in the windows and doorways. Talk about laws that are difficult to enforce![271]

As time went on, the members of the yacht club whose parents had summer places at Fenwick, decided to build a station at Folly Point within walking distance of their family's baronial summer cottages. Morgan Bulkeley's two sons—Morgan, Jr. and Houghton—had joined the Hartford Yacht Club, as had James Goodwin's boys—Frankie and James—and a number of other members of the Fenwick community. In February of 1900, the Hartford Yacht Club raised $5,000 to build Fenwick Station. Morgan Bulkeley leased—probably in fee simple—several acres on Folly Point to the club; the members, of course, made ex-Gov. Morgan Bulkeley an honorary member. By July of 1900, the Fenwick Station was completed. Besides dockage, the Folly Point station had kitchen, bath, and bunk facilities for those who did not have cottages at Fenwick.

From 1880 to 1888, Morgan Bulkeley had served as Hartford's mayor and he loved taking long walks about town. While enjoying these reveries, he smoked big, black Havana cigars that became his trademark. Ambling along, he constantly stopped to talk with friends. Nothing happened in the city without his knowledge. In politics, one of his best friends, Republican Gideon Winslow, ran a butcher shop on the corner of State and Front streets—the true heart of the tenderloin. When Morgan Bulkeley served as governor, from 1889 to 1893, Bulkeley appointed Gideon Winslow his dairy commissioner—though Winslow didn't want the job and rarely showed up for meetings. If Morgan Bulkeley wanted information about the tenderloin, he picked up the phone and talked to Gideon Winslow. Bulkeley knew all about the hotels and saloons with backroom operations, as well as the houses of ill repute—and they gave him pause.

Bulkeley also knew about the gambling dens, but he couldn't care less about gambling because he spent so much time betting on the trotters at Charter Oak Park in West Hartford. Bulkeley didn't only bet the horses, he sat on the board of directors of Charter Oak Park and judged races when he could. He loved horses and participated in racing any way possible.

Prostitution was different. The Bulkeleys were a religious family. When they first arrived in Hartford in 1847, the Bulkeleys walked from their rented rooms over the Aetna Fire Insurance building in Statehouse Square down to South Church at the corner of Buckingham Street. Later, their walk was cut in half when they joined the Pearl Street Congregational Church. Judge Bulkeley died in 1872 and Morgan took over his father's house on Washington Street. At that time, he returned to the South Congregational Church. The Bulkeleys could trace their roots all the way back to Rev. Peter Bulkeley who establish the Town of Concord, Massachusetts, with the blessings of Boston's Rev. John Cotton—credited with naming the faith "Congregationalism."

Beyond their religious status, the Bulkeleys were patriots. Throughout American history, the Bulkeleys always fought in the nation's wars. Hartford native J. P. Morgan and his first cousin, James Goodwin, paid substitutes to take their places in the Civil War. Meanwhile, Frankie Goodwin entered Divinity School, securing a deferment just months before the shelling of Fort Sumter. Judge Bulkeley's three sons—Charlie, Morgan, and Billy—served in the war. In 1864, Capt. Charles Bulkeley died on Battery Garesche, a heavy-artillery fortification defending Washington.

In one last way, Morgan Bulkeley was quite different from the other captains of industry in Hartford and a truly admirable human being. Bulkeley had no prejudices of any kind toward other people. His home swarmed with Irish immigrants, working as domestic servants, seamstresses, and cooks. His stable hands and coachmen were Irish immigrants. At Aetna Life, Morgan Bulkeley hired Pat McGovern, a genius with numbers. McGovern was born in County Cavan, Ireland and never got past sixth grade. Pat McGovern also became Morgan Bulkeley's right-hand man in politics and his bagman as well.

One of the Irish seamstresses in the Bulkeley home became so close to Morgan's mother, Lydia Bulkeley, that the woman was buried next to Lydia in the family plot at Cedar Hill Cemetery. Bridget McCormick received the same lavish head stone as the rest of the family, which read: "Bridget McCormick, Born in Ireland; Friend And Confidante Of Lydia Bulkeley For Over Forty Years." A visitor to Cedar Hill Cemetery would have to look long and hard to find such a thing in the family plots of other wealthy Hartford families. Morgan Bulkeley, Billy Bulkeley, and their sister, Mary Bulkeley Brainard, made these arrangements.[272]

While other presidents of large companies in town had white chiefs of staff, Morgan Bulkeley hired Charles Custis, a mountain of a black man from Norfolk, Virginia, who was born into slavery in 1859. Custis wandered to Hartford with a minstrel show and stayed because of a winter blizzard. Soon, he became the night elevator operator at Aetna Life on Main Street (corner of Atheneum Way). Morgan Bulkeley admired Charles's courtly manners and sound judgment, so he made Custis his chief of staff. Custis stayed with Aetna Life for sixty-two years and worked directly for Morgan Bulkeley from 1888 until Bulkeley's death in 1922. From 1922 to 1950, Custis served as chief of staff for Bulkeley's nephew and successor, Morgan Bulkeley Brainard.[273]

Meanwhile, Edward and Adelia Habenstein always catered Morgan and Fannie Bulkeley's parties at their home on Washington Street. Edward

Habenstein was a German immigrant, who with lightning speed became the most prominent confectioner in town. Habenstein threw the most lavish tasting parties at his shop on Pearl Street whenever he came up with a new medley of pastries, cookies, chocolates, tarts, cakes, pies, sweets, and other melt-in-your-mouth delights. He was a brilliant caterer, restaurateur, and impresario, as well as a gifted confectioner. Besides catering for the most prominent families in Hartford, the Habensteins catered the Governor's Balls at Foot Guard Hall on High Street too.

During the decade before it burned, the Hartford Bridge had become problematic. The bridge had seven spans resting on six piers, but the third span from the west had weakened so much that it bowed toward the south, showing a "deviation of two feet."[274] There were two sets of trolley tracks traversing the bridge, but the sections were all in such poor condition that the bridge commissioners would not allow two trolley cars on the same span at one time."[275]

As the bridge burned, many people suspected arson, but it seemed far more probable that some cigar or cigarette started the blaze as smokers cast their butts away recklessly. Alternatively, it could have started from the sparks given off by the trolley tracks or the electric wires overhead. Had a persistent danger resulted in the complete destruction of the bridge?

The loss of the bridge caused a great deal of inconvenience and business suffered to some degree. Besides the obvious vehicle and passenger traffic, the electric companies that strung their lines atop the bridge would suffer lost revenues.[276] The old bridge that had connected Hartford with eastern Connecticut since 1818 went up in a sheet of flames and the stone piers alone remained. All of electric service east of the river ended, and the Manchester, East Hartford, and Glastonbury trolley cars stood where they were when the wires broke. The electric lines were worthless until power could be restored.

The city had bought out the owners of the bridge in 1889 and made the passage free. Now the bridge commissioners wasted no time addressing a myriad of problems. The first step was to have the Berlin Iron Bridge Company build a temporary bridge just north of the old piers. Scheduled to begin right after the fire, Atty. Charles Cole of the Berlin Iron Bridge Company called to say that the work would not be feasible "until the state paid what was already due."[277]

The excitement of the bridge fire didn't last long. Soon, two ferries— the *Schuylkill* and the *F. C. Fowler*—were brought upriver and placed in service. At the same time, a new controlling authority was organized—The Connecticut River Bridge & Highway Commission. The work associated with building a new bridge and sculpting new approaches in two towns seemed so massive that it could never be done without a governing body. From the very start, it was understood that ex-Gov. Morgan Bulkeley would head the commission. Bulkeley, the President of Aetna Life Insurance Company, had enjoyed elective office, but he had also earned the reputation as a man who could get things done.

On the flip side, Morgan Bulkeley had a nasty status in political circles. Throughout the United States, he had the notorious reputation as a vote buyer. That said, once he got into office, his administrations were notable for a complete lack of corruption. Bulkeley had to buy votes to get into office because of a weak resume. As a boy, he was a poor student and never even graduated from high school. His time in the Civil War appeared lackluster too, highlighted by three months of idleness in Suffolk, Virginia. He never smelled powder. When Judge Bulkeley died in 1872, Morgan

Bulkeley ascended to the presidency of Aetna Life and developed into an excellent businessman and a gifted administrator.

In spite of Morgan Bulkeley's complete lack of racial or religious prejudices, he harbored a quiet bias against the demimonde. During his years as mayor, he watched the number of brothels grow yearly. The city's biggest and most important commercial strip, State Street, had become overrun with headstrong madames, preening young prostitutes, and sporting houses that ran the gamut from lavishly-appointed pleasure palaces to repugnant sinks of iniquity. Bulkeley knew all about the girls hanging out the windows of the houses, embarrassing his sons and their friends as they walked through the tenderloin to the Hartford Yacht Club. While mayor, he saw brazen madames wage war on good police officers. In his first year as mayor, Morgan Bulkeley watched as the perfidious Carrie Farnham brought charges against Officer Lawrence Keegan after a legitimate raid on her State Street bordello. Since Carrie Farnham intended to call respectable family men to the stand—men who could never show their faces in court—the matter embarrassed everyone and put Mayor Bulkeley in an ugly bind. Ultimately, the council had to dismiss Lawrence Keegan from the police force. Yes, Morgan Bulkeley had a bias against the half-world.[278]

On July 3, 1895, the new Bridge & Highway Commission met in Morgan Bulkeley's office at Aetna Life on Main Street. Among other things, the commissioners drew lots to determine each member's length of service and officially elected Morgan Bulkeley president of the new body. The following Tuesday, Bulkeley and three of his fellow commissioners got in his carriage and drove down Morgan Street to inspect the remains of the old bridge. From the start, there were two camps, headed in opposite directions. One group wanted to investigate the fire and attach some kind of responsibility for the destruction, while a second cluster wanted to skip the post mortem and move forward. Since Morgan Bulkeley headed this latter group, there never was an investigation of the fire. Instead, the commissioners spent all of their time building a temporary bridge.

On June 11, 1895—twenty-five days after the bridge fire—the temporary bridge opened for electric trolley cars, teams of horses, and pedestrians. With a little luck, maybe the temporary bridge would last until the new Hartford Bridge was finished. Wishful thinking aside, this temporary bridge carried the seeds of its own destruction. Obviously, a temporary bridge had to be built, but the commission erroneously decided to use as little money as possible on the temporary bridge, saving the lion's share of their funds for the permanent bridge. As a result, the first temporary bridge lasted a scant seven months.

By December 1895, the Connecticut River was completely clogged with ice, jeopardizing the peers of the temporary bridge. By December 12, the safety of the temporary bridge turned so questionable that the Berlin Iron Bridge Company had to put "defenders" up on the pilings to protect them from the ice blocks. Teams were not allowed to use the bridge, only passengers.

Just before Christmas, 1895, a 200-foot section at the middle of the bridge gave way. Weakened by high water and the awful pressure of the ice flow, the compromised pilings collapsed. With much creaking and groaning, the large center span wrenched itself away from its supports and toppled into the river. All traffic between Hartford and East Hartford stopped.[279]

At this point, the Bridge & Highway Commission voted not to build another temporary bridge, but to put everything into a permanent bridge; hopefully, it could be built in record time. As if to punctuate this decision, in March 1896, heavy rains and warm weather swelled the rivers and streams in the state to a fifty-year high and the remainder of the temporary bridge disappeared downstream.[280]

Good arguments were probably made for the grand push directly to the permanent bridge, but the public would have none of it. They rounded on Morgan Bulkeley like jackals. Bulkeley and his commissioners had to reconsider. After chasing bids for a month, the contract for a new temporary bridge went to the Berlin Iron Bridge Company for $37,000.

Work on the second temporary bridge began on May 1, and the bridge opened for use on June 12, 1896. Some guardrails were yet to come, and the piers were still to be ballasted with stone, but the bridge could withstand traffic. The structure consisted of nine spans erected on eight piers, plus two abutments.[281]

People were in carriages, on foot, bicycles, carts, and trolley cars, moving east with great delight. The crowd bubbled in a jubilant mood, since it had been thirteen months since fire swept away the old bridge. Alternatively, there existed a dreary emptiness at the base of Ferry Street, where the ferryboats *Nellie, Schuykill, Fowler,* and *Cora* had worked doggedly to meet the needs of people. At 2:35 p.m., Morgan Bulkeley and the city's elected officials participated in a grand ceremony. With no little fanfare, they cut a ribbon at the approach of the temporary bridge. Histrionics and hoopla aside, the ceremony was shot through with irony: all this pomp and circumstance for a temporary bridge that the public expected to be needed for less than a year? Of course, only in a perfect world would that have been the case, but such were the expectations.

As if the city needed more trouble, critics were quick to criticize the bridge building efforts in Hartford. Simply put, there were five town— Hartford, East Hartford, Manchester, East Windsor and Glastonbury—who benefited the most from the bridge and were merged together to pay for it. It sounded fair, but Glastonbury argued that the Bridge and Highway Commission had not been legally created—and couldn't force Glastonbury to pay a dime. A court challenge followed and Glastonbury lost in the Connecticut Supreme Court of Errors. Undeterred, Glastonbury took the case all the way to the U.S. Supreme Court. Almost three years later, the U. S. Supreme Court held that the state had the right to merge the five towns to build and maintain the Hartford Bridge. Therefore, the commission had indeed been legally created. During this three-year impasse, the commission did no work at all.[282]

Owing to this legal delay, bids for the new bridge were not solicited from interested parties until late March 1899. [283]

Meanwhile, in April 1896, the citizens of Hartford elected the Democratic Mayor Miles Preston, who did nothing to ameliorate the condition of vice in the Capitol City. By the time Preston finished his first term in March 1898, reporters wrote, "At the present time, there are 2,500 prostitutes within the confines of the Capitol. Over thirty houses of ill fame are running under the protection of the mayor, the police commissioners, and the police department . . . houses of assignation do a thriving business on every corner. The situation is appalling and no one questions but what a change is sadly needed."[284]

When the *Bridgeport Sunday Herald* adopted the cleaning up of Connecticut's Capitol City as an intrastate drama, it didn't seem to matter that the newspaper wrote in the florid style of the day, because its managing editor, Richard Howell, was respected among his peers as a first-rate journalist and editor. Howell started as a newspaper cartoonist and later became an editor. So said, Howell had a soft spot in his heart for good newspaper art and hired some of the best artists, caricaturists, and cartoonists in the business. The *Bridgeport Sunday Herald* and the *Waterbury Sunday Herald*—where Howell was also the managing editor— were newspapers that were great fun to read. Not surprisingly, the *Bridgeport Sunday Herald* had the highest readership in Connecticut, and that fact could not be ignored by the pompous Yale grads in Hartford.

Therefore, when the *Herald* laid out the number of brothels and gambling joints in the Capitol City, the scandal was more than a first-rate public relations firm could handle. Naturally, the denizens of Hartford cried foul and slammed the *Herald's* articles as "sensational journalism," but the rank smell of low tide lingered.

The *Herald* maintained that the fault lay with a "pool of influence" somewhere within the hierarchy of the city, for "it must require some influence to run a house of prostitution for years without molestation . . . . If a stranger . . . wishes to engage in this business, he must see some person who is on the inside, and then the business can be 'fixed.' How much money is required . . . has never been stated. . . . but this is the year of investigations and the incoming legislature should appoint a committee for the purpose of prying into a few facts, and their first tour of duty should commence in Hartford. They would not be in session very long before the taxpayers learned of . . . strange methods of business, which have been employed . . . for years.[285]

A little while later, the Bridgeport newspaper bore down, "Hartford at present is a disgrace to the good old Nutmeg State, and unless the authorities . . . awaken to this fact, the deserved censure will soon come from all sides. The city is overrun with the lowest class of fallen women to be found in the country, and the streets after nightfall are lined with young and old specimens, who openly solicit on street corners . . . . These women dress as loud as possible and "prostitute" is plainly stamped all over their anatomy. Their actions are so bold that even the young libertines of the town turn from them in disgust."[286]

When pressed in the past, authorities in Hartford asserted that it would be impossible to drive these prostitutes from the streets. Though the statutes against streetwalking, soliciting, and prostitution were clearly on the books—and the fines and jail terms spelled out clearly—enforcement wasn't easy. As the days and weeks passed, it became clear that the situation had been set in concrete by so many decades of indifference.

So emboldened were the streetwalkers that a respectable woman would not use the streets at night without a male escort. Even men could not walk the main thoroughfares without being accosted by the brazenfaced young women of the demimonde, who promised a memorable trip to a house of assignation. The police department's seeming lack of interest had reached such an outrageous level that a stranger asked, "Do the police lay in with these women?"[287]

In a way, it seemed almost humorous to hear uninformed people malign the police when talking about the freedom of the tenderloin. A great example of the kind of cop walking the beat in Hartford's tenderloin was Officer James Francis Lally. Among the toughs, "Pud" Lally had a reputation as the most feared officer. James Lally, with his older brother John, ran away from home in County Westmeath, Ireland when he was fourteen. The brothers sailed to America and joined the navy, during the early part of the Civil War. Both of them were on the *Monitor* when it fought the *Merrimac* at Hampton Roads, Virginia in March 1862. Sadly, James Lally's brother, John, was blown to bits during the battle and James eventually completed his service and mustered out. By working hard and saving his money, he brought his parents, brother, and sisters to America. Lally worked a number of different jobs on the railroad before becoming a

Hartford policeman in August 1889. At the time, gang initiation included "trimming" a cop. But Lally never fell for that nonsense and managed to stay on his feet. He had a fabulous sweep with his right arm, a move that could deliver the force of another man's best punch. Lally was probably the handiest man in the department with his fists and could deflect a "knockdown" better than anyone else.[288]

Officer James F. Lally

One of the greatest standup fights in department history took place on State Street one afternoon and involved Sgt. John Butler—once the amateur heavyweight boxing champion of New England. Butler was so strong that he didn't bother to take a "billy" with him on rounds. He once said, "I'm afraid to hit a man with a billy because I'm afraid I'll kill him." That afternoon, Butler worked near the corner of State and Market Streets and had a run-in with the Manion brothers—both of them the apotheosis of toughness. Sgt. Butler kept knocking them down, but they kept getting back up. He just couldn't land a knockout blow on either of them. James Lally, strolling farther down State Street, saw the crowd gather and got to the scene as fast as he could. Lally raised his billy only twice, landing withering blows on the heads of the Manions, one by one. When they next saw daylight, the Manions were in separate cells at the police station.

James Lally made good as the "subduer of toughs," but he acted like a true gentleman with respectable people. When he died of heart trouble in 1906, his wife, Mary, and his five children held his funeral mass at St. Joseph's Cathedral on Farmington Avenue.

Here's the point: Was James Francis Lally afraid to do his duty? Not hardly. Was he afraid of the characters of the demimonde? Laughable. A good businessman like Tom Hollister would never cause problems for a cop, but even if a self-centered sport like Billy West decided to make trouble, he wouldn't stand a chance against James Lally. True, there were some tough foreign proprietors on the lower end of State Street, but nothing James Lally couldn't handle.

SGT. JOHN BUTLER

Lastly—at the end of the Gilded Age, killing a police officer was unthinkable. Even if a man killed a policeman by accident, the smartest thing he could do was take his own life. Cheating Connecticut's traveling gallows was possible for a brief time, but realistically the killer's life was over. A sample of the tenor of the times: Two wardens at the Connecticut State Prison at Wethersfield, Daniel Webster and William Willard, were killed by inmates in 1862 and 1870, respectively. Both assailants were tried and hanged within months of the murders.

For some, there existed great irony in Hartford's uncontrollable vice. The Capitol produced all of Connecticut's laws, but the Capitol City appeared to be the most lawless and immoral city of its size in the country. Many felt that there wasn't another city of Hartford's size in the United States that harbored such a large number of fallen women and allowed them to do as they pleased. Still, while the ruckus bothered the men in control of the Capitol City, there was a strange reluctance to make any changes. Wrongly, there were those who thought the catalyst should be the Hartford police. Many an argument erupted from the false premise that the police could simply arrest the scofflaws and close the brothels. Others felt that Judge Albert Bill of the police court should start using jail sentences to mete out justice. However, jail sentences had been doled out sparingly up to this time and had accomplished nothing. One final wrong-headed idea involved the state legislature. What if the General Assembly allowed cities and towns to license houses of ill fame? This one final legal maneuver suited some, but was clearly a step in the wrong direction.[289]

Hartford Police Court Judge Albert F. Bill
Circa 1898

Many cities laid out red light districts in an effort to keep houses of prostitution separated from respectable neighborhoods. In 1882, a Los Angeles city ordinance made it "unlawful for any person to open, keep, maintain, or carry-on within the limits of the City of Los Angeles, any bawdy house, or place of ill fame, or prostitution, or to reside or live in any house of ill fame." However, the population of Los Angeles between 1880 and 1900 skyrocketed from 11,000 to 102,000, and the explosion in the number of bordellos caught everyone flat-footed. In an effort to protect the business district, the Los Angeles Common Council forbade bordellos inside of the block bounded by Fort (Broadway), Los Angeles, First, and Fourth Streets. Eventually, the council fashioned a red light district that was essentially a square between Alameda Street on the east, Broadway on the west, and First and Third Streets on the north and south. So said, to the northeast of this red light district, about 200 prostitutes lived and worked on Schaefer Street near Union Station. Schaefer Street no longer exists as the city closed the disorderly houses and bulldozed the whole area in 1909, adding nicely to the valueless middens of history. Still, when archeologists unearthed a privy in this area in 2008, about 200 medicine bottles were found, including bottles of *Darby's Prophylactic Fluid,* a common type of health formula used in houses of ill repute. At that time, *Darby's Prophylactic Fluid* was manufactured by Z. H. Zeilin & Co. of Philadelphia. . . .The rubble also included douche formularies and gynecological paraphernalia.[290]

The tenderloin district of San Francisco was in the North Beach and Embarcadero districts (Barbary Coast) near the water. The city fathers tried to keep prostitution between Larkin, Market, Church, and Eighteenth Streets—and also extending down to the waterfront. In the 1870s, they fashioned an even smaller red light district between Kearny, Stockton, Market, and Broadway Streets. This proved too tight an area since houses of ill fame kept popping up between this red light district and the waterfront.[291]

"Storyville," was New Orleans's red light district from 1897 to 1917. Named after Alderman Sidney Story, who wrote the necessary guidelines and legislation to control prostitution within New Orleans, this sixteen-block district was bounded by North Robertson, Iberville, Basin, and St. Louis Streets. (Recent maps show the Storyville District to the east of the original red light zone—between the French Quarter and Interstate 10.)

The red light district in Chicago was called The Levee because of its proximity to the wharves on Lake Michigan. The Levee District consisted of four blocks in Chicago's south loop area, between 18th and 22nd streets. From 1880 to 1912, prostitution boomed in the Levee District, but police eventually closed it down in the wake of a blistering vice commission report.

Every large city had a red light district and it isn't necessary to identify all of them. Suffice it to say that, during the Gilded Age, prostitution was almost universally regarded as a necessary evil; and perhaps even uncontrollable. Once again, authorities in all cities came to the conclusion that, with prostitution, they could ignore it, embrace it, or seek some middle ground. The red light districts were an attempt to secure the middle ground.

There were two notable attempts at licensing and legitimatising prostitution during the Gilded Age. The first was in Saint Paul, Minnesota, a city whose police force appeared ineffectual until after the Civil War. The second case was in St. Louis, Missouri, where prostitution was legalized in 1870.

Saint Paul, Minnesota had attempted to register prostitutes, beginning in 1865. Though this system of regulating prostitutes collapsed in less than twenty years, the influence of the system continued in Saint Paul's "under the hill" district well into the twentieth century. Though people are under the impression that Ordinance No. 10—the regulation of prostitutes in Saint Paul, Minnesota—ended in the early 1880s, the effects of the experiment lingered for decades thereafter.

In 1900, the *Saint Paul Globe* wrote, "This plan [of regulating prostitutes] was to apply not only to known houses of ill fame, but to the . . . lost creatures of the street. This subject is not a palatable one for newspaper discussion . . . and the city papers informally agreed to avoid mention of the plan while it was being experimented upon. It soon became manifest that it was an intolerable nuisance, and under the protection, afforded the number of immoral women to increase until nearly 200 were registered as "rumors" alone—not counting the inmates of recognized houses of ill fame. But this was not the worst of it. Protected by their licenses, these creatures became bolder and bolder, until they actually came to solicit in the very doorways of respectable businesses, and defied the police to restrain them. The system is still involved, and its evils unabated, notwithstanding the complaints that have been made."[292]

St. Louis, Missouri broke with the rest of the United States on July 5, 1870 when its common council passed the Social Evil Ordinance, legalizing prostitution. Half-a-dozen doctors were recruited to examine prostitutes, hopefully screening out the diseased women and admitting them to the Social Evil Hospital. The plan envisioned funds for this hospital coming from the registration fees and fines collected during the routine business of legalized prostitution. At first blush, St. Louis seemed well on its way to becoming a prostitution utopia. Sadly, historians will never know whether or not St. Louis's plan was good or bad because, in 1874, the Missouri General Assembly nullified the ordinance. Folks said, "the law received almost unanimous endorsement of the doctors of medicine in the state, but quite as unanimously the condemnation of the doctors of divinity."[293]

No matter what experiments were tried in the Gilded Age, during the period from 1907 to 1917, houses of ill repute came under a great deal of pressure to close. "Of forty cities investigated in the spring and summer of 1917, four had never established limits within which prostitutes were permitted to openly conduct their business, twenty-six had closed their red light districts, and ten cities still had them."[294]

As out-of-town newspapers grew bolder in their quest to expose and stamp out the immoral houses in the Charter Oak City, they sent sketch artists to Hartford in an effort to produce renderings of these houses "in which debauchery and crime were carried on during every hour of the passing days." They howled, "Where are the church people who claim to be anxious to save men's souls? What are city officials doing after they took an oath to suppress crime and bring offenders to the bar of justice? The capital needs cleansing and needs it badly." [295]

"To Chief of Police Bill, it is hard to say anything. . . . He has been chief of police for some years and has almost absolute control of the seventy or eighty patrolmen . . . . No man can question Chief Bill's honesty or integrity. . . . Are his hands tied by the click of politicians who are in power?"[296]

"At Wells Street, within a stone's throw of the finest capitol in New England, stands a house built on modern architectural lines. The building is well maintained . . . .The red blinds and the well-kept lawns and flower gardens, would attract the eye of a stranger; they would ask what well-to-do citizen resides in that domicile? In front of the house flows . . . the Park River. . . . And still further to the westward stands the capitol."[297]

"This house is so centrally located and so well patronized by the aristocrats, that it could not do business without the knowledge of the entire police department . . . .The artist who wished to get a sketch of the house and grounds, stopped a blue-coated guardian of the peace and quietly asked him where it was. The officer said, 'First house off of Mulberry Street on Wells Street. I think the number is seventy-six.' Then the policeman smiled and went on his way."[298]

Hartford wasn't the only city where the police knew every house of ill repute—and probably availed themselves of the inmates' services. In 1892, Salt Lake City's Chief of Police Arthur Pratt organized an "onslaught on the dives of vice . . . arresting keepers of houses of ill fame, inmates, and their patrons until the register at the police station recorded the names of fifteen keepers of houses of prostitution, forty-one inmates, and twenty-four visitors. . . . Among the latter was Capt. John J. Donovan, arrested at Lillie Evans's resort on East Third South Street."[299] (Pratt and Donovan didn't get along, and Chief Pratt used this little scheme to humiliate Donovan.)

The argument . . . by some well-known officials remained "let it run. It's a respectable place, and places of this sort are a necessity and they cannot be licensed, so let respectable houses go for the good of the community."[300]

The newspapermen in Bridgeport made a cogent point here. Bridgeport had a reputation as the most immoral city in Connecticut when it came to houses of assignation—fleabag hotels where soiled doves brought customers. Well and good, but when it came to the open acceptance of brothels, no municipality in the state could hold a candle to the Capitol City. Slicing the baloney a little on the thin side, one reporter noted, "In Bridgeport, the vice and immorality is light and frothy; in Hartford, it eats at the very roots of society from the highest to the lowest. . . . Hartford's immorality results . . . from its shifting population. State officials are coming and going all the time, and when the legislature is in session, there is a large transient population in the Capitol City."[301]

As the public became more and more anxious for information about the new Hartford Bridge, Morgan Bulkeley finally released a truncated version of his overall plan to transform the whole East Side of town.

In February of 1902, a New Bridge meeting commenced at the Hartford Board of Trade. The room seated about two hundred, but quickly it was standing room only. As different matters were discussed, it quickly became clear that everyone wanted a stone bridge. The Connecticut River Bridge and Highway Commission presented plans for the new bridge and its approaches. On the tables were huge architectural models of the plans under consideration.

Morgan Bulkeley made a few points. Firstly, the bridge must be erected at the same spot where the old bridge stood and the Hartford terminus must be at Morgan Street (because the state only owned the land where the old bridge stood). Secondly, $500,000 was provided for the erection of the bridge and the improvement of the causeway in East Hartford. This improvement alone would take half the money, and the other half was not enough to build the bridge.

The first plan envisioned an approach to the bridge coming diagonally from Morgan Street to the police headquarters on Market Street—then on to Main Street. This choice was the most expensive. The second option provided for the approach to run from Morgan Street to State Street. This offered a much wider approach to the bridge. A third scheme provided an approach from Morgan Street through State and Commerce Streets. (These three plans are simplified, but each involved huge changes to the landscape, including bulldozing buildings, moving railroad tracks, and so forth.)

The commission was hampered in all its plans by the fact that the General Assembly had fixed $500,000 as the cost of the bridge and the five towns that benefited most were expected to pay for it. Hartford's share was $379,000. In an odd arrangement, Hartford also received half of the tax money paid to the state by the trolley companies using the bridge. Out of these funds, the commission had constructed the temporary bridge and the causeway in East Hartford. The only way to raise more money was for the people of Hartford to pay more. Naturally, the commission wanted to know whether or not the citizens of Hartford would accept this.

Morgan Bulkeley then told of the various kinds of bridge structures and their costs—from a girder bridge that would cost about $750,000; to a steel arch bridge at $880,000; and lastly, a stone bridge that would run $1.6 million. These figures did not include the cost of approaches in Hartford and East Hartford. Depending on the approach accepted, a sum between $750,000 and $1,357,000 had to be added to the cost of the bridge. Most people wanted a stone bridge, with a total price tag of about $3 million. (Author's note: Massive cost overruns were rare in the early part of the twentieth century, but Morgan Bulkeley undoubtedly sensed that the work he had in mind could not possibly be completed for the sums that were being discussed.)

The upriver cities and towns were positively rabid when it came to the "draw" in the bridge so that upriver navigation would remain a viable dream. (By lifting the draw, boats could pass *through* the new bridge.) Under the laws of the United States, a bridge cannot be placed across a navigable stream without a draw, unless the war department gives permission. If a draw had to be used, it would add considerably to the expense of the new Hartford Bridge.

Morgan Bulkeley saw it this way: "Of the ten bridges between here and Springfield, only one had a draw. Besides, the river couldn't be navigated above Hartford by any boats that couldn't slip under the arch of the new bridge—as the span would be forty feet above low water mark. The draw issue was a dead letter.[302]

At the next meeting of the common council, resolutions were adopted to appropriate $1 million for a stone bridge across the Connecticut River and $709,000 for the approach from the city. Both matters had to be submitted to vote of the people.[303]

On March 11, 1903, the *Courant* reported that the bridge commissioners had reached a definite decision: the new bridge would be made of stone.[304] At one-fifth of a mile, it would be the largest stone arch bridge in the world.

The most fascinating part of the construction of the new stone arch bridge involved the caissons. To imagine a caisson, think of an upside-down shoebox, without a lid. Secondly, pretend that the shoebox is made of very thick wood and the top is layered to a thickness of three feet. Lastly, imagine that there is only six feet of headroom in the finished wooden caisson.

The man in charge of the caisson work was engineer Walter C. Ritner, who worked on the caissons at the New York and Brooklyn ends of the East River Bridge (Brooklyn Bridge). In the simplest form, at the Brooklyn Bridge, Ritner had to go down 96 feet, whereas, at Hartford he would only have to go down 60 feet to hit bedrock. However, there were only two massive piers at the Brooklyn Bridge, each requiring a caisson measuring 88 feet by 144 feet. For the Hartford Bridge, Ritner would have to sink eight caissons, each measuring 22 feet by 103 feet. After the final caisson was built and the men were digging out the earth from under it, eight caissons would be working in unison.

To build these caissons, Ritner brought by boat three million feet of southern pine to the site. Since the biggest sloop on the river could only handle a half-million board feet of lumber, it took six massive sloops to get the lumber in place. Each of these sloops drew eight feet of water, and the water at the center of the river—near the Hartford Bridge site—was only twelve feet deep.

As the caissons were completed—including their three-foot thick tops—concrete was poured on top to push the massive pile of wood to the bottom of the river. Then, twenty men went inside the caisson and dug it down to bedrock. Laborers on the Brooklyn Bridge got only $3.50 for a three-hour day, which was all they could work because of nitrogen narcosis—"the bends." The ordinary laborers in the caissons at the Hartford Bridge received $2.50 for an eight-hour day. At a depth of fifty-five feet, the workday dropped to six hours and the hourly wage rose to $2.75. The men reached $3.00 when the concrete work began in the caisson.[305]

On March 1, 1904, the caisson work began. The first trolley car would not cross over the bridge until November 29, 1907.

Concurrent with the work on the new stone bridge, the Connecticut River Bridge & Highway Commission began a huge municipal renewal program. As Morgan Bulkeley sought to clean up the avenues to the new Hartford Bridge, he began knocking down buildings with the enthusiasm of a little child. The repugnant waterfront neighborhoods that had festered like open ulcers for a century came tumbling down. Ferry, Kilbourn, Commerce, Pleasant, and Charles Streets—as well as sections of Talcott,

Grove and State Streets—were all slated for destruction. A new avenue, Connecticut Boulevard—running along the waterfront and forming a "T" at the entrance to the new bridge—would take their place.

The newspapers documented each demolition as if the city were losing the mansions and country houses of highborn Victorian noblemen. "One brick building at the extension of the Charles Street has been torn down, and a building at the corner of Front and Pleasant Streets is now being torn down. Some of the families have been given fifteen-day notices to get out. It is estimated that fully 300 families will be obliged to move from buildings required for the bridge, the approach, and the boulevard."[306]

For four years, this process continued, as a part of town that had long ago outlived its usefulness, came under the bulldozer's blade. Humorously, some of the very properties that had become notorious, even wicked, were mourned alongside those with a sliver of redeeming social value. For some odd reason, the public had the vast butter soft heart of a woman when it came to lost causes and condemned neighborhoods.

In a phrase, Morgan Bulkeley was a live-and-let-live kind of man. If most people were happy with the way vice was handled, then he could live with it. That said, with the new Hartford Yacht Club rising from the waters of the Connecticut River, and State Street designated as the most important approach to the new Hartford Bridge, he could see that the time had come for massive changes in the city. These changes did not coalesce in Morgan Bulkeley's brain overnight.

Several years before the old covered bridge burned, there were efforts afoot to replace it. However, when the bridge went up in flames in May 1895, the matter was predictably moved to a front burner. Even so, Morgan Bulkeley still had about eight years from the fire to the beginning of construction on the new bridge. This gave him the time he needed to coordinate a complete upgrade in Hartford's East Side, together with the construction of the new Hartford Bridge. In the end, it was as if the bishops proclaimed "On all of the major approaches to the Hartford Bridge, there will be no brothels."

Chapter 8

The End of an Era

After Tom Hollister's death in 1894, Jennie's health declined more each year. She was only fifty-two when her husband passed away, but her constitution wasn't what it should have been. Even her signature on Tom Hollister's estate papers—unlike her earlier copperplate flourishes—showed a weak and trembling hand, suggesting a much older woman.

Jennie and Tom Hollister had only been married for sixteen years, but these were comfortable and successful times. After Tom Hollister's passing, not only could Jennie see huge changes coming to Hartford, but she had a better understanding than most, thanks to conversations with her high-powered patrons. The massive urban renewal taking place on the East Side would not immediately affect Wells Street, but Jennie knew enough people at City Hall to know that Hartford's war on vice would eventually blanket the whole city. It was only a question of time.

In the last few years of the 1890s, Jennie did some traveling with her old friend and mentor, Angeline Start. They took trips to New York, Boston, Old Point Comfort—at Hampton Roads, Virginia—and a few other places. They thoroughly enjoyed each other's company. Jennie was now doing better financially than Angeline Start, who seemed to have less cachet than a barn swallow. Undoubtedly, this bothered Angeline Start since she had five years on Jennie Hollister and had given the younger woman her start.

In addition to continuing the Hollisters' business, Jennie continued as the charitable soul she had always been. Her obituary in the *Courant*—a paper not enamored of those in the prostitution business—spoke volumes. "Her death caused more comment than is usually the case when a woman of the half-world is called before her Maker. But Jennie Hollister was an extraordinary woman. She was charitable to a considerable degree and was beloved by many poor unfortunates who knew when they heard of her death that they had lost the best friend they had on this earth."[307]

Dr. Harlan P. Cole and his son, Dr. Hills Cole—homeopathic surgeons and gynecologists, with an office in the old Cheney building on Main Street—were Jennie Hollister's physicians. A few years earlier, Dr. Hills Cole had diagnosed her with a "fatty heart," and that was given as the cause of Jennie's death on Sunday, April 29, 1900. Since the allopathic physicians—the forerunners of today's medical doctors—believed in harsh treatments, including intestinal purging with calomel and vomiting induced with tartar emetic, homeopaths often achieved better results with their gentler methods. Patients, especially women, preferred the homeopaths' milder techniques. Therefore, it makes perfect sense that Jennie Hollister gravitated toward homeopaths despite her husband's preference for an allopathic physician.[308]

Family and friends attended Jennie Hollister's funeral at 76 Wells Street on Thursday, May 3, 1900, and she was laid to rest the same day at Cedar Hill Cemetery next to her husband, Tom Hollister, his parents

Joseph and Louisa Hollister, and his sister, Addie. The family monument in Section 5, Lot 147 at Cedar Hill is quite impressive and ringed with smaller stones for the individual family members.

At her death, Jennie Gertrude Hollister suddenly had a middle name. With all the games Jennie played with her name throughout her life, this one *might* be the most curious. The name Gertrude appears frequently in the nineteenth century Hollister genealogy. It is not an Irish name. It seems that Jennie McQueeney made one final name change—to Jennie Gertrude Hollister—presumably because she liked the sound of it. This may be thought of as the perfect exit for a member of the half-world, whose members had more aliases than bank robbers in the Old West and never tired of reinventing themselves.[309]

Though Jennie wasn't yet sixty, she had outlived her mother, father, and four siblings. Beyond that, Tom Hollister had already made bequests to his two surviving sisters, large enough sums to last them the rest of their lives. It seemed that the three daughters of Bridget McQueeney Mahon of Hartford, Timothy McQueeney's sister, were Jennie's only kin. The first of these three, Anna Mahon, was so painfully shy that her name never appeared in the papers. The last two women, the widows Bridget Mahon Luckingham of Hartford and Mary Mahon Dalton of Waterbury, came to the fore. They were first cousins of Jennie Hollister.

Just when it seemed that they were the only heirs, Judge Arthur Eggleston, with the help of the chief of police in Cleveland, Ohio, located an uncle, Francis "Frank" McGuire, who was the brother of Jennie Hollister's mother, Jane. Born in 1832, Frank McGuire was seventeen years younger than Jennie's mother. "He was born in Ireland near where [Jennie] Hollister was born and came to the United States in 1849." When Frank emigrated, he took the *Abeona* from Liverpool, with four of his siblings and landed in New York on December 7, 1849. They all went to Providence first and Frank worked as a laborer. Then he found a job in New York as a butler in a private home, and lastly served as a waiter at the Stillman House in Cleveland where he remained for over thirty years.[310]

McGuire wasn't much of a talker, but told Judge Eggleston quite a bit about the McGuires and McQueeneys of Dublin. McGuire explained, "His father, mother, and all of his siblings were dead now. Many of them didn't marry and those that did never had children."[311]

Frank McGuire was sixty-eight, never married, and suffered from kidney problems and cirrhosis of the liver. He last visited Jennie Hollister two years ago in Hartford. After Frank McGuire finished his interview with Judge Eggleston, he drew up a will. If McGuire should die unexpectedly, he would still be the heir to his niece Jennie's estate, and his will would direct all of Jennie Hollister's funds to beneficiaries of Frank McGuire's choosing.

With these legal matters resolved, Frank McGuire went to live with his niece, Mary Dalton, and her four children in Waterbury. Speaking of Mary Dalton, Frank McGuire told Judge Eggleston, "She is a child of a sister of the father of Mrs. Hollister."[312] (Bridget McQueeney Mahon was the younger sister of Timothy McQueeney, and she and her Irish-born husband, Patrick, came to America shortly after Jennie's family.)

No sooner had Frank McGuire put matters in order, than he took sick. At this point, the money had not yet passed to Frank McGuire because the estate was still in the process of settlement. On November 26, 1900—only seven months after Jennie Hollister's passing—sixty-eight-year-old Francis McGuire passed away in Waterbury from Bright's disease.[313]

Before the discovery of Frank McGuire, the death of such a successful madame touched off a scavenger hunt for her will. The Wells Street property was turned upside down and, finally, Judge Arthur Eggleston sheepishly announced that he had the will; it was admitted to probate on May 8, 1900 without opposition.

Jennie's last will and testament seemed a simple enough document, executed on April 26, 1893, with only four bequests: Firstly, Jennie gave $150 in trust to her husband, Tom Hollister, . . . "The money to be paid annually to Bishop Harkins of Providence, Rhode Island, to take care of Lot 16, Section 6 at St. Francis Catholic Cemetery in North Providence, Rhode Island." (The final resting place of her beloved sister, Catherine "Katie" McQueeney, who was laid to rest in 1875.)[314]

Secondly, Frank McGuire was to receive $1,000. Thirdly, her cousin Anna Mahon was given "all of Jennie's books and family pictures, but no pictures of Jennie Hollister, nor the oil painting of Jennie's sister, Katie." Fourthly, the rest of Jennie's estate, both real and personal, went to her husband, Thomas Hollister.[315]

Probate Judge Harrison Freeman asked for the amount of the personal estate in order to set bond for the administrator. No one knew, so Fred Holt of the Connecticut Trust Company agreed to help. Holt said that the personal estate was between $12,000 and $14,000, mostly in bonds. After entertaining requests for an administrator, Judge Freeman assigned J. Gilbert Calhoun, and at the suggestion of Judge Arthur Eggleston, set bond at $15,000. Appraisers of the estate were also appointed and Angeline Start was asked to continue watching the Wells Street property.

After Jennie's funeral, the young prostitutes working at 76 Wells Street—Lillian Brown, Ida Miller, Edith Blane, and Jennie Smith—took their personal belongings and left the house. The only two items they were not allowed to take were a pair of talking parrots. Angeline Start knew the birds belonged to the girls, but she refused to let the parrots leave the premises. Of course, the idea of talking parrots in a brothel is rife with humor—and maybe that's why Angeline didn't want them to leave. What if these seemingly innocent parrots had been trained to say, "Welcome back, Governor Bulkeley?" Angeline Start had enough imagination to realize that the talking parrots were as good as two little kegs of dynamite. Whether or not the parrots could actually speak remains a titillating mystery. In any event, common sense suggests that the parrots got their necks wrung and wound up in the Connecticut River.[316]

On May 21, 1900, the appraisers—Fred Holt and Joseph Buths—announced that Jennie Hollister's estate amounted to 37,996.92. (In 2014 dollars, that would be more than \$3.4 million.)[317]

The most obvious problem with Jennie's 1893 will was that events on the ground had changed. By the time Jennie Hollister passed away, three of her beneficiaries were already dead. Tom Hollister died in 1894; Anna Mahon passed away in 1898; and now Frank McGuire had expired. If Frank McGuire had not drawn up a will just after Jennie's death, the only two people left to inherit Jennie's estate, were her two first cousins—Bridget Mahon Luckingham of Hartford and Mary Mahon Dalton of Waterbury.

When Frank McGuire's will was probated in Waterbury, there were no surprises. Frank simply divided the money equally between Jennie Hollister's cousins—the two women mentioned above. A good guess is that Frank honored the \$150 request to maintain the gravesite of Catherine "Katie" McQueeney at St. Francis Catholic Cemetery in North Providence because he was eventually buried there too![318]

While Frank lived, the administrator, J. Gilbert Calhoun, gave McGuire \$50 a month just to make his last days comfortable. After the bills were paid, all monies received for the house, land holdings, furniture, personal items, bank accounts, and bonds went to the beneficiaries of Frank McGuire's estate.

At this point, two legal dramas took wing. The first was a claim brought against the estate by the Main Street undertaker, Charles Dillon, who was denied payment for services rendered, on the grounds that his bill was exorbitant. The second matter was a suit brought against the estate by Jennie's old friend, Angeline Start, of Warwick, Rhode Island.

On June 13, 1900, about two weeks after Jennie Hollister's remains traveled to Cedar Hill Cemetery, undertaker Charles Dillon presented a bill for $1,116 to administrator J. Gilbert Calhoun. The amount of the bill—and the fact that Mr. Calhoun had flat-out told Dillon that he was trying to get rich off one funeral—practically sent both parties in search of dueling pistols. Calhoun refused to pay the bill and told Dillon that if he insisted on receiving $1,116, he would have to sue the estate.[319]

In fairness to Charles Dillon, Jennie Hollister asked to be buried in the best possible manner, and her relatives gave Jennie a funeral rivaling that of European royalty. The undertaker's bill reflected this. For example, the casket—white oak, hand carved, full trim, silk lined, pillow to match, plate and engraving, with . . . hand-carved handles to match—cost almost as much as the ordinary working man's cottage.[320] So said, everyone has a little larceny in their hearts and the manner in which Jennie Hollister made her money may have played havoc with Charles Dillon's sense of fairness. Whatever the case, Dillon wanted exactly what he had billed.

One sanguine note emerges from Dillon's bill. The undertaker had to engage a hearse, plus fourteen carriages, to transport the casket and mourners to and from Cedar Hill. Not to present this as a historical fact, but the number of carriages suggests that there were more than fifty people at Jennie Hollister's funeral, when one would expect just a few curiosity seekers. Then again, Jennie always showed great generosity—paying the bonds of Ada Leffingwell, Carolyn Webster, and some of the other young prostitutes who needed her help. She may indeed have had more friends than circumstances suggest.[321]

The undertaker, Charles Dillon, was a fighter, while J. Gilbert Calhoun had a reputation as a conscientious lawyer. The *Courant* noted, "a case of this type—whereby an undertaker had to sue for payment of his bill—was so rare, the outcome might indeed be interesting."[322]

Eight months later, in the middle of February 1901, the dust-up between Dillon and Calhoun was resolved. Just before the trial was to begin in superior court on Tuesday, February 12, 1901, Charles Dillon dropped his suit for a settlement of $750. Between the reduced settlement and the legal expenses, Charles Dillon was probably the only one who didn't make a killing when Jennie Hollister passed away. [323]

Before Frank McGuire breathed his last, Jennie Hollister's old friend, Angeline Start, hired Hartford Attorney Sidney E. Clarke to lodge a claim against the estate. "For assistance, counsel, and advice rendered Mrs. Hollister in the conduct of her business by Mrs. Start, from October 1894 down to the time Mrs. Hollister died, April 29, 1900, Mrs. Angeline Start wanted $15,000." This struck one newspaper as spurious because [Jennie Hollister] never needed any advice or counsel."[324]

The *Courant* felt obliged to mention, "Mrs. Start formerly conducted the Cedar Mountain House on the New Britain road in this city. She now conducts the Hillside Hotel near Providence."[325] (Once again, the *Courant's* Editor in Chief Charles Hopkins Clark, a Yale-educated Republican of irritating righteousness, couldn't resist the opportunity to tell his readers that Mrs. Start was involved in prostitution.)[326]

The administrator, J. Gilbert Calhoun, received the suit on December 27, 1900. Angeline Start's lawyers were a distinguished pair. Sidney Clarke was an 1881 Yale Law School graduate and former chairman of the Hartford Democratic Town Committee, while Attorney Charles Wilson was not only a member of the Rhode Island bar for twenty-five years, but was Judge Advocate General of Rhode Island from 1887 to 1898. At present, he was a senior partner with Wilson, Gardner & Churchill of Providence. [327]

Judge Arthur Eggleston and Attorney Hugh O'Flaherty represented Attorney J. Gilbert Calhoun, the administrator of Jennie Hollister's estate.

The trial got underway in superior court on Tuesday, May 21, 1901, with Judge Alberto T. Roraback on the bench. Angeline's first motion seemed the weightiest. She made a claim against the estate for $15,000 owing to a promise allegedly made to her by Jennie and Tom Hollister. Angeline Start, upon taking the witness stand, was asked by her attorney, Charles Wilson, to detail the promise. Angeline said that during one of her visits to 76 Wells Street, about three weeks before Tom Hollister's death, he said to her, "Angie, should I die, I want you to give up your business, and come here and live with Jennie, and care for her, and I will have her promise to give you this house and furniture should she die before you." Angeline claimed that Tom Hollister then called Jennie into the room and asked her to promise to carry out this request. Angeline averred that Jennie said, "I will promise." Thomas Hollister died on December 27, 1894, and at least in Angeline Start's mind, the promise had value even though Angeline did not sell her business and move in to care for Jennie.

To bolster her claim, Angeline proceeded to characterize the many services that she had rendered to Jennie in the years after Tom Hollister's death. Firstly, she accompanied Jennie on trips to New York, Boston, Old

Point Comfort, and other places—for a total cost of $750. Secondly, she rendered care and nursing advice in the conduct of Mrs. Hollister's business.

Angeline said that in 1898, she received from Mrs. Hollister, by mail, a demand note for $20,000 in which the consideration mentioned was "love and sympathy." On her next trip to Hartford, Angeline asked Jennie Hollister why she sent the note. Jennie said simply that she wanted Angeline to have it. But Angeline claimed she told Jennie that she did not want the note, as she (Angeline) might die and Mrs. Hollister might then be annoyed and inconvenienced by it. Apparently, Angeline tore up the note in Jennie's presence. Jennie then told Angeline that a will would be executed, bequeathing to Angeline the house and furnishings at 76 Wells Street.

Judge Eggleston, on behalf of the administrator, began the cross-examination. Angeline said that she got acquainted with Mrs. Hollister about 1861 and with Tom Hollister about 1863. She admitted having run a disreputable house in association with Bill Prentice, then her husband. When Prentice died in 1873, Angeline continued to run the house. Angeline said that she and her new husband (Joe Start) now kept a hotel in Warwick, Rhode Island. Asked if it was a roadhouse, Angeline maintained that she did not know what a roadhouse was.

Attorney Charles Wilson made a number of objections at different times during Angeline Start's testimony. Wilson claimed that the questions had drifted too far afield and had nothing to do with the claim at hand. Judge Roraback saw it differently. Since he had allowed the plaintiff's lawyers considerable latitude on the direct examination, now he wanted to find out all he could about the parties involved and the nature of the service, as $3,000 a year for five years seemed a large sum. Eggleston continued.

In answer to Judge Eggleston's next line of questioning, Angeline admitted that when Tom Hollister died, his horses, blankets, bridles, snaffle bits and other stable equipment were given to her husband (Joe Start). Angeline admitted quietly that Jennie had been kind to her.

"She clothed you, didn't she" asked Judge Eggleston? Angeline began to split hairs, saying that Jennie had not clothed her, but that she (Angeline) had received some old clothes at different times from Jennie.

While Angeline Start gave testimony on the direct, Attorney Wilson put in evidence an envelope, in which it was claimed the "demand note" was sent to Angeline in Rhode Island.

On the cross-examination, Judge Eggleston drew from Angeline the fact that she found the envelope in Jennie Hollister's desk just recently. Angeline was also forced to admit that her bill of particulars wasn't accurate. She claimed in the bill that she sold a house in Providence to be in a position to care for the deceased, when in fact she did not own a house at the time. She sold only some secondhand furniture.

Angeline's other attorney, Sidney Clarke, called Fred P. Holt, the superintendent of the safety vault department of the Hartford Trust Company on Main Street in Hartford. Holt admitted that Jennie Hollister talked to him about preparing a will. Holt admitted that Angeline Start's name appeared among the proposed beneficiaries, but that the will had never been prepared.

Annie Wilson, a black domestic servant in the Wells Street house, said that Mrs. Hollister was sick a great deal after Mr. Hollister died and Mrs. Start visited the house often. The witness told Judge Eggleston that Jennie Hollister often gave things to Angeline Start.

Jessie Lansing, who for more than seven years was housekeeper for Jennie Hollister, told Attorney Clarke that Angeline Start visited at the house a great deal after Mr. Hollister died. Mrs. Lansing also said that she thought when Angeline Start came to the house, the visits were solely of a social nature. Mrs. Hollister often gave Mrs. Start clothing, and when they went on trips together, Mrs. Hollister told her (Jessie Lansing) that she (Jennie) always paid Angeline Start's expenses.

The last witness, Mrs. William Goodrich of Hartford, said that she was acquainted with Jennie Hollister. She had visited her home and saw Angeline Start at the home as well. Annie Goodrich lived on Kingsley Street—in the tenderloin—with her husband, William, a clerk with the post office. The Hollisters may have known William and Annie Goodrich from the days when Jennie and Tom Hollister ran the Bange mansion.

At 10 o'clock the next morning, Judge Eggleston said he had nothing more and the proceedings were closed. [328]

About a week later, on May 27, 1901, Judge Roraback awarded Angeline Start $800 with costs.[329] Roraback wrote "As Mrs. Start had left her bed and board at least eight times a year for three years or more to wait on Jennie, and that if the latter had promised to leave Angeline the house and furniture at 76 Wells Street, then Mrs. Start was entitled to secure monetary consideration."[330]

Since Angeline promised her lawyers one half of whatever the court allowed, she was about $400 ahead of the game. This paid the attorneys well for coming to Hartford and fighting the case for the effervescent, little Angeline Start. Jennie Hollister's friends considered Angeline mean-spirited for suing the estate of a dead woman. As a result, Angie Start lost face with many folks who were usually friendly toward her. People believed that Angeline did not sue for the money, but for the satisfaction, and to get under the skin of the rightful heirs. Without question, Jennie intended Angeline Start to be one of the beneficiaries of her estate. Unfortunately, Jennie died unexpectedly, which in part accounts for all the lawsuits. That said, litigation over Jennie Hollister's estate had finally come to an end.[331]

Jennie's housekeeper, Jessie Lansing, teamed up with Grace Howard in the management of the Bange mansion and never missed a beat. Grace Howard once said famously, "I run the most reputable house of ill-repute in the city." Grace bought out Jessie Lansing, before the latter woman's death, but when the winnowing out process had run its course, and the sporting houses in town were closed for good, Grace Howard lost everything.

Probably the most exciting episode in the life of the Bange mansion happened after Billy West moved to Norwich and Grace Howard had control of the old place again. On December 27, 1902, a couple of young gunmen—William Rudolph, a.k.a. "The Missouri Kid," and George Collins, a Hartford Dutch Point terror—used nitroglycerine to blow a safe at the Bank of Union, Missouri, and absconded with $14,500 in cash. Almost immediately, the bank's proprietors hired the Pinkerton Detective Agency to bring the outlaws to justice. Sometime during the next couple of days, in an ugly shootout, the bank robbers killed Detective Charles J. Schumacher. At length, a piece of paper surfaced, linking George Collins with Hartford, Connecticut. The Pinkertons contacted Hartford's Chief of Police Cornelius Ryan and an around-the-clock surveillance of the Capitol City was organized. Sure enough, Rudolph and Collins showed up at a boardinghouse near the corner of Asylum and Trumbull Streets. For a little excitement, during the evening hours, the two went to Grace Howard's pleasure palace.

Chief Ryan and the Pinkerton detectives were well in command of the situation, but were determined to apprehend the robbers on the street instead of risking a shootout inside a bordello. They managed to grab Collins on State Street, but had to go into Grace Howard's place to get William Rudolph. The police jumped Rudolph before he could pull his gun, but he still put up a vicious fight. Rudolph was in his early twenties and looked like a stripling, but he was deceptively strong. Detective John Butler, a heavyweight boxer, described "the Kid's" physique as something on the order of cast iron. Detective Garrett Farrell later said that he did everything in his power, but couldn't control Rudolph. With his very last ounce of strength, Detective Butler got a half Nelson hold on Rudolph's head and neck, finally subduing him. When the dust settled, Rudolph and Collins were in cells at the Hartford police station. Ten days later, they began the long train ride back to Missouri.

The two murderers were tried and convicted in separate trials. Collins was hanged on March 24, 1904. Rudolph's hanging was postponed a number of times—once because the execution date was too close to St. Patrick's Day—but, eventually, he met his maker on May 8, 1905. The hanging did not break Rudolph's neck, so he flopped around on the end of the rope for thirteen minutes before his body came to rest. One has to wonder if these malfunctions happened by design when a lawman was murdered.

Grace Howard surely saw the climax of the case in the newspapers, but the constant movement in the tenderloin occupied her time almost to the exclusion of all else. After all the *sturm und drang* of Jennie Hollister's death, and the lawsuits that followed, a local saloonkeeper, Edward McKernan, purchased 76 Wells Street for $14,000, aided by a $6,500 mortgage from Society for Savings. Faster than a madame could say "straw man," the property plopped into the hands of J. Gilbert Calhoun, administrator of Jennie Hollister's estate. Calhoun, in turn, sold it to Ada Leffingwell for $14,000 cash. This chicanery was designed to keep the public wondering who bought the property and whether or not 76 Wells Street would continue as a parlor house. Of course, the legal gymnastics fooled no one.[332]

In the middle of 1900, Ada Leffingwell was wooing Grace Howard to take over her Arch Street property, but eventually sold it to Grace Morton for $12,000. Ada Leffingwell moved her furniture in broad daylight from Arch Street to Wells Street, but the newspapers wondered— "Did Ada pay $14,000 for a place—specifically built as a house of ill fame—without speaking with Chief of Police George Bill? Did Ada give Chief Bill the impression that she intended to use a 6,000-square-foot brothel as her own private residence? How could Ada simply ignore the Saint Patrick's Day raid of 1899?" All great questions, but no good answers were forthcoming.

Whatever behind-the-scenes drama transpired, Ada Leffingwell's most heart-felt dream became a reality. By owning 76 Wells Street, Broken-nosed Ada became Jennie Hollister—albeit for just eighteen months until her own passing.

On November 16, 1901, forty-year-old Adella E. Curtis Alvord Leffingwell died at 76 Wells Street of pelvic peritonitis. The local papers were loathe to waste ink on Ada, but finally relented and printed obituary snippets that were almost the same size as those of Jennie Hollister. Besides her $10 fine in the 1895 *faux*-raid for selling liquor, the police raided Ada's place at 5 Arch Street only twice in fifteen years. In August 1892, Judge McConville fined Mrs. A. E. Alvord (Ada E. Leffingwell) $100 for keeping a house of ill fame, and she was fined the same in the 1899 St. Patrick's Day bloodbath.

In Massachusetts, Ada had a mother and sister, so without even a feeble wave of the hand to her many friends and admirers in Hartford, a hearse whisked her remains off to the Oak Grove Cemetery in Springfield. Ada may not have been much, but she was a profound inspiration to the millions of "also-rans" throughout the land.[333]

The glory days at 76 Wells Street were clearly over when a small article appeared in the classified section of the *Courant* on December 9, 1901—

Auction. Central Real Estate.

76 Wells St. Saturday, December 14, 1901.

By order of the probate court, to settle the estate of Adella E. Leffingwell, deceased. The premises, 76 Wells Street, 17 rooms, steam heat, excellent repair, brick barn. . . 108 feet on Wells Street and 200 feet deep.

—Bestor Auctioneers.[334]

The Saengerbund, a German singing society, bought 76 Wells Street from Ada Leffingwell's estate on October 12, 1902. The Saengerbund remodeled the building, adding a beautiful auditorium in 1910. The singing group used the old parlor house as a clubhouse until 1927 when they dedicated a new place at 266 Washington Street. The 76 Wells Street property was demolished a year later and the land added to a huge parcel— between Main, Gold and Wells Streets—cobbled together for Bushnell Towers and the Metropolitan District Commission's new headquarters.[335]

When the old Hollister place (Saengerbund Clubhaus) on Wells Street was purchased in 1928, the wrecking ball wasted no time reducing Hartford's marquee pleasure palace to rubble. Eventually, every single building on Mulberry Street disappeared and the whole area became just another pleasant memory—with a German accent. The Heublein Hotel, Poli Theatre, and City Hotel also surrendered as progress coldly and cruelly marched on.[336]

The business of running houses of ill fame threw off ancillary jobs and created new firms. In the years when the top of State Street represented the heart of the tenderloin—with its high-end collection of bordellos—there existed an immense need for laundry services. It tasks the imagination to think of a madame running a busy bawdy house and doing the laundry too. The sheets had to be changed after each session, not to mention the towels and linens that piled up endlessly in the course of a routine day. The Chinese residents of the city spotted this overarching need and started laundries in the area. They weren't allowed to become citizens, but they could work as resident aliens. Based on the number of Chinese laundries in and around State Street, it should come as no surprise that, as organized prostitution went into a death spiral, the area became the center of Chinese life in Hartford. In fact, by 1908, that whole block—from Statehouse Square to Front Street—became the city's Chinatown. The Shanghai Restaurant—the first, and best, eatery of its type opened on the second floor of 163 State Street, Frank Russell's old saloon-brothel, and that building became the target of a long string of opium raids as one vice replaced another.[337]

The biggest dilemma with prostitution was that the madames and their inmates were arrested regularly, but they merely paid their fines and returned to work. The women thought that if the court simply collected money in lieu of licensing fees, there was nothing to worry about. Once in a blue moon, one of the madames—feeling particularly abused by the police court—appealed her case in superior court. However, the expenses of lawyers and court costs were prohibitive; better to pay the fine in police court and go back to work.

In 1904, Hartford's Prosecuting Attorney J. Gilbert Calhoun made a few comments about the disappearance of the toughs from Hartford and he introduced some interesting points. Calhoun admitted that there was less crime now than at any time he could remember. He reminisced: "Ten years ago, there were many more [toughs] hanging out on the East Side . . . and they were frequently before the police court . . . for theft . . . for robbery . . . violence . . . .The police are more vigilant . . . . The interest in sailing and the Hartford riverfront has lessened the number of toughs. . . . Lastly, woman "rounders" began to disappear as, two or three years ago, county commissioners looked to eradicate saloons with backroom operations."[338]

Now the city concentrated on closing the houses of ill fame. It was as if, four decades after the Civil War, the public finally got its conscience back. However, for the moment, they let gambling and liquor violations slide. The gamblers conducted so many card and dice dens, the totality of the heap cannot be enumerated. If Chief of Police William Gunn got the word from the mayor, his forces would be busier than ever. Poker rooms were located on nearly every big block, and policy offices were more numerous than saloons. Chinamen love fan-tan and played it day and night right under the noses of the police. A book on the races was made every day in a centrally located saloon.

Meanwhile, Pearl, Allyn, and Trumbull Streets were overflowing with streetwalkers. These women weren't a bit shy; they hung onto a man like a prizefighter hung onto a foe. The women smelled of cheap wine and beer, and pestered every man until they could get one to buy them a drink of rum.

Despite raids, and efforts to put legal pressure on the property owners, by 1905 the bordellos in the tenderloin were still doing a lively business. On State Street, the team of Grace Howard and Jessie Lansing were working well together at the Bange mansion while near carbon copies of their operation ran at 167 and 169.

CHIEF WILLIAM GUNN

Farther down the street sat the French district, where "foreign places" brought vice to a whole new level. Robberies, fistfights, and knifings were standard fare for the truly wicked places down by the river. The women were of the lowest order, and their behavior shocked everyone; depravity became them.

One of the brothel business's foundations was the constant replenishment of young girls. The white slave traffic was at its worst in the degenerate area of the tenderloin around Front Street.

In the middle of the Gilded Age, a Nashville newspaper editor did a creditable job delving into the white slavery business. Wrote the newspaperman, "A notorious landlady among the demimonde was among those who went from Nashville to witness the scene at Murfreesboro. The object was to replenish her establishment. . . . The large number of young girls from the country offered an attractive field for the procuress . . . . As long as humanity remains what it is . . . there will be found men and women whose hearts . . . unchecked by morality . . . will work the ruin of young girls . . . .[339]

No matter what the clergy, the mayor, and the public thought of prostitution, the white slave trade was essential if the houses were to stay in business. Since the average length of service of a prostitute in a brothel was between two and four years, every place needed a steady supply of young prostitutes.

In the 1840s, political demagogues used the term "white slavery" to win votes by suggesting that shiftless, uneducated whites should be sold into slavery. After the Civil War, the term white slavery surfaced in many ways, but rarely in reference to young girls sold into prostitution. White slavery was used to describe inhumane working conditions and the status of women in the home—unpaid, overworked, lonely, and hopeless. So said, true white slavery—underage girls forced into prostitution—appeared so ugly that newspapers shied away from it.

In Norwalk, Connecticut, on Sunday, Novembers 14, 1842, two New Yorkers, David and Elizabeth Valentine, "did with force & arms willfully, maliciously, and feloniously entice & decoy away for the purposes of prostitution from & out of the lawful charge & custody of John Malloy . . . a certain female child of the name of Jane Day [sic] who was then under the age of twelve years &c. . . ."[340]

The Valentines were members of a religious community in Kakiat, Rockland County, New York (near Ramapo). On February 2, 1842, the jury found David and Elizabeth Valentine guilty and they were sentenced to two- and five-year terms, respectively, in the Connecticut State Prison at Wethersfield. The warrants were signed on March 1, 1842 and they began serving their sentences immediately.

But consider this—nothing about the arrest, trial, imprisonment, or release of the Valentines appeared in any newspaper in the United States! The first telegraph transmission wasn't until 1844 so the information wasn't available to the fourth estate. So said, even in the second half of the nineteenth century, cases of kidnapping for prostitution were rarely found in print. It wasn't until the first decade of the twentieth century that white slavery became front-page news.

In the West, citizens sometimes took a hands-on approach to white slavery. "In 1887, James Miller, from Volcano, California, came to [Los Angeles], bringing with him a bright girl, fifteen years of age, who he claimed to be his wife. . . . He attempted to place her in a bordello in Los Angeles. But from this place, she was temporarily rescued by the police. A party of indignant citizens, in disguise, waited upon Miller, escorted him to the bank of the river, and gave him a thorough coating of tar and feathers, as good a one as mortal man has ever received before. He was then warned not to be seen in the city."[341]

The White Slave Traffic Act—better known as the Mann Act—is a federal law passed by Congress on June 25, 1910. A little-known fact is that Connecticut was the first state in the country to win a prosecution under the Mann Act. Connecticut's pit bull State's Attorney for Hartford County, Hugh "Mead" Alcorn, convicted a dozen people under the Mann Act, and some of the guilty got sentences as long as ten years. Alcorn also revived an old law—the Confirmed Criminal Statute (indeterminate sentence statute)—whereby sentences of up to thirty years could be given to three-time losers. This made Connecticut an especially uninviting place for criminals to do business. In March 1910, a two-bit robber, Timothy Sheedy, got a sentence from three to thirty years! "The news of the conviction . . . reached New York where the majority of the professional crooks . . . came from, and when it was [learned] what was being done . . . this section was concluded to be a good place to keep away from."[342]

Articles about the white slave traffic in connection with houses of ill repute simply were few and far between in the nineteenth century. It wasn't until the early part of the twentieth century that stories appeared in newspapers castigating the social evil of enticing young girls into lives of prostitution.

There has been a kidnapping law on the books in Connecticut since 1830, which has served well even in white slavery cases as early as 1842. It is curious that in all of the cases of white slavery—from 1842 to 1912—the prison terms matched those prescribed by this law—just as they did in the David and Elizabeth Valentine case described earlier. The law states—

> Every person who shall kidnap, or forcibly or fraudulently carry off, or decoy, out of the state, any free person or persons entitled to freedom, or shall arrest or imprison a free person, or persons entitled to freedom, or knowing such person to be free, or entitled to freedom, with the intent to have the person carried out of the state, or to be held in slavery or service against his will, shall suffer imprisonment in the Connecticut state prison for a term not less than two nor more than five years, and pay a fine not to exceed five hundred dollars. . . .

People in the white slavery business knew how to be careful. At the first sign of trouble, they put their operation in mothballs. But for those who continued in the trade, the business of bringing young girls into the brothels became known as the "cadet system." This term goes back to the Revenue Marine Service, better known as the Revenue Cutter Service, established in 1799 for the proper collection of import and tonnage dues, as well as to aid in the observance of navigation laws. In 1876, Congress adopted a measure to appoint cadets to fill vacancies that occurred in the line. The cadets' pay sat below that of the third lieutenants.[343]

Big city police and fire departments used a cadet system as well, but it fell out of favor. In New York, it proved unworkable as the pay of seasoned workers shot through the roof. The pay of cadets crippled everyone, so the cadet system was abandoned.

In New York, the Herman brothers of Hartford, Albert and Jacob, were arrested for procuring young girls. Louise Tinkham, a Hartford girl, was a victim of the Herman brothers' attempt to make some easy money. According to George Titus, New York's Chief of Detectives, Albert and Jacob Herman had been extensively engaged in enticing girls from Hartford to New York, supplying the disorderly houses of the big city. In this case, Titus said that the brothers took the girl to New York on the Hartford boat Monday night [August 26, 1901] and sold her to the proprietor of a West Side bordello.

Louise Tinkham was a tall, pretty girl, with black hair and black eyes, but only seventeen years old. Before she went away, Louise shared a room in a boarding house with a cousin. Additional dispatches from New York said that the Herman brothers were held on bail of $1,500 each and Louise Tinkham landed in the House of Detention.[344]

During New York's 1893 Lexow Committee hearings on police corruption, the information collected by Rev. Dr. Charles H. Parkhurst's City Vigilance Committee was sensational and salacious, opening the public's eyes as nothing else could. Parkhurst and other reformers worked tirelessly to end the cadet system. After the Lexow revelations, the public's gentle sensibilities took a back seat to the exposure of vice and newspapers began to publish the facts.

Whether it be a man, a woman, a couple, or a group, the business of gathering young girls for the houses of ill fame was highly lucrative and as secretive as any business on earth. A proprietor would happily boast about how much money his place made last year, but he wouldn't say a word about the source of his young inmates. The subject was just too unsettling, except for the moral cripples who worked in this trade.

The biggest of all the white slavers in Hartford was the Italian immigrant Pasquale "Patsy" Fusco. He owned a grimy saloon—with a backroom operation—at 70 Talcott Street (corner of Front Street) on the lower East Side. When arrested, Patsy Fusco stated that 135 girls—seventeen and up—were delivered from New York to Hartford each year. At the same time, nationwide 60,000 new prostitutes were needed annually. Patsy Fusco also said that the Mann Act (1910) cut into the number of New York girls that could be procured, but he could get all he wanted from Connecticut.[345]

Pasquale "Patsy" Fusco

Under enormous pressure, Fusco admitted that he had a connection on New York's Upper East Side—Morris and Lena Cohen—who furnished girls to brothels in Connecticut and a number of cities in New York State. Patsy Fusco, and another Hartford madame Jennie Luretta, went to New York as star witnesses against Morris and Lena Cohen, and the couple received two- and five-year sentences, respectively. Morris also paid a $5,000 fine. Patsy Fusco's legal problems continued and he eventually disappeared—probably fleeing to Italy. For turning state's evidence, Jennie Luretta received a suspended sentence.[346]

The Hartford police had nothing to do with the biggest decisions regarding vice. This can be said with one caveat—to a man, the Hartford police knew about, and hated, the cadet system and the work of the white slave traffickers. It was a conundrum; while the police liked Jennie and Tom Hollister, accepted their Christmas presents—and probably even frequented their parlor house—the same officers hated the very foundation of the Hollisters' business. That said, a madame like Ethel Graves of the New England House was always treated like a leper because she openly tried to advance the cadet system.[347]

As Morgan Bulkeley and the rest of the bishops decided the best course for the city, there were a few key institutions of city government where they needed help. The mayor and the common council were no problem and the police would do what the mayor said. The real progress, or lack thereof, lay with the court system. A legal challenge to the Bridge Commission's authority had already set the project back three years and the last thing they wanted was a reprise of that mess.

The Hartford Police Court was where all the petty crime of the city reached a resolution. When Chief of Police Walter Chamberlin gave his first annual report to the common council, the city only had a population of

29,152—yet there were 435 arrests for drunkenness, 80 for breach of peace, 47 for assault, 22 for theft, and 1 for keeping a house of ill fame. By 1900, the city had a population of 80,000, and all of these numbers had more than tripled.

Easily one of the toughest jobs in the court system was that of judge of police court. While a judge's tenure could be rewarding and even inspiring, police court was pure hell. Not only did the judge have to deal with the dregs of society—drunks, brawlers, prostitutes and thieves—but now the judge of police court had to close thirty brothels. This last piece of business would force more than 200 madames and prostitutes out on the street.

What happens to old prostitutes? What happens when a prostitute's youth, beauty, skills, and stamina have abandoned her? In a Baltimore study of 256 aged prostitutes, it was found that only 30 percent of old prostitutes married, lived with men, or worked some legitimate job. The rest died or disappeared. Since this data is fairly intuitive, the judges who closed down the bawdy houses knew that suffering would follow. The job of police court judge was one of the nastiest jobs in town and about to get worse.[348]

Judge Albert C. Bill of the police court was an honest and capable man, but he had been in the job since 1895 and would turn forty soon. If he stayed on the bench in 1903, he would complete eight continuous years at the head of the Hartford police court. It should be remembered that the original police court statute of 1851 envisioned judges serving just a single year. The bishops felt it was time for a change. They needed someone younger to do the gut-wrenching work needed to turn the city around as the Hartford Bridge came on line in early 1908.

Edward J. Garvan was born in East Hartford on May 17, 1871 to state Senator Patrick Garvan. Edward attended Hartford Public High School,

Yale University, and graduated from Yale Law School in 1896. He was a Catholic, but a Republican. When he had completed his education, Judge Arthur Eggleston took a shine to Edward Garvan and made sure that he met the right people, including Attorney J. Gilbert Calhoun, who partnered with young Edward Garvan for ten years. The two maintained offices on Main Street.[349]

Garvan was exactly what the bishops wanted, and in March 1893, Judge Edward J. Garvan took over the police court. He was thirty-one.

When Judge Garvan took the bench at the police court, behind the scenes he made it clear to the new Chief of Police, William Gunn, exactly what he wanted. The job required both men to work closely together, so Gunn wasted no time getting down to business. Chief Gunn and his men put together a raid of six houses of ill fame. On a Sunday night in December 1903, between 7 and 8 o'clock, the police swooped down on six houses of ill repute and arrested thirty-four women and two men, bringing them to the station house in carriages, sleighs, and a patrol wagon. They were all released on bonds. The madames arrested included Grace Howard, Lena Wooley, Grace Morton, Anna Castaybert, and Clara and Minnie Simmons. (Since this case did not make it to superior court, one assumes the cases were dismissed or settled for an undisclosed amount in fines.)[350]

Judge Garvan dealt with every kind of criminal case under the sun, with a preponderance of drunkenness, thefts, and assaults. But on January 30, 1905, he was confronted with another proprietor of a house of ill repute. He paused and then proclaimed, "I'm opposed to the idea which is entertained by the proprietors of immoral houses. They . . . think . . . they can appear in police court, plead guilty, pay a fine as a sort of tax . . . and then go right back to business." To convince them that the idea was an erroneous one, Judge Garvan sentenced Louise Duval, for conducting an immoral house on Commerce Street, to three months in jail. Mary Sherman and Gabrell Shenot, who were charged with being inmates of the house, were each fined $10 and costs, "after the judge had given them to understand that they would be sentenced to jail if brought into court at any future time." It was 1905 and Judge Garvan's toe had slipped into the water.[351]

JUDGE EDWARD J. GARVAN

Clearly, Garvan didn't have the stomach to send a dozen madames to jail after only twenty months on the bench. Given the choice, he would have loved to complete the task with a series of baby steps, convincing brothel owners to close up shop on their own. The sentencing of Louise Duval to jail for three months—and putting the fear of God into her inmates—was a move in that direction. Unfortunately, Judge Garvan's break with the past didn't create a big enough splash.[352]

Four months later, on Saturday April 7, 1906, Judge Garvan faced another batch of messy cases. Some of the allegedly guilty parties were said to be proprietors; others claimed they were only married to proprietors; still others claimed they were merely frequenting houses of ill repute. Judge Garvan gave out a mixed bag of sentences, but was clearly frustrated, as he said, "In the past, these people have been brought into court and fined . . . then returned to the . . . same business."[353]

Judge Garvan knew what he had to do. At this point, he'd had more than three years' experience on the police court, but was still fighting an inner battle with the iniquities of the law—the revolving door, the depraved people who ran the bordellos, and of course his part in callously throwing so many people out onto the street. It was one thing to accept the job of closing the sporting houses and quite another to actually do it.

When Ethel Graves came before Judge Garvan that Saturday morning, the "Queen of the Madames" got the worst treatment any member of the demimonde had ever gotten. Besides being fined, the gay and festive Ethel was sentenced to thirty days at the Syms Street jail. Ethel's lover, Dick Hyland, got the same. Though the amount of time given to Ethel Graves was less than that given to Louise Duval a year earlier, it represented a huge sentence because Ethel Graves ranked so high in the demimonde and always had the best lawyers. The point was to make something stick.[354]

Ethel Graves was a prominent character in Bohemia for years, and knew enough to keep a man, plus a few high-priced lawyers, at her side. For years, Ethel Graves's lover was "Tudor" Adams. He spent three fortunes on Ethel, who was in her prime and irresistible. After Tudor went broke, Ethel transformed herself from a chrysalis into a butterfly by opening the New England House at the bottom of State Street. It was the lowest form of brothel, where dissolution trumped eroticism. Dick Hyland, a young sport—with a wife and kids in Middletown—met Ethel's needs and moved in with her.

Ethel Graves and Dick Hyland appealed their cases to superior court, putting great faith in their lawyers. The superior court was thrust into an unenviable position. If the court didn't come down hard on Ethel Graves and Dick Hyland, the other keepers of bawdy houses would rightly sense judicial weakness. Judge Garvan's initiative would go up in smoke. That said, the black-robed, high priests of the superior court knew exactly what was happening. The Hartford Bridge would be completed in early 1908, so closing the houses in the middle of 1906 seemed like inspired timing. Mayor William Henney, Judge Edward Garvan, and Chief of Police William Gunn were not acting on a whim. They had the most powerful backing imaginable.[355]

On June 6, 1906, Ethel Graves and Dick Hyland entered the courtroom of Judge Ralph Wheeler, originally from New London. Wheeler was a Democrat, who graduated from Yale in 1864 and was accepted into the New London bar in 1867. Wheeler served in the state Senate in 1874 and served as mayor of New London during Morgan Bulkeley's controversial holdover term as governor—from 1891 to 1893. Morgan Bulkeley's successor in the governor's office, Luzon Morris, appointed Ralph Wheeler to the superior court in 1893. Wheeler was an astute jurist. Future governor, Simeon Baldwin, wanted to put Wheeler on the Connecticut Supreme Court in 1915, but Wheeler died before that could happen. Suffice it to say, Judge Ralph Wheeler had no trouble helping Hartford drive out the lingering vice that threatened to tarnish the city's otherwise bright future.

After hearing Ethel Grave's motion in superior court, Judge Ralph Wheeler, through his long flowing white beard barked, "Ethel Graves, stand up! . . . . I will fine you $75 plus costs, with the understanding that you get out of the city and never return to do business in these parts." In his turn, Dick Hyland got the same fine and ejection order. Given the options, the couple decided to take flight. Ethel sold the New England House to a friend and didn't even arrange for future residuals, a common practice in the business. [356]

At the New England House, the inmates were just waiting for the storm to blow over. They assumed that business would return to normal. Whoever bought the New England House should have done well, except that Morgan Bulkeley had already decided that the New England House was one of the many sinks of iniquity that would be bulldozed to make way for the approach to the Hartford Bridge. Over the critical years of building and opening the bridge, it's obvious that certain members of the demimonde were slow to understand the powerful forces allied against them.

By early 1907, the houses of ill fame in the tenderloin were still running flat-out. Though there were raids and the fines kept going up, the proprietors had dug in their heels. Judge Garvan's legal machinations dragged along in desultory fashion through the spring of 1907, with the completion of the new Hartford Bridge in sight.[357] The bell rope was still lifting the monk, but the bishops could wait no longer; they were out of time.

Owing to a raid on ten houses of ill repute on Saturday night and Sunday morning, July 6-7, 1907, Judge Edward Garvan had a most unusual sight in his courtroom on Monday morning. Sitting and standing about the court room were almost a hundred women in their very best Sunday-go-to-meeting clothes, and most of the costumes were as loud as trolley gongs. The girls of the demimonde apparently wanted Judge Garvan to get the full libertine experience. The shocking colors and general mayhem made it seem more like another German-American orgy at the Auditorium than a sobering legal entanglement. But Judge Garvan wasn't moved, for his intention was to turn up the heat on the madames and their girls. Turning his chair slightly toward Chief of Police Gunn, he cleared his throat and began. Judge Garvan didn't want one syllable lost, so he conversed loudly in open court with Chief Gunn—

Garvan: I want to ask you the reason for these raids. Do you intend to stop this vice or to let these people . . . continue?

Chief Gunn: Anytime a warrant is given to me, I shall execute it.

Garvan: Then you consider it the duty of the prosecuting attorney to issue a warrant for you to raid these places?

Gunn: I do. Yes sir.

Garvan: Prosecuting Attorney Harrison Freeman. I would like to ask you the object of these raids. Is it the sincere purpose to keep State Street and [other] streets free from vice?

Freeman: It is the sincere purpose to clean State and [other] streets, and to keep them clean. There is to be a Boulevard along the west side of the river, and trolley cars are to run up State Street. It is the sincere purpose to keep the street clear of [brothels].

Garvan: If it is the sincere purpose to stop this vice . . . the court will assist all that it can.

Judge Garvan then fined, and sent to jail for three months, all the madames caught in the latest raid. . . . All of these women posted bonds and then covered the fines of their inmates. As far as the jail sentences, they would take their chances in superior court. For the time being, they had loads of money and passed out plenty of gold $20 certificates in the payment of fines and court costs. The money collected came to $1,537.[358]

Over thirty women of the half-world, the Bohemian inmates of the houses "in the Ward," left Hartford. The girls could not be induced by the madames to remain anywhere near the Capitol City. Judge Garvan and Chief Gunn thoroughly frightened the girls and these footloose members of the half-world held their collective breath until their trains cleared city limits.[359]

Judge Garvan showed an enormous amount of nerve. There had been many raids over the past forty years, but never before had a judge given three-month jail sentences to ten well-established madames. Judge Garvan caused a shock wave through the tenderloin that resulted in the wholesale exodus of prostitutes. It probably wasn't consistent to send all the older madames—women who had been before the court many times—to jail for three months, but Morgan Bulkeley had a schedule to keep. Almost every house of ill repute—with the exception of a few truly outlaw French houses on Front Street—were badly crippled by Judge Garvan's order.[360]

Six of the ten madames appealed their cases to the criminal division of the superior court. When their cases, at last, found their way into superior court, it was a lovely Wednesday morning, and the women were bedecked in diamonds and their finest apparel—but it made no difference. After hearing from their attorneys, Judge Howard J. Curtis sentenced them all to three months in jail. Grace Howard, Grace Morton, Kate Lamphere, Laura Phillips, and Clara and Minnie Simmons from Providence, were taken into custody. It may not have completely sunk in at the time, but when at length they got back to their houses, it would be only to pack their bags and say goodbye to four bare walls. Hartford wasn't an open city anymore.

Many of the madames and proprietors of resorts in the city were through. They could see what was coming down the road. For example, Grace Howard—who seemed to have more pluck than ten women—fled

Hartford for good in May 1908. She "purchased a New London place and installed new girls. She admitted that she did so for the purpose of making a good investment of a little money and New London was the only city in New England where houses of ill repute were practically guaranteed immunity from prosecution."[361]

The *coup de grace* delivered by Judge Garvan that Monday morning wasn't a surprise to Morgan Bulkeley and the other bishops. The first trolley car crossed over the new Hartford Bridge on the afternoon of November 29, 1907—only four and a half months after the big raid. Since the nastiest job in the world was complete—and the cars were using the new bridge—Judge Garvan tendered his resignation to Governor Rollin S. Woodruff on December 5, 1907, to take effect on January 1, 1908. Garvan served almost five years as judge of the police court. With Judge Garvan's resignation to take effect on January 1, 1908, one wonders if he assured Morgan Bulkeley that he would stay on the bench until 1908—the bridge's scheduled completion date. The chronology supports this conclusion.[362]

On Christmas Day 1907 the temporary bridge closed, and all traffic—walkers, teams and trolleys—had to use the new bridge over the Connecticut River.[363] The bridge cost $1,600,000. When the cost of the approaches was added in, the total came to $3,000,000. (Since this number was compiled in early 1908, when significant work on the waterfront remained incomplete, the final tally was likely much higher.)[364]

On his last day, Judge Garvan walked blindly into a huge party in his courtroom. His bench was covered with American Beauty roses and Judge Walter Clark presented him with a handsome silver loving cup. The courtroom swelled with well-wishers—Mayor William Henney; his father, Hon. Patrick Garvan; six pastors from the biggest churches in town; state Senator Patrick McGovern; a dozen of the finest attorneys in the city; and another two dozen businessmen and dignitaries from all around the area. Judge Clark presented the cup to Judge Garvan and gave a little speech—

> You've been at the head of this court for nearly five years. You took it at a time when . . . . the legislature . . . passed the probation law so that it fell to you . . . to appoint the first probation officer for this court . . . .There is no brighter page in the history of the . . . police court, than that which records your administration.

Edward Garvan had done what no judge before him was able to do, but he paid a high price. Judge Garvan had developed bleeding ulcers of the stomach and complications set in fast. He fought the battles as they came, but lost the war on March 4, 1910 when he died at his home on Farmington Avenue. He was thirty-eight.[365]

A quick study of the friends and co-workers at Judge Garvan's retirement party is enlightening. There were six clerics, a dozen prominent attorneys, and quite a few businessmen. But where were the bishops? Morgan Bulkeley sent his political sidekick, Patrick McGovern—still an actuary at Aetna Life, but now also a state Senator. The Goodwins were always the biggest taxpayers in Hartford because they owned so much real estate. In addition to the United States Hotel and many other rental properties, they owned a wide swath of farmland on the west side of Hartford—just waiting to be cut up into building lots. This land would someday become Woodside Circle, Goodwin Circle, Scarborough Street, Terry Road, Woodland Drive, Westerly Terrace . . . the list can hardly be enumerated. Didn't the Goodwins benefit by the elimination of bordellos in Hartford? So where were Frankie and James Goodwin? Where were the Dunhams, who owned Willimantic Linen and Hartford Electric Light

Company? (In fairness, the principal ownership of Hartford Electric Light had been transferred to Morgan Bulkeley, Billy Bulkeley, Thomas Enders, A.C. Dunham and three other Hartford men in 1884.)[366] Where was James Goodwin Batterson, the president of Travelers Insurance Company—the man with the largest private library in town, and a fine rolling estate at Albany Avenue and Vine Street?

REV. FRANCIS "FRANKIE" GOODWIN

A list of the wealthiest members at The Hartford Club on Prospect Street—almost all Republicans—would render a good sampling of the bishops. Many years ago, most of the members had lunch in the grillroom as opposed to the main dining room. In this smaller venue, there sat a huge, round wooden table in the middle of the room, surrounded by smaller tables that seated from two to six diners. Very few people ever dared sit at the big table. The men who thought of themselves as the wealthiest and most influential men in town were the ones who used this central table. The most prominent members ate there when they chose, but no one at the club ever uttered the word bishop.

After all the city's brothels had been closed, the members of the Federation of Churches and the local pastors did an enormous amount of back-slapping as they suffered under the delusion that they had done it all. Actually, in 1895—right after the old wooden covered bridge burned—Morgan Bulkeley's Bridge Commission conferred with city authorities and "emphatically insisted that every street approaching the bridge—that trolley cars, carriages, and automobiles used for a traffic way—should be free from brothels." [367]

The immediate effect of the displacement of so many houses of ill fame was like squeezing a balloon. Closing the bagnios in the heart of the tenderloin guaranteed that new brothels would spring up in other parts of the city, as the police predicted. Hicks Street, always considered a lovely residential street filled with respectable families on the north side of Bushnell Park, got its first two houses of ill repute about this time—at 22 and 46. The police closed them quickly.

Potter Street was deep "in the Ward," and packed with day laborers—mostly Irishmen and Italians. Full of rented tenements, it seemed a fairly easy place to start a house of ill repute. Once again, the police were forced to close down these new houses apace. In effect, the period from 1907 to 1911—when virtually every immoral house in the city had been closed down—was an uncertain time, when the final outcome wasn't known. While Judge Garvan's sentences in July 1907 should have been enough to close down the tenderloin, it was uncertain what the final outcome would be. Could the city stamp out all the brothels, or would forty years of uninhibited vice prove too much to overcome? [368]

Naturally Judge Garvan's jail sentences shocked everyone, but it must be kept in mind that the people of the tenderloin had no other skills. For this reason, and because the houses were so lucrative, some of them would fight Judge Garvan's edict to the bitter end. While it may have looked like the houses of ill repute would all be closed by the time Morgan Bulkeley's new bridge opened, the mop-up operations lasted through 1911. Even from 1912 through 1917, bawdy houses popped up here and there, but the police kept on top of the situation.

Another huge consideration in Hartford's clean-up in the first decade of the twentieth century, was the city's police force. When organized in 1860, Hartford's population at that time was 29,152, and there were only 8 sworn officers—including the chief. While the work of eliminating prostitution ground to completion just before 1910, the population of the city was 98,915, and the police force had swollen to 123 sworn officers. In other words, the population of Hartford rose 237% while the number of sworn police officers rose 1450%!

What accounts for such a huge disparity? There are three trends to consider. Firstly, in 1860, there were ten houses of ill fame. By 1900, there were thirty, an increase of 200%. However, including streetwalkers, houses of assignation, and backroom operations, the growth rate of the sex industry was more like 400%. Any way you cut it, prostitution in the Capitol City was out of control.

Secondly, city and town hiring practices always favored veterans. With Civil War soldiers and sailors still abundant in Hartford, the entire nation was crushed by the Panic of 1873—and a decade-long depression followed. Without question, all of the municipal departments were quickly loaded to the gunwales with veterans of the Civil War. This *may* have started an unprecedented climb in hiring at the police department that went unchecked until long after 1910.

Lastly, for almost a half century, everyone—from the members of the common council to the day laborers in the river wards—ignored prostitution, gambling, and liquor law violations. Did the bishops know that the time would come when respectable citizens would demand an end to vice? Would breaking age-old habits take a large and powerful police force? One guesses that someone in the city noticed the huge increase in police officers long before 1910. Regardless of how the matter was dissected, solely from a manpower perspective, the police department was never in a better position to crack down on vice.

JAMES G. BATTERSON

Judge Garvan's jailing of ten madames in July 1907 was about as powerful as the law gets, but as alluded to earlier, the Gilded Age sex industry just couldn't be dismantled that easily. It was like trying to put out a root fire in a forest; you never knew where the fire would pop up next. Judge Garvan sent dozens of young girls running from the city, but the madames were still there—with rent bills to pay.

Besides the accumulation of pressure from the Law and Order League, the Federation of Churches, as well as the courts, newspapers and citizens groups—large and small—the Women's Suffrage Group also helped by mobilizing housewives. In Hartford, Dr. Thomas N. Hepburn, a Scottish-American urologist at Hartford Hospital, was married to civic activist, Katherine "Kit" Martha Houghton Hepburn. (Kit eventually had six children, including the actress Katherine Houghton Hepburn, who was born in 1908.)

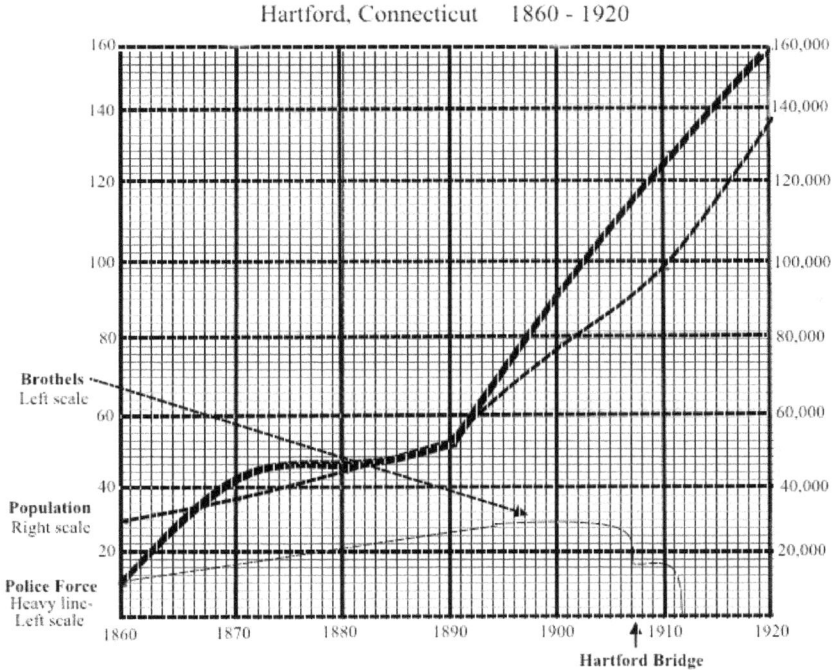

Hartford, Connecticut   1860 - 1920

Kit Hepburn championed the entire spectrum of cutting-edge feminist issues of her time, from family planning to women's suffrage. In the first decade of the twentieth century, Kit became deeply concerned with prostitution. While Dr. Hepburn led a lifelong campaign against venereal disease, Kit fought against white slavery, the unspeakable underpinning of the sex business. One finds it curious that Dr. and Mrs. Hepburn were such avid social reformers in their adopted home, while their housing situation bespoke uncertainty. The Hepburns rented houses from 1904 until 1919, when they purchased their first home on Laurel Street. Did it take them fifteen years to make up their minds about Hartford?

Kit Hepburn gave public addresses on the white slave traffic and prostitution to women's groups who were shocked at the frankness of her words. Nevertheless, Mrs. Hepburn talked openly about "Patsy" Fusco and his trafficking in white slaves, and brought the whole matter out of the darkness. The Women's Suffrage Group cannot be given all the credit, but the pressure generated by all of these groups was what brought action. While about ten cities in the United States still had red-light districts even after the First World War, closing the brothels in Hartford by 1911 must be viewed as an estimable achievement.

After two feckless Republican mayors—William Henney (1904-1908) and Edward Hooker (1908-1910)—Democratic Mayor Edward L. Smith became the city's chief executive in April 1910. Immediately, representatives of various organizations besieged him to finish the clean up of the city.

By the end of 1911, public opprobrium breached the dam of inactivity, and Mayor Edward Smith decided that tolerance had run its course. On Friday, December 29, 1911, Mayor Smith ordered Chief of Police William Gunn to close all the remaining houses of ill fame at once. Chief Gunn lost no time in executing the orders. At the end of a long day's work, Chief Gunn summarized the action for the press—

"The mayor has instructed the chief of police to close every house in this city that is reputed to be a house of ill fame. These instructions were executed today. . . . In giving them, the mayor has the full and undivided support of the board of police commissioners. He feels that whatever affect this policy may have upon the broad social question of prostitution, it cannot fail to have a deterrent effect upon the white slave traffic. [369]

MAYOR EDWARD SMITH

Completing the interview, Mayor Smith said that he would issue any further orders that became necessary for a full and complete obedience to the spirit and letter of the law. He said that a vigorous campaign would be waged against streetwalking, houses of assignation, and other forms of vice as they exist . . . in Hartford. . . .[370]

Mayor Smith then appointed a fifteen-member vice commission and a vice squad. This commission compiled a massive amount of information. In 1913, this data was published in book form. Among other things, it said that the police department was free from graft or complicity in the conditions that had existed. However, the time had come for a change in the policy of laxity in these matters, and the order of suppression should continue in force. After the commission had published its work, the vice squad continued its efforts, making many arrests, conducting raids, and keeping the lid on vice.

Owing to the American Social Hygiene Organization, the Wasserman Test (1906) and Dr. Paul Ehrlich's discovery of Salvarsan (1909), it became apparent that red light districts did not dampen vice and disease, but rather led to the proliferation of both.

Between 1910 and 1917, forty American cities ran vice studies, which showed that between 60 and 75 percent of all prostitutes had venereal infections. In Baltimore, infected prostitutes ran to 96 percent. Based on the information unearthed by these vice commissions, approximately 200 American cities—including virtually every one with a population over 100,000—closed their red light districts. The notorious Barbary Coast in San Francisco and the arrogant Storyville in New Orleans both disappeared by 1917.[371]

In the years after the War of the Rebellion, when the nation was sick with grief, the average person couldn't care less about prostitution, gambling, or drinking. If a woman lost her husband in the war, what would she care if her neighbor placed a bet on a horse or took a drink on Sunday? She wouldn't, and the same applied to prostitution. For almost a half century, America grieved. Then as the melancholic mourning period came to a close, the country pulled itself back together.

Slowly, the machinery of vice was broken down. In some smaller cities like Hartford, the houses of ill fame closed down just before the First World War. The houses in the larger cities lasted until World War I was almost concluded. No matter how the matter is analyzed, 1917 marked the end of an era. The people of America regained their moral consciences and the houses of ill fame closed. Throughout this period, there was widespread speculation as to whether or not the houses of ill repute would remain closed. They did, and of course, white slavery ended. However, vice never goes away forever because human nature is constant. Whenever a brothel strikes a low-class character as a good business opportunity, a new house of ill repute pops up. The place does a brisk business until the bishops tell the mayor to have the police close it down.[372]

Appendix A

Hartford Houses of Ill Fame (Taken from Police Raids) — 1850-1917

Albany road	N. J. Snow - 1857
Albany road	Dorrance Cadwell (1862)
76 Ann Street	Matilda (née Bridget Troy) Elliott
74 Ann Street	Mary Barnard (née May Smith)
Ann Street	Simmons sisters from Providence - 1898
Allyn Street	Minnie Greene –1904
111 Allyn Street	Henry Brown - 1907
5 Arch Street	Ada Leffingwell - 1885-1900 Grace Howard - 1900-1902 When Jennie Hollister died on April 29, 1900, Ada bought 76 Wells Street for $14,000. Ada died on November 16, 1901. Grace Morton - 1902-1906 Kate Edwards - 1907
116 Asylum Street (Foster Block)	Howard and Marie Parsons
255 Asylum Street	National Hotel - Julia Anderson - 1906
142 Grove Street	Grace Lombardi - 1902
146 Grove Street	Belle Young and Julia Fitzgerald
22 Hicks Street	Charley Cusick
24 Chapel Street	Wm. Roberts - 1907

39 Chapel Street	Adelaide Young
17 Charles Street	Joseph Ferrante - 1897
34 Chestnut Street	John Corrington
22 Commerce St.	John Stoszek - 1900
101 Commerce St.	Mary Bernard - 1902
103 Commerce St.	Benjamin Benjamins - 1904
109 Commerce St.	Louise Duval
133 Commerce St.	Grace Gorman
253 Commerce St.	Sarah McKennan
36 Elm Street	B. A & Jane Davis
Exchange Hotel	Peter Suzio - 1899
Ferry Street	Minnie Pease - 1880
32 Ferry Street	Julia Ann Harlow-1852 Mary Ann Atherton-(a.k.a. Polly Ann) - 1863 John Bertrand & Lewis Tracy-1883
46 Ferry Street	Mrs. Jacob Jordi - 1876
49 Ferry Street	Bartholomew Mahoney -1883
55 Ferry Street	Charles Johnson Ada Jackson
76 Ferry Street	River House - "the great red hotel by the river" James Wilson - finished building in 1871 Mary Ann Atherton (Wilson)-1871-1901
10 ½ Ford St	Gertrude Burnham - 1898

	May Smith
6 Ford Street	Minnie Greene - 1902
	Wallace Peterson
70 Front Street	Joe Cronin - saloon - backroom
88 Front Street	Joe Emmons's saloon - backroom
184 Front Street	Napoleon Champagne saloon - brothel
278 Front Street	John Mack & Emma Smith - saloon - backroom
Front Street	Laura Peck (near New England House) - 1860
Front Street	Rosa St. Germaine
327 Front Street	Frederick Bedlow and Margaret Goodrich
352 ½ Front Street	May Marquette – 1910
526 Front Street	Pasquale "Patsy" Fusco (crnr. Talcott Street)
585 Front Street	Pietro and Jennie Madeneso – rest. - backroom
17 Gold Street	Yee Tan
26 Gold Street	Sarah Andrews - 1873
Grove Street	Delia Pluff
Grove Street	Margaret Delaney
Grove Street	Josie Perry
Grove Street	Mamie Doyle
136 Grove Street	Louise Duval - 1912
142 Grove Street	Grace Lombardi

22 Hicks Street	Charles Cusick
46 Hicks Street	Dora Crossler
43 Kilbourn Street	Jennie Taylor's - Tom Hollister bought 43 Kilbourn Street from John Meek in June 1867. Hollister knew Jennie 'Taylor' McQueeney well and rented the place to her. The police arrested Jennie for keeping a house of ill fame there in 1868. Later, she changed her name to Jo Bullock and started a new house at 21 Sheldon Street.
47 Kilbourn Street	Joseph Barney (left Hartford after arrest)
136 Main Street	Frank & Carrie Rose Stahl – massage front - backroom
232 Main Street Hotel Alexander	Helen McIsaacs
217 Main Street	City Hotel - back room - T.F. "Jim" Callahan
483 Main Street	Grace Howard - 1898-1900
Main Street, Upper	Mary Barnard (née May Smith)
Main Street, Upper	New England Cafe- (opp. Fourth Cong. Church)
Main Street, Upper	Joe Weeks- 1866
577 Main Street	Woodruff Cadwell-1866
755 Main Street	Antoine Germaine
1094 Main Street	Elliott House-Matilda (née Bridget Troy) Elliott
1160 Main Street	Elizabeth Gray - 1916
1233 Main Street	Quincy House - Timothy Foley - 1901

1246 Main Street	Mary Schick - 1914
4 Market Street	Joe Weeks
22-28 Market Street	1851 Lafayette House (1st class hotel) 1860 Lafayette House . . . Joseph Clark, later Wm. Stratton 1868-Woodruff Cadwell buys the property-$13,000 1868 Central House . . .Dorrance Cadwell, hotel keeper 1875 Derby House . . ..Augustus Derby 1878 prop. reverts to Cadwell. . . When Frank Cadwell dies on Oct 17 1879, age 27, his wife Lizzie Cadwell runs the place until 1882. In the meantime, Lizzie Cadwell buys out Jennie and Tom Hollister at 165 State Street in 1883. 1882 Revere House W. A. Newton 1890 Revere House Mrs. Isaac Van Wagner 1891-1901 Columbia House . . . Timothy F. Meagher (N.Y.-Spfld.) Aug. 1, 1902- Columbia House torn down.
138 Market Street	Grace Morton Mary Montagne -1906
253 Market Street	Julliette Kenard
261 Market Street	Emmanuel Valenti - 1912
304 Market Street	Samuel Herrop
306 Market Street	Belle Meech
Market Street	Gertrude Burnham – 1898
Market Street	Hannah Coogan
87 Morgan Street	Wm. C. and Belle Daley, saloon - backroom–1866

89 Morgan Street	John Clough - saloon - backroom
13 Mechanic Street	Adolph 'Duffy' Pluff and Della Pluff
Mulberry Street	Pat Phlelan's saloon - back room
1008 Park Street	Mary "May" Wing-1900
Pearl Street	Isaac Warriner- 1865
81 Pleasant Street	Lillie "Swamp Angel" Taylor - 1900
30 Portland Street	Louis Hamkahib - 1911 Margaret Hamkahib
10 Potter Street	Annie Russell - 1907
16 Potter Street	Catherine Collins - 1894 Jeremiah Mahoney - 1896 Belle LeClare - 1907
82 Potter Street	Elizabeth Benedict - 1904
Prospect Street	Brower House (crnr. 25 Central Row) - Wm. "Bill" Crowley and his partner, Morgan Sherman . . . (later Hotel Climax- men only, but women were imported in droves.)
18 Sheldon Street	Maria Coffee - 1895
21 Shelton Street	Jo Bullock (Jennie Hollister)
107 State Street	Frank Russell's saloon
137 State Street	Caroline Webster- 1899
163 State Street	Maria Jacob's place (with her husband Henry)-1895 Adolph and Minnie Russell, Anna Castaybert Anna Castaybert –1899

May Minor - 1900
Laura Phillips

165 State Street   Tom Hollister- 1866-1874
                    Tom Hollister & Jo Bullock- 1875-1883
                    Lizzie Cadwell's-1883-1894
                    Grace Howard & Billy West- 1893-1896
                    Billy and Cora West-1896-1900, then Billy West
                    to Norwich.
                    Jessie Lansing - 1902
                    Grace Howard - 1902-1907
                    Tony Mousette's Boulevard Hotel - 1908

167 State Street   J. E. Durant's – 1874
                    Charles Rosenthal – 1875 – saloon - backroom
                    "Diamond Lucy" Chapman - 1877-87 (to New
                                                        Haven)

169 State Street   Liz Cadd
                    Daniel Dolancy - 1900

171 State Street   May Curley

179 State Street   Carrie Farnham -1880

181 State Street   Mary Montagne - 1894
                    Carolyn Webster - early 1895
                    Grace Morton
                    Clara Simmons- 1903

191 State Street   Julia Jaquith - 1893
                    May Cadwell - 1898
                    Lillian Stanley -1899
                    "May" Smith
                    Lena Wooley- 1903
                    Belle St. Clair -1907

193 State Street   Emma Kealey-1899
                    Minnie Simmons- 1903-1907

197 State Street	Louise Clark - 1906
	Gussie Smithian -1907
218 State Street	Kate Lamphere
245 State Street	New England House . . .Ethel Graves (later with Dick Hyland)
246 State Street	Mary Elliott - 1896
	Eva Beck - 1899
253 State Street	Charley Patterson's- 1874 - (crnr of Commerce)
	Nellie Roach
261 State Street	Blanche Russell- "Canadians, Italians, Irish, Swedish"
	Thomas F. & Nellie Somers - 1893
	Mrs. Herman Hunnebuck
263 State Street	Joe Weeks & Chas. Andrews - saloon - backroom
265 State Street	Mrs. Herman Hunnebuck -1896
269 State Street	Daniel Delaney, a.k.a. Amos Delurie - 1895
State Street (lower)	May Alton - 1906
State Street	Kate Pratt's - 1874
Statehouse Square	American Hotel - backroom
28 Temple Street	Mrs. Martha Johnson's
	Rodney & Minnie McGinnis -1898
38 Temple Street	William C. Dwight's saloon - backroom
44 Temple Street	W. W. Hunter's - saloon - backroom
46 Temple Street	Toot's place, H. B. & Toots Goodale
52 Temple Street	Hibbert "Hub" Smith's saloon - backroom

65 Temple Street   Mrs. Rudolph Davis's, saloon - backroom

Trumbull Street   Grace Howard and Harry Arnold-1896-1898

110 Ward Street   Mabel Hotchkiss - 1914

22 Water Street   Allen Wesley & Julia Sullivan - 1893

135 Wells Street   Franklin & Minnie Cadwell - 1874

114 Wells Street   Charles Thompson -1886
Mary Bernard (a.k.a. Mary Smith) - 1903

76 Wells Street   Thomas & Jennie Hollister- 1883 -1900
Adella Leffingwell - 1900-1901

48 Wells Street   Joseph Longworth's saloon - backroom

305 Windsor Street   John & Josephine Starzick

309 Windsor Street   Gustav Stavel

Woodland Street   Frank Cadwell's - 1874

Other keepers -   Lewis Cook - 1874
Joanna Cunningham - 1867
Charles Hill - 1874
John Mack & Emma Smith - 1874
Catherine Ricard - 1862
Augustine Sherlock - 1866
Charles Winter - 1866
Jennie Luretta – 1910

Author's Notes

Introduction

[1] Hartford Land Records, Hartford City Hall, Main Street, Hartford, Vol. 187, p. 297, June 2, 1882; "Pen and Ink Sketches of the Brothels of Sin . . .," *Bridgeport Sunday Herald*, May 31, 1896, 11.

[2] "Pen and Ink Sketches of the Brothels of Sin . . .," *Bridgeport Sunday Herald*, May 31, 1896, 11.

[3] Letter from Mark Twain to *Alta California*, dated September 6, 1868. Section "Hartford—The "Blue Laws."

Chapter 1 – Jennie McQueeney of Dublin

[4] FamilySearch.com (LDS); Ancestry.com; US Census Reports, 1850, 1860, 1870, 1880, 1900.

[5] US Census Reports, 1850, 1860, 1870, 1880, 1900; Vital Records, Connecticut State Library, 231 Capitol Avenue, Hartford, CT; Passenger Ship's Manifests, NARA, Ancestry,com.

[6] "Frank McGuire Found In Cleveland," *Hartford Courant*, May 22, 1900, 5.

[7] Miller, 35.

[8] Jones, 1906, 286-294.

[9] Dudley-Edwards, R; Williams, TD. *The Great Famine, Studies in Irish History 1845-52.* Dublin: Lilliput Press, 1956, (Reprinted 1997); Miller, 282.

[10] Miller, 291-293; *Revenue, Population & Commerce,* London: Oxford University Press, 1850.

[11] Ibid; "Riot in Glasgow," *The United Irishman,* March 11, 1848, 67; "Riots in Edinburgh," *The United Irishman,* March 11, 1848, 67; "Riots in London . . . ," *The United Irishman,* March 11 1848, 67.

[12] Hyde, 1975, *passim.*

[13] New York Passenger Lists, 1820-1957, Ancestry.com;

[14] "Editorial Article 2—No Title," *Hartford Daily Courant,* September 19, 1838, 2; Geer's Hartford City Directories, 1850-1855.
Note: A skilled machinist in a manufactory could make about $400 annually. Thus, weekly earning in the early 1850s would have been about 7.69; in 1900, median weekly earnings were $9.40; and, in 2014, median weekly earnings had blossomed to about $784. Keep in mind that weekly median earnings represent only one guide to dollar conversion through the decades. The 1850-dollar must be multiplied by 102, and the 1900-dollar by 83, to reach a reasonable value of past wages and prices.
Bureau of Labor Statistics, U.S. Department of Labor, *The Editor's Desk,* Median weekly earnings, 2004–2014 on the Internet at

http://www.bls.gov/opub/ted/2014/ted_20140423.htm (visited *September 25, 2014*).

[15] "The Working of the Law ," *The United Irishman,* February 26, 1848, 37.

[16] "The Poor Law," *The United Irishman,* March 18, 1848, 82.

[17] "State Prosecutions," *The United Irishman,* March 25, 1848, 101.

[18] Ibid.

[19] "Meeting of the Irish Confederation," *The United Irishman,* May 27, 1848, 235.

[20] "The Coercion Act—The Law of Dublin".—*The Irish Felon,* July 22, 1848, 66.

[21] Préteseille, Landry. *The Irish Immigrant Trade to North America: 1845-1855.* Master's Thesis, Centre d'Etudes Irlandaises de l'Université Rennes 2, Haute Bretagne.

[22] Ibid.

[23] "Frank McGuire Found," *Hartford Courant,* May 22, 1900, 5.

[24] Ibid.

[25] Greenhill & Giffard 1974, 14.

[26] "Common School Report…," *Hartford Daily Courant,* February 20, 1845, 2.

[27] Ibid.

[28] Southworth, Eve. *Drunken Sailors and Fallen Women: The New London Whaling Industry and Prostitution, 1820-1860,* (2005).History Honors Paper, 1.

[29] Weaver, Thomas, 1901, 5-11.

[30] Sanger, 1858, 484; "Diamond Lucy Chapman," *Bridgeport Sunday Herald,* October 2, 1904, 11.

[31] "Real Estate Transaction 1—No Title" *Hartford Daily Courant,* July 23, 1868, 2; "Article 6—No Title," *Hartford Daily Courant,* October 7, 1862, 2; "Old Lafayette House," *Hartford Courant,* August 1, 1902, 5.

[32] "Conclusion of Windsor Locks Murder Trial," *Hartford Daily Courant,* May 13, 1872, 2.

[33] U. S. Census Records, 1850, 1860; In the cemetery plot at St. Francis Cemetery in North Providence, R.I. that Jennie Hollister bought for her favorite sister Katie McQueeney, she only allowed two others to be buried there. Both were uncles of hers: Francis "Frank" and Alexander McGuire.

[34] "City Police Court," *Hartford Daily Courant,* August 11, 1860, 2.

[35] "A Strange Affair," *Hartford Daily Courant,* November 10, 1882, 2.

[36] "City Police Court, "*Hartford Daily Courant,* March 2, 1852, 2.
A skilled mechanic at Colt's Patent Fire-Arms in the mid-1850s made about $7.69 a week. In 1900, median weekly earnings were $9.40; and, in 2014, median weekly earnings had ballooned to $784. Therefore, to reach a reasonable value of past wages and prices, the 1850 dollar must be multiplied by 102 and the 1900 dollar by 83.
Bureau of Labor Statistics, U.S. Department of Labor, *The Editor's Desk,* Median weekly earnings, 2004–2014 on the Internet at http://www.bls.gov/opub/ted/2014/ted_20140423.htm (visited *September 25, 2014*).

[37] Death Certificate, City of Hartford, "Jennie G. Hollister," Connecticut State Library, 231 Capitol Avenue, Hartford.

[38] "Money and Business," *Hartford Daily Courant,* March 23, 1860, 2.
[39] Kneeland, George, 1913, 244-245; Woolston, 68-69.
[40] "Police Matters," *Hartford Daily Courant,* October 27, 1865, 2.
[41] "Article 3—No Title, "*Hartford Daily Courant,* December 23, 1863, 2.
[42] "Editorial Article 4—No Title," *Hartford Daily Courant,* December 24, 1863, 2.
[43] "Article 8—No Title," *Hartford Daily Courant,* March 29, 1864, 2.
[44] "Article 1—No Title," *Hartford Daily Courant,* December 23, 1863, 2.
[45] "Article 8—No Title," *Hartford Daily Courant,* August 2, 1858, 2.
[46] Woolston, 1921, 52.
[47] Ibid.
[48] "Widening of Market Street," *Hartford Daily Courant,* January 16, 1856, 2; "Article 3—No Title," *Hartford Daily Courant,* December 23, 1856, 2.
[49] "Article 6—No Title," *Hartford Daily Courant,* December 5, 1856, 2; "Article 3—No Title," *Hartford Daily Courant,* March 1, 1858, 2.
[50] "Money and Business," *Hartford Daily Courant,* March 23, 1860, 2.

Chapter 2 – Entering The Oldest Profession

[51] "After 'Jo' Bullock's Cash," *Bridgeport Sunday Herald,* September 16, 1900, 10.
[52] U.S. Census Records, 1850, 1860; "Death of Thomas Hollister," *Hartford Daily Courant,* December 28, 1894, 3; Ancestry.com.
[53] "Death of Thomas Hollister," *Hartford Daily Courant,* December 28, 1894, 3; "Wanted," *Hartford Daily Courant,* Nov, 19, 1855, 1.
[54] Ibid.
[55] "Arrested Fifty Times," *Bridgeport Sunday Herald,* September 16, 1900, 10.
[56]"Common Council—December 8," *Hartford Daily Courant,* December 9, 1845, 2; "Common Council—January 26," *Hartford Daily Courant,* January 27 1846, 2.
[57] "Police Court," *Hartford Daily Courant,* July 2, 1851, 2.
[58] "Court of Common Council—May 26," *Hartford Daily Courant,* May 27, 1851, 2; "Police Court," *Hartford Daily Courant,* July 2, 1851, 2; "Public Acts," *Hartford Daily Courant,* July 14 , 1851, 2; "Common Council—November 10," *Hartford Daily Courant,* November 11, 1851, 2.
[59] "City Meeting," *Hartford Daily Courant,* October 22, 1851, 2.
[60] "City Police Court," *Hartford Daily Courant,* February 6, 1852, 2.
[61] Geer's City Directory, 1899. On May 11, 1862, Boston Police Officer James T. Hill was attacked by toughs. Officer Hill was forced to pull his revolver and kill one of his attackers. ("Attack on Policeman," *Hartford Daily Courant,* May 12, 1862, 3.) Regardless of the date when police officers were officially allowed to carry firearms, it is clear that in New York, Boston, Hartford and many other

cities, revolvers—usually .32 caliber—were carried long before the police commissioners gave permission.

[62]"Police Headquarters," *Hartford Daily Courant,* March 14, 1865, 2; "New Police Headquarters," *Hartford Daily Courant,* March 24, 1870, 2; "New Police Building," *Hartford Courant,* March 16, 1897, 8.

[63] "Walter P. Chamberlin," *Hartford Daily Courant,* Nov. 21, 1870, 2.

[64] Ibid.

[65] Ibid.

[66] "Article 8—No Title," *Hartford Daily Courant,* February 22, 1859, 2.

[67] Ibid; "Walter P. Chamberlin," *Hartford Daily Courant,* Nov. 21, 1870, 2.

[68] Murphy, 2010, 2.

[69] "Report . . First Quarter of Police Force," *Hartford Daily Courant,* October 24, 1860 , 2.

[70] "Short Paragraphs," *Hartford Daily Courant,* July 31, 1860, 2; "Article 17—No Title," *Hartford Daily Courant,* July 31, 1860, 2.

[71] "Article 12—No Title," *Hartford Daily Courant,* January 23, 1862, 3.

[72] "Article 5—No Title," *Hartford Daily Courant,* July 21, 1862, 2.

[73] "All Sorts," *Hartford Daily Courant,* March 7, 1866, 2.

[74] Fishkill, New York, on the Hudson River above the city, was as close as the great railroad magnates would allow an out of town road to get to New York City. For a number of years, trains could move goods and passengers as far south as Bridgeport, from whence they would transfer everything onto steamships to complete the journey into New York City.

[75] U.S. Census Reports, 1850, 1860, 1870, 1880.

[76] U.S. Census Records, 1850, 1860, 1870, 1880, 1900, 1910, 1920. Providence City Directories, 1860-1927. Rhode Island Birth, Death, and Marriage Records; 1860-1930.

[77] "After 'Joe' Bullock's Cash," Bridgeport Sunday Herald, September 16, 1900, 10; It has been written that Angeline ran the Cedar Mountain House with Joe Start, her second husband, but this cannot be true. Angeline did not marry Joe Start until 1885, after Jennie "Taylor" McQueeney was running her own houses of prostitution for eighteen years. Angeline may have run the Cedar Mountain House while she was married to Billy Prentice—and this is where Jennie "Taylor" McQueeney got her start. The math works, but there is no corroboration for this chronology of events.

[78] "Saint Louis," *The Dallas Herald,* August 4, 1881, 6; Index to deaths in the *Saint Louis Globe Democrat,* 1881, http://www.slcl.org/content/index-deaths-saint-louis-globe-democrat-1881-m (accessed 7-18-2014)

[79] "Mrs. Start's Claim," *Hartford Courant,* May 22, 1901, 4.

[80] "The Shaw-Carstang Case . . . ," *Evening Star* (repr. *The Herald, N.Y.),* April 5, 1860, 1.

[81] Ibid.

[82] "New York City . . . ," *Hartford Daily Courant,* March 18, 1886, 3.

[83]"Jo" Bullock's Wine Closet," Bridgeport Sunday Herald, May 26, 1895, 11.

[84] Porter, Daniel L. Porter, 1466-67.

[85] "This Woman Made Happy," *Bridgeport Sunday Herald,* June 2, 1901, 10.

[86] U.S. Census Records, 1900.

[87] Hartford Land Records, Connecticut State Library, 231 Capitol Avenue, Hartford. Vol. 122, p. 453, June 27, 1867; Vol. 129, p. 426, March 20, 1868; Vol. 129, p. 426, March 28, 1870;

[88] Ibid;

[89] "Police Court," *Hartford Daily Courant,* May 15, 1868, 2; Woolston, 1921, 94; Howard Woolston's statistics regarding madames are based on U. S. Department of Justice statistics.

[90] "Article 4-No Title," *Hartford Daily Courant,* January 27, 1864, 2. Mary Ann Atherton's first recorded arrest was in 1864 and she was still in the business when she died in 1901. Always operating houses of ill fame in the squalor of Ferry Street, for all of her long career, she was without a doubt, the oldest and most notorious madame in Hartford.

[91] "General News" *Marshall City Republican,* "May 3, 1867, 1.

[92] U.S. Census Reports, 1870, 1880; Geer's City Directory, 1867.

[93] Dr. William Sanger's book *History of Prostitution* was published in 1858, but he began his research in 1855; Woolston, 1921, 20-21; Baldwin, 1999, 83.

[94] Woolston, 1921, 59-60.

[95] Ibid; "Police Intelligence," *Hartford Daily Courant,* August 26, 1870, 2; "Mr. Joseph Weeks In Jail," *Hartford Daily Courant,* January 23, 1873, 2; "The Courts," *Hartford Daily Courant,* February 12, 1873, 2; Hartford & Vicinity," *Hartford Daily Courant,* November 3, 1873, 2; "Police Intelligence," *Hartford Daily Courant,* March 24, 1874, 1; "Police Court," *Hartford Daily Courant,* September 28, 1874, 2; "The Courts," *Hartford Daily Courant,* February 12, 1881.

[96] "Police Intelligence," *Hartford Daily Courant,* August 26, 1870, 2.

[97] Ibid.

[98] "Action of the Police Board," *Hartford Daily Courant,* May 30, 1871, 2.

[99] "The Police Scandal," *Hartford Daily Courant,* September 9, 1874, 2.

[100] "The Chief of Police… ," *Hartford Daily Courant,* May 23, 1871, 2.

[101] "The Police Force… ," *Hartford Daily Courant,* November 8, 1871, 2.

[102] "The Police Board," *Hartford Daily Courant,* November 21, 1871, 2; "Vindication," *Hartford Daily Courant,* April 26, 1875, 2; "Steps Down And Out," *Hartford Daily Courant,* October 17, 1881, 2.

[103] "Williams A Witness," *Hartford Courant,* December 27, 1894, 1; "A Stubborn Witness," *Hartford Courant,* December 28, 1894, 1.

[104] Ibid.

[105] "A Pension for Williams," *Hartford Courant,* May 25, 1895, 1.

[106] "Police Court," *Hartford Daily Courant,* August 1, 1866, 2.

[107] Beers, 343; "Recollections of Forty Years in Connecticut Politics," *Hartford Courant,* October 25, 1914, E21-23.

[108] Ibid.

[109] Murphy, Kevin, *Fighting Joe Hawley* (2014) 192.

[110] Woolston, 23.

[111] Woolston, 24-25.

Chapter 3 – A Different Tack

[112] Connecticut General Statutes, 1796; Hartford: Hudson & Goodwin 1805, 216, 30, Connecticut State Library, 231 Capitol Avenue, Hartford.

Re: Nathaniel Hawthorne's 1850 book *The Scarlet Letter*— Scholars have searched forever for cases of actual branding with the letter A, which might have happened in the 17th and 18th centuries and the matter is cloaked in mystery. However, the following article courtesy of the Lane Memorial Library in Hampton, New Hampshire, sheds as much light on the subject as exists in 2014.

While there has been no shortage of studies on Hawthorne's literary borrowings in *The Scarlet Letter*, little has been found concerning historical sources of the letter *A* itself and virtually nothing has been uncovered concerning adulterous figures in Puritan history who might have been the prototypes of Hester Prynne and the Reverend Arthur Dimmesdale. We do know that by 1838, when an early version of Hester appeared in "Endicott and the Red Cross," Hawthorne was aware of the 1694 law enacted in Salem that required a woman convicted of adultery to wear a capital *A* sewn conspicuously on her garments. Although the appearance of this law so late in the century might seem anomalous to the 1634 setting of "Endicott and the Red Cross" or to the 1642-49 setting of *The Scarlet Letter*, we may easily resolve the discrepancy by assuming either that Hawthorne had been influenced instead by the early seventeenth-century case of Goodwife Mendame, sentenced to wear an *AD* on her sleeve, or that, contrary to his usual practice, he felt the need in this instance to take liberties with the historical record. . . In three separate sources, Hawthorne could have read about a woman who . . . had the letter *A* branded upon her. Perhaps just as curious, this woman was married to a former Puritan minister who had been previously censured for adulterous behavior. Hawthorne was undoubtedly acquainted with the fall of this Puritan divine, the implication being that the adultery of the Reverend Dimmesdale was not entirely the product of Hawthorne's irreverent imagination after all. As the scholarship on Hawthorne's historical works has consistently revealed, the "Actual and the Imaginary" do indeed meet, and "each imbue[s] itself with the nature of the other. . . ."

The case of the woman branded for adultery first appeared in the records of York, in what is now Maine. Dated 15 October 1651, the entry reads: "We do present George Rogers for, & Mary Batchellor the wife of Mr. Steven Batcheller minister for adultery. It is ordered by ye Court yt George Rogers for his adultery with mis Batcheller shall forthwith have fourty stripes save one upon the bare skine given him: It is ordered yt mis Batcheller for her adultery shall receive 40 stroakes save one at ye First Towne meeting held at Kittery, 6 weekes after her delivery & be branded with the letter A." (Beside that entry, written in the same hand, is the notation, "Execution Done." It appears that Charles Edward Banks, in his *History of York, Maine* (1935), recognized the connection between Hawthorne's novel and this case, for he refers to Mary Batchellor's branding in a section titled "The Scarlet Letter.")

    http://www.hampton.lib.nh.us/hampton/bachilerscarletletter.htm (Accessed November 1, 2014)

[113] Connecticut General Statutes, 1854; New Haven: T. J. Stafford, printer, 1854, Revision 1866. 266-67. Connecticut State Library, 231 Capitol Avenue, Hartford.

[114] Hartford Land Records, Connecticut State Library, 231 Capitol Avenue, Hartford. Vol. 138, p. 134, April 18, 1871; Vol. 150, p. 142, May 23, 1873.

[115] "Births, Marriages and Deaths, Vital Statistics, Hartford, CT," Connecticut State Library, 231 Capitol Avenue, Hartford.

[116] U.S. Census Reports, 1870, 1880.

[117] Sanger, 158, 524.

[118] Woolston, 1921, 66.

[119] "The Girls," *Cincinnati Daily Star,* July 25, 1878, 1.

[120] "Births, Marriages, and Deaths," Connecticut State Library, 231 Capitol Avenue, Hartford.

[121] "The Rev. Samuel A. Davis," *Hartford Courant,* March 18, 1897, 5.

[122] Ibid.

[123] "Article 5—No Title," *Hartford Daily Courant,* November 1, 1860, 2.

[124] "The Rev. Samuel A. Davis," *Hartford Courant,* March 18, 1897, 5.

[125] "Births, Marriages, and Deaths," Connecticut State Library, 231 Capitol Avenue, Hartford; "John E. Higgins. . .," *Hartford Courant,* December 11, 1900, 7.

[126] "Death of Thomas A. Hollister," *Hartford Courant,* December 28, 1894, 3.

[127] "Brothels Must Go," *Bridgeport Sunday Herald,* May 22, 1898, 68.

[128] Ibid.

[129] *48ᵗʰ Annual Report of the Park Commissioners of the City of Hartford, Hartford, Connecticut,* the Smith – Linsley Co., 1908, 8-17, State Archives, Connecticut State Library, 231 Capitol Avenue, Hartford. Bushnell Park was accepted by the voters in 1854, but not officially dedicated until 1868.

[130] Ibid; Baldwin, 1999, 20-29.

[131] "Soap & Candle Making Business," *Connecticut Courant,* August 15, 1810, 5; "Nichols & Humphrey," *Connecticut Courant,* November 12, 1822, 4.

[132] "Obituary: Lemuel Humphrey," *Hartford Daily Courant,* October 7, 1881, 2.

[133] Hartford Land Records, Hartford City Hall, Main Street, Hartford, Vol. 187, p. 297, June 2, 1882; "Pen and Ink Sketches of the Brothels of Sin . . .," *Bridgeport Sunday Herald*, May 31, 1896, 11.

[134] "Hartford's Immorality," *Bridgeport Sunday Herald,* May 31, 1896, 11.

[135] Ibid.

[136] Hartford Land Records, Connecticut State Library, 231 Capitol Avenue, Hartford. Vol. 26, p. 58, January 9, 1806; Vol. 42, p. 306-7, September 25, 1822; Vol. 185, p. 701, April 12, 1882; Vol. 187, p. 297, June 2, 1882; Vol. 198,

p. 30, March 25, 1885; "Obituary 1—No Title," *Hartford Daily Courant,* August 20, 1853, 2; "Atlas of The City of Hartford and the City of West Hartford," Springfield: L. J. Richards & Co., 1909; "Atlas of Hartford," Springfield: L. J. Richards & Co., 1896; City Atlas of Hartford –1880, Philadelphia: G. M. Hopkins, C.E., 1880. Maps courtesy of the Connecticut State Library, 231 Capitol Avenue, Hartford.

[137] "Fire Loss 1—No Title," *Hartford Courant,* November 29, 1886, 2.

[138] Hartford Land Records, Vol. 228, p. 649, March 27, 1894, Connecticut State Library, 231 Capitol Avenue, Hartford.

[139] Murphy, Kevin, 2010, 176; Murphy, Kevin, 2014, 137-8.

[140] "Hartford . . . Then and Now," *Hartford Courant,* March 31, 1957, SM13.

[141]"A Full Dock," *Hartford Daily Courant,* June 3, 1895, 3.

[142] "Strike at Miss ADA's," *Bridgeport Sunday Herald,* April 11, 1897, 18; "Obituary, Adella E. Leffingwell," *Hartford Courant,* November 18, 1901, 4; U.S. Census Records, 1900.

[143]" No. 5 Arch Street Raided, *Hartford Courant,* August 23, 1892, 1; Hartford Land Records, City Hall, Main Street, Hartford, Vol. 226 p. 707, April 29, 1893.

[144] Ibid.

[145] Ibid.

[146] Ibid.

[147] Ibid.

[148] U.S. Census Reports, 1850, 1860, 1870, 1880, 1900, 1910, 1920, 1930; Ancestry.com; FamilySearch.com (LDS); Geer's City Directories 1845-1863; "Hartford Fifty Years Ago," *Hartford Daily Courant,* January 14, 1857, 2; "City Intelligence," *Hartford Daily Courant,* November 16, 1863, 2; "Article 7—No Title," *Hartford Daily Courant,* November 17, 1863, 2; "Article 4—No Title," *Hartford Daily Courant,* January 27, 1862, 2; "The Riverfront To Lose Landmark," *Hartford Courant,* December 16, 1904, 5; "Deaths: Mary Ann Atherton (Sept 25)," *Hartford Courant,* September 26, 1901, 5.

[149] "Waterfront Once Busy Place," *Hartford Courant,* June 27, 1908, 11.

[150] "Four Fires," *Hartford Daily Courant,* March 2, 1885, 2.

[151] "Tenderloin in Tears," *Hartford Courant,* March 17, 1899, 1.

[152] No Title, *Boston Evening Transcript,* August 15, 1883, 2.

[153] "The River Front To Lose Landmark," *Hartford Courant,* December 16, 1904, 5; Landmarks Torn Down By Commission," *Hartford Courant,* November 29, 1907, 15.

Chapter 4 – The Demimonde

[154] "Caused Consternation," *Bridbeport Sunday Herald,* June 7, 1896, 11.

[155] Rosenzweig, 1983, 95.

[156] Baics, 2001, 54.

[157] Baics, 2001, 65.

[158] "'Diamond Lucy' Chapman," *Bridgeport Sunday Herald,* October 2, 1904, 11.
[159] Ibid.
[160] "Died In Agony," *Bridgeport Sunday Herald,* October 2, 1904, 3.
[161] "Death of Lucy Chapman," *Bridgeport Sunday Herald,* September 28, 1904, 4.
[162] "Fight In A House of Ill Fame," *Hartford Daily Courant,* February 18, 1878, 2.
[163] "House of Ill Fame Raided," *Hartford Daily Courant,* March 25, 1878, 2.
[164] "Honoring The Dead," *Hartford Courant,* October 10, 1891, 2.
[165] "Lucy Chapman's Case," *Hartford Daily Courant,* June 25, 2014, 2.
[166] "Society of the Sinners," *Bridgeport Sunday Herald,* March 14, 1897, 8.
[167] "Raid of Miss Chapman," *Bridgeport Sunday Herald,* January 3, 1897, 9.
[168] " A Gilded Den." *Bridgeport Sunday Herald*, March 27, 1898, 6.
[169] "Prindle Street Reformed," *Bridgeport Sunday Herald,* May 8, 1898, 7.
[170] "Lucy Chapman's Career Closed," *Bridgeport Sunday Herald,* February 15, 1903, 1.
[171] "Death of Lucy Chapman," *Bridgeport Sunday Herald,* September 28, 1904, 4; "Died In Agony," *Bridgeport Sunday Herald,* October 2, 1904, 3.
[172] "The Girl of the Period," The Charleston Daily News (repr. from London Saturday Review), April 18, 1868, 1.
[173] Ibid.
[174] Ibid.
[175] Ibid.
[176] Ibid.
[177] "The Latest Folly," *Evening Star (DC),* September 27, 1879, 1.
[178] Ibid.
[179] Ibid.
[180] Ibid.
[181] "Auditorium Sold…," *Hartford Courant,* February 25, 1905, 12.
[182] "Change of Location," *Bridgeport Sunday Herald*, January 29, 1899, 11.
[183] "Masquerade Ball," *Hartford Courant,* January 24, 1899, 11.
[184] "The Malley Trial, " *Hartford Daily Courant,* May 2, 1882, 2.

Chapter 5 – Tom Hollister's Passing

[185] The 1880 map of G. H. Hopkins C. E (Philadelphia) and the 1896 map of L. J. Richards & Co. of Springfield, Massachusetts, show very nicely the differences of the footprints between Lemuel Humphrey's old home on Maiden Lane, and the Hollister's creation of a parlor house at 76 Wells Street, Hartford. Also, the layout of the old Hollister place and the changes the Hartford Saengerbund made in 1910 can be gleaned from "New Building For Saengerbund," *Hartford Courant,* March 11, 1910, 4. (Jennie Hollister died on April 29, 1900 and the Hartford Saengerbund bought the house from Ada Leffingwell's estate on October 12, 1902.) The maps mentioned earlier can be seen at the Connecticut State Library, 231 Capitol Avenue, Hartford.

"The District Telephone," *Hartford Daily Courant,* January 27, 1879, 2,

[186] "AUCTION, AUCTION," *Hartford Courant,* December 10, 1901, 7; "New Building For The Saengerbund," *Hartford Courant,* March 11, 1910, 6.

[187] Ibid.

[188] Woolston, 1921, 132.

[189] Sanger, 1858, 549-556.

[190] Woolston, 1921, 64-5.

[191] Kneeland, 1913, 8.

[192] "Death of Lucy Chapman," *Bridgeport Sunday Herald,* September 28, 1904, 4; "Died In Agony," *Bridgeport Sunday Herald,* October 2, 1904, 3.

[193] Sanger, 1858, 549-556.

[194] "Death of Thomas A. Hollister," *Hartford Courant,* December 28, 1894, 3.

[195] "The Late E. M. Reed," *Hartford Courant, "* March 15, 1892, 4; Murphy, Kevin, 2010, 34.

[196] "Death of Thomas A. Hollister," *Hartford Courant,* December 28, 1894, 3; "Death of Thomas B. Seymour," *Hartford Courant,* September 4, 1868, 2; "Will of Thomas A. Hollister," *Hartford Courant,* January 11, 1895, 4.

[197] "After Jo Bullock's Cash," (*Bridgeport Sunday Herald,* September 16, 1900, 10.)

[198] Thomas A. Hollister," *The Hartford Weekly Times,* January 3, 1895, 6; Cedar Hill Cemetery, Lot 147, Section 5, Maple Avenue, Hartford.

[199] "History of the Sixteenth Connecticut Volunteers," http://www.gutenberg.org/files/31867/31867-h/31867-h.htm (Accessed August 30, 2014).

[200] "Doctoring in the Field of Battle," *Hog River Journal,* Spring 2007; Chemetzky, Jules. *Jewish American Literature" A Norton Anthology.* New York: W. W. Norton & Co., 2001, 94-5; "Dr. Nathan Mayer," *Bridgeport Sunday Herald,* July 11, 1912, 4.

[201] "Thomas A. Hollister," *Bridgeport Sunday Herald,* December 30, 1894, 11.

[202] "Will Prefer Charges. . .," *Hartford Courant,* April 9, 1895, 4; "Complaint Against Westcott," *Hartford Courant,* April 24, 1895, 6; "Westcott Wanted Delay," *Hartford Courant,* May 25, 1895,6; "Westcott Sued For Divorce," *Hartford Courant,* June 7, 1900, 4.

[203] "East Hartford News," *Hartford Courant,* June 6, 1895, 9.

[204] Section 5, Cedar Hill Cemetery, Maple Avenue, Hartford.

Chapter 6 – To Every Season

[205] "Barnum's Great Show Coming," *Hartford Courant,* April 25, 1887, 2; "Barnum," *Hartford Daily Times,* April 29, 1873, 2.

[206] "The President 'Ducking,'" *New York Times,* December 29, 1889, 5.

[207] U.S. Census Reports, 1850, 1860, 1870, 1880, 1900.

[208] FamilySearch.org; U.S. Census Reports, 1850, 1860.

[209] U.S. Census Reports, 1850, 1860, 1870, 1880, 1900; FamilySearch.org; "Billy West's Ambition," *Bridgeport Sunday Herald*, December 18, 1898, 35.

[210] FamilySearch.org; "Solicits Shady Business," *Bridgeport Sunday Herald*, May 19, 1895, 11.

[211] FamilySearch.org; "Officer Down Memorial Page," www.odmp.org/officer/12424-special-deputy-marshal-henry-smith (accessed June 26, 2014)

[212] Ibid.

[213] "Jo Bullock's Wine Closet," *Bridgeport Sunday Herald*, May 26, 1895, 11; "Hartford's Immorality," *Bridgeport Sunday Herald*, May 31, 1896, 11.

[214] U.S. Census Reports, 1850, 1860, 1870, 1880, 1900; FamilySearch.org; "Solicits Shady Business," *Bridgeport Sunday Herald*, May 19, 1895, 11; "Shadows From A Sundial," *Bridgeport Sunday Herald*, May 7, 1899, 10; "Death of A Well-Known Minstrel," *Hartford Courant*, February 17, 1902, 1.

[215] "Solicits Shady Business," *Bridgeport Sunday Herald*, May 19, 1895, 11;

[216] "One More Blasted Bud," *Bridgeport Sunday Herald,* March 3, 1895, 11.

[217] Ibid.

[218] Ibid.

[219] "The Problem Solved…," *Hartford Courant*, January 8, 1902, 6; "Says Bank Has Run…," *Hartford Courant,* March 30, 1906, 13.

[220] Ibid.

[221] "Maggie Doyle's Chum," *Bridgeport Sunday Herald,* May 22, 1898, 93.

[222] "Protesting Innocence To The Last…,"*The Evening Independent,* July 30, 1915, 1; "New York Murder…," *Eugene Register-Guard,* July 16, 1962, 4.

[223] Ibid; "Billy West's Ambition," *Bridgeport Sunday Herald,* December 18, 1898, 35; "With Her Lover," *Bridgeport Sunday Herald,* May 22, 1898, 11.

[224] Ibid.

[225] Ibid.

[226] "Brothels Must Go," *Bridgeport Sunday Herald*, May 22, 1898, 68.

[227] "Billy West's Ambition," *Bridgeport Sunday Herald*, December 18, 1898, 35; "Shadows From A Sundial," *Bridgeport Sunday Herald,* August 21, 1898, 10.

[228] "Hartford's New Tenderloin, "*Bridgeport Sunday Herald,* August 21, 1898, 35.

[229] "Law and Order League," *Hartford Daily Courant,* November 19, 1884, 2; "Strikes at South Norwalk" *Hartford Daily Courant,* September 1, 1886, 4; "Law and Order League," *Hartford Daily Courant,* November 19, 1884, 2; "Organized For Business," *Hartford Courant,* November 21, 1893,2.

[230] "Police Captains Vindicated," *Bridgeport Sunday Herald,* February 3, 1901, 7.

[231] "Where is the Law and Order League?" *Bridgeport Sunday Herald,* June 14, 1896, 10.

[232] "Drug Stores Raided," *Hartford Courant,* January 13, 1902, 1; "Fourteen Raids," *Hartford Courant,* February 16, 1903, 9.

[233] "Foote Makes A Raid," *Bridgeport Sunday Herald,* February 22 1903, 10.

[234] "State Police Bill," Hartford Courant, March 11, 1903, 8; May, 1903—House Bill 247, (State police), Longo, Jerry. Connecticut State Police. Charleston, SC: Arcadia Publishing, 2005, 7.

[235] "Tenderloin in Tears," *Hartford Courant,* March 17, 1899, 1.

[236] Ibid.

[237] Ibid.

[238] Ibid.

[239] Ibid.

[240] "Tenderloin in Tears," *Hartford Courant,* March 17, 1899, 1: "New Haven Athletic Club," *Bridgeport Sunday Herald,* February 20, 1898, 10.

[241] "Brass City Full of Bad Blondes," *Bridgeport Sunday Herald*, July 31, 1898, 25.

[242] Miller, Eleanor M. and Romenesko, Kim and Lisa Wondolkowski . *Prostitution in the United States. Westport, CT, Greenwood Press, 1993*.n.p.; Woolston, 25-26.

[243] "Highest Fine Ever Paid," *Bridgeport Sunday Herald,* July 16, 1899, 7.

[244] "By Authority," *Dallas Herald,* June 15, 1872, 1.

[245] "Laws That Harm The State," *The Memphis Daily Appeal,* July 4, 1868, 1.

[246] "City Ordinances," *The Louisiana Democrat,* October 30, 1895, 1.

[247] "Metzler Gets His Dose," The Indianapolis Journal, August 29, 1903, 1.

[248] "The Chinese Must Suffer," *Daly Alta California,* March 16, 1890, 8; "Judgments Affirmed," *San Francisco Call,* May 17, 1890, 2.

[249] "Shadows From A Sundial," *Bridgeport Sunday Herald*, May 7, 1899, 10.

[250] Ibid.

[251] Ibid.

[252] Ibid; US Census Records, 1900, 1910, 1920; "Divorce Decrees," *The Day (N.L.),* February 20, 1914, 7.

[253] "Brothels Must Go," *Bridgeport Sunday Herald*, May 22, 1898, 68.

[254] "Buried The Liquor," *Bridgeport Sunday Herald,* August 20, 1899, 9; Rocky Hill Center Historic District, http://www.livingplaces.com/CT/Hartford_County/Rocky_Hill_Town/Rocky_Hill_Center_Historic_District.html, (Accessed September 3, 2014)

[255] Sanger, 1858, 487.

[256] "Syphilis From 1880 to 1920: A Public Health Nightmare And The First Test Of Medical Ethics," http://www.uri.edu/artsci/com/swift/HPR319UDD/Syphilis.html (Accessed October 18, 2014); http://www.cdc.gov/std/stats/sti-estimates-fact-sheet-feb-2013.pdf (Accessed October 18, 2014)

[257] "Bristol's Sarsaparilla," New York Daily Tribune, September 10, 1842, 1.

[258] "Kidwell's . . .,"Daily Evening Star (DC), March 15, 1854, 1; "Samaritan's . . .," Daily Evening Star (DC), February 26, 1867, 1; Rosadalis," Charleston Daily News, June 5, 1869, 1; "Dr. Mott's . . . .," Evening Star (DC), June 14, 1871, 1; Cuticura . . . ," Memphis Daily Appeal, October 7, 1879, 1; "Acker's . . .," Benham Weekly Banner (TX), March 17, 1886, 1; "Africana," Anderson Intelligencer (SC), September 1, 1897, 1.

[259] "U.S. Public Health Service Syphilis Study At Tuskegee," http://www.cdc.gov/tuskegee/syphilis.htm, (Accessed 7-18-2014)

[260] "Salvarsan," The Sun (NY), February 13, 1914, 1; "Efficacy and Use of Salvarsan," Bismarck Daily Tribune, November 28, 1911, 1.

[261] Benedek, Thomas D. MD. History of the Medical Treatment of Gonorrhea. (paper) University of Pittsburgh. http://www.antimicrobe.org/h04c.files/history/Gonorrhea.asp (Accessed 7-21-2014) "High Death Rate. . .," Hartford Courant, February 14, 1917, 17.

[262] State Census Figures. Office of Connecticut's Secretary of State.

[263] "Notorious House Raided Monday," Bridgeport Sunday Herald, February 18, 1906, 6; "Raids Were Evidently Preceded By Tips," Bridgeport Sunday Herald, December 3, 1906, 6..

[264] "Highest Fine Ever Paid," Bridgeport Sunday Herald, July 16, 1899, 7.

[265] "Highest Fine Ever Paid," Bridgeport Sunday Herald, July 16, 1899, 7.

Chapter 7 – Two Random Events

[266] "Hartford Yacht Club," Hartford Courant, April 24, 1895, 6; "How The Fire Raged," Hartford Courant, May 18, 1895, 1.

[267] Hartford, Conn. As A Manufacturing, Business and Commercial Center. Published by the Hartford Board of Trade, 1889. (Printed by Case, Lockwood & Brainard Co., Hartford, CT. 20-45.

[268] Ibid.

[269] "Hartford Yacht Club," Hartford Courant, April 24, 1895, 6.

[270] "Bombarded By Boys," Bridgeport Sunday Herald, May 22, 1898, 56.

[271] "Three Of A Kind," Sacramento Daily Union, September 23, 1892, 3.

[272] Records of Cedar Hill Cemetery, Maple Avenue, Hartford.

[273] U.S. Census Records 1850, 1860, 1870, 1880, 1900, 1910, 1920; Records of Cedar Hill Cemetery, Maple Avenue, Hartford; "Attendant To Aetna Life Head…," Hartford Courant, April 10, 1938, 6; "C. L. Custis Of Aetna Life Dies at 90," Hartford Courant, October 8, 1910, A10.

[274] "New Bridge, Sure," Hartford Courant, August 20, 1894, 5.

[275] "The Bridge's Weakness . . . ," Hartford Courant, January 3, 1895, 3.

[276] "The End Of The Bridge," Hartford Courant, May 18, 1895, 8.

[277] "Old Bridge Gone," Hartford Courant, May 18, 1895, 1.

[278] "Police Commissioners," Hartford Daily Courant, August 4, 1880, 2.

[279] "The Bridge Gone," Hartford Courant, December 23, 1895, 1.

[280] "Disastrous Flood," Hartford Courant, March 2, 1896, 1.

[281] "New Temporary Bridge," Hartford Courant, June 13, 1896, 5.

[282] "Briefs in Bridge Suit," Hartford Courant, April 22, 1897, 7; "Bridge Law Sustained," Hartford Courant, May 3, 1898, 3.

[283] "New Dry Bridge," Hartford Courant, March 22, 1899, 3.

[284] "Frisbie or Preston, Which?" Bridgeport Sunday Herald, March 27, 1898, 21.

[285] "Citizens' Eyes Open," Bridgeport Sunday Herald, December 16, 1894, 9.

[286] "Hartford's Awful Shame," *Bridgeport Sunday Herald*, August 4, 1895, 10.

[287] Ibid.

[288] "Lally, Subduer of Toughs, Dead," *Hartford Courant,* December 29, 1906, 13.

[289] "Hartford's Awful Shame," *Bridgeport Sunday Herald*, August 4, 1895, 10.

[290] "Ordinance No. 224." *Los Angeles Herald,* April 24, 1886, 1; "Evidence Of Seamy Past Dug Out In Downtown LA," http://articles.latimes.com/1996-05-31/news/mn-10475_1_archeological-evidence, (Accessed 7-28-2014); Sharpless, Megan. *Unity in Numbers: The Archeology of the Demimonde (1840-1917).* (paper) University of Wisconsin, Senior Thesis, May 2008.

[291] "A Special Charge," *Daily Alta California,* April 13, 1872, 1; Kerr, Courtney. Geographical History of Prostitution in San Francisco. Journal of Urban Affairs, San Francisco State University, 1994, 54.

[292] Some More Valuable Expert Testimony . . ." *St. Paul Globe,* April 20, 1900, 1 (From *Dispatch* editorial, January 26, 1900)

[293] Cott, Nancy F. (Ed.). *Prostitution,* (Munich: K.G. Saur Verlag, GmbH & Co., Walter De Gruyter, Inc., 1993, 219; Woolston, 1921, 29-30.

[294] Woolston, 1921, 104.

[295] "Hartford's Immorality," *Bridgeport Sunday Herald*, May 31, 1896, 11.

[296] Ibid.

[297] Ibid.

[298] Ibid.

[299] "Yesterday's Sensation," *Salt Lake City Herald,* February 7, 1896, 1.

[300] Ibid.

[301] Ibid.

[302] "New Bridge Meeting," *Hartford Courant,* February 8, 1902, 7.

[303] "The City Government," *Hartford Courant,* March 25, 1902, 9.

[304] "It Is To Be A Stone Bridge," *Hartford Courant,* March 11, 1903, 10.

[305] "Caisson Work Begins," *Hartford Courant,* March 2, 1904, 3.

[306] "Work On The Bridge," *Hartford Courant,* August 7, 1903, 4.

Chapter 8 – The End Of An Era

[307] "Wealth Did McGuire No Good," *Bridgeport Sunday Herald,* December 2, 1900, 11.

[308] Murphy, Kevin, 2013, 52-3.

[309] "Obituary 6—No Title," *Hartford Courant*, April 30, 1900, 8; Cedar Hill Cemetery, Lot 147, Section 5, Maple Avenue, Hartford.

[310] "Frank McGuire Found In Cleveland. . . .," *Hartford Daily Courant*, May 22, 1900, 5; Passenger Lists – Ancestry.com; U.S. Census Records, 1850, 1860, 1870, 1880, 1900.

[311] Ibid.

[312] Ibid.

[313] "Frank McGuire Sick", *Hartford Daily Courant*, June 14, 1900, 2; "Mrs. Hollister's Estate," *Hartford Daily Courant*, October 11, 1900, 4; "Francis McGuire Dead," *Hartford Courant*, November 28, 1900, 3.

[314] "Will & Inventory of Jennie G. Hollister," April 26, 1893, Connecticut State Library, 231 Capitol Avenue, Hartford; Hartford Land Records, Connecticut State Library, 231 Capitol Avenue, Hartford, Vol. 222, p. 604, July 1, 1892; Vol. 264, p. 203, February 7, 1899.

[315] Last Will and Inventory of Jennie G. Hollister, April 26, 1893, Connecticut State Library, 231 Capitol Avenue, Hartford.

[316] "Jennie Hollister's Will," *Hartford Courant*, May 8, 1900, 4; "Mrs. Hollister's Estate" *Hartford Daily Courant*, October 11, 1900, 4; "Will of Mrs. Jennie G. Hollister," *Hartford Daily Courant*, May 5, 1900, 5; "Will of Mrs. Jennie G. Hollister," *Hartford Daily Courant*, May 5, 1900, 5. .

[317] There are a million ways to compare wages and cost of living numbers over the decades, so the author has simply gone by average weekly wage in 1900 and in 2014. Using government statistics, the average weekly paycheck in 1900 was $9.40, and in 2014 it is $848.00. In other words, the weekly wage has risen by a factor of 90 times. Therefore, the roughly $38,000 that Jennie Hollister left in 1900 would be worth $3,420,000 today. This does not include the value of health and retirement benefits, paid sick days, vacations and maternity leave, none of which existed in 1900. Nor does it take into account the whopping debt of the US government in 2014, all of which could value Jennie Hollister's estate much higher in today's dollars.

[318] "Wealth Did McGuire No Good," *Bridgeport Sunday Herald*, December 2, 1900, 11; Report of Joan McNulty of the Diocese of Providence, Rhode Island. Dated: June 9, 2014; "Frank McGuire Will", *Hartford Daily Courant*, December 7, 1900, 16.

[319] "An Undertaker's Bill…" *Bridgeport Sunday Herald*, June 24, 1900, 9; "Mrs. Hollister's Burial," *Hartford Courant*, June 19, 1900, 5.

[320] Ibid.

[321] Ibid.

[322] Ibid.

[323] "Hollister Funeral Bill," *Hartford Courant*, February 13, 1901, 5.

[324] "After Jo Bullock's Cash," *Bridgeport Sunday Herald*, September 16, 1900, 10.

[325] "Claim Against Mrs. Hollister's Estate," *Hartford Courant*, September 14, 1900, 4.

[326] Murphy, Kevin, *Water For Hartford*, 2010, 56-162.

[327] "S.E. Clarke, East Hartford Lawyer Dies," *Hartford Courant*, July 10, 1935, 4; Marquis, Albert Nelson, 1915, 1164; "Mrs. Start Sues Hollister Estate," *Hartford Courant*, December 28, 1900, 4.

[328] "Mrs. Start's Claim: She Wants $15,000 From The Hollister Estate," *Hartford Courant*, May 22, 1901, 4.

[329] "Mrs. Start Gets Judgment For $800," *Hartford Courant*, May 28, 1901, 16.

[330] Ibid.

[331] "Received An $800 Verdict," *Bridgeport Sunday Herald*, June 2, 1901, 10.

[332] "Investigation Promised by Mayor," *Bridgeport Sunday Herald,* October 21, 1900, 11; "Mrs. Hollister's Property Sold", *Hartford Daily Courant*, July 12, 1900, 14.

[333] "Obituary, Adella E. Leffingwell," *Hartford Courant,* November 18, 1901, 4.

[334] "Classified Ad 3—No Title," *Hartford Courant,* December 9, 1901, 7.

[335] "Hartford . . . Then and Now," *Hartford Courant,* March 31, 1957, SM13.

[336] "Saengerbund Has Semi-Centennial…" *Hartford Courant,* January 13, 1908, 13.

[337] "Hartford, Connecticut: Landmarks…," http://hartford.omaxfield.com/citycenter/eastside1959.html. (Accessed August 8, 2014); "White Women Found…," *Hartford Courant,* December 9, 1914, 1.

[338] "The Tough Is Going," *Hartford Courant,* May 11, 1904, 3.

[339] "Recruiting The Demimonde," The Pulaski Citizen,(repr. from Nashville Banner), March 4, 1880, 1.

[340] Trial Record. February 2, 1842, 83. Fairfield County Superior Court, Connecticut State Library, 231 Capitol Avenue, Hartford.

[341] "Tarred and Feathered," *Los Angeles Daily Herald,* October 15, 1887, 1.

[342] "Making Hartford County Too Hot For The Criminals," *Hartford Courant,* June 28, 1914, X2

[343] "Revenue Marine Cadets," *Lancaster Intelligencer,* June 9, 1881, 1.

[344] "Hartford Girls Lured," *Hartford Courant,* August 29, 1901, 1.

[345] Address given by Katherine Houghton Hepburn, wife of Dr. Thomas N. Hepburn, on April 15, 1914 at the National Association of Collegiate Alumni in Philadelphia and published later by the Connecticut Women's Suffrage House in Hartford.

[346] "Patsy Fusco Is Recalled," *Hartford Courant,* August 13, 1917, 6; "White Slave Case Before Grand Jury," *Hartford Courant,* October 18, 19111, 2; "Mrs. Cohen Gets Five Years In Prison," *Hartford Courant,* October 31, 1911, 15.

[347] "Ethel Graves Required By Law. . .," *Bridgeport Sunday Herald,* June 10, 1906, 8.

[348] Woolston, 1921, 76.

[349] "Judge Garvan Dead," *Hartford Courant,* March 5, 1910, 2.

[350] Police Make Raids," *Hartford Courant,* December 7, 1903, 12.

[351] "Keeper of Immoral House," *Hartford Courant,* January 31, 1905, 3.

[352] Ibid.

[353] "Must Check Social Evil," *Hartford Courant,* April 9, 1906, 6.

[354] "Ethel Graves and Dick Hyland . . .. ," *Bridgeport Sunday Herald,* April 15, 1906, 8.

[355] Ibid.

[356]"Ethel Graves Required By Law . . . ," *Bridgeport Sunday Herald,* June 10, 1906, 8.

[357] "Bridge Commission Gets Land North of State Street: City Will Ultimately Own Large Part Of Riverfront," *Hartford Courant,* December 7, 1905, 3.

[358] "Police Raid Ten Resorts," *Hartford Courant,* July 8, 1907,1; "City Treasury Got A Big Find," *Hartford Courant,* July 9, 1907, 7.

[359] A Twenty Year History," *Bridgeport Sunday Herald*, July 14, 1907, 20.

[360] Ibid.

[361] "City Of New London…," *Bridgeport Sunday Herald,* May 17, 1908, 21.

[362] "First Car Crosses Over . . . ," *Hartford Courant,* November 30, 1907, 1.

[363] "Temporary Bridge Is Now Closed," *Hartford Courant,* December 26, 1907, 4.

[364] "Cost of New Bridge," *Hartford Courant,* February 21, 1908, 8.
Hartford had to pay $2,104,000 and towns on the east side of the river $105,000, for a total of $2,309,000, and the Bridge Commission had income from other sources, which was being used.

[365] "Judge Garvan Dead," *Hartford Courant,* March 5, 1910, 2.

[366] Murphy, Kevin, 2010, 95.

[367] "Pastors Take Credit," *Bridgeport Sunday Herald,* July 14, 1907, 19.

[368] "Resorts Everywhere," *Bridgeport Sunday Herald,* September 1, 1907, 11.

[369] "Mayor Smith Begins Anti-Vice Crusade," *Hartford Courant,* December 30, 1911, 1.

[370] Ibid.

[371] Woolston, 1921, 54-55; Social Hygiene, Vol. 4, The Passing of the Red Light District, Mayer, Joseph, 197-209.

Acknowledgements

This book presented a unique challenge—fleshing out the lives of some of the most marginal characters of the Gilded Age. The madames, prostitutes, streetwalkers, runners—and a huge cast of supporting characters—made every effort to maintain low profiles. Just as Jennie Hollister made sure that no pictures of her survived, so it was with other members of the demimonde. For the most part, they lived fast, died young, and were almost forgotten forever.

As always, I first must thank my parents, Bob and Mary Murphy, for giving me life, a first-class education, and a million incidentals along the way. I have used these words before, but I don't know how to say it any better.

Along the same lines, I would like to thank a dear friend, Jody Galvin, who edited the final manuscript. It's a mystery where these guardian angels come from, but I can assure you it is above my pay grade.

Once again, I am grateful for the help and patience of the staff at the Connecticut State Library, particularly Carolyn Picciano, Jeannie Sherman, Mel Smith, Jerry Seagrave, Kevin Johnson, Glenn Sherman, Maria Paxi, Steve Rice, and Kristi Finnan.

Also at the Connecticut State Library, I would like to thank Connecticut State Librarian Kendall F. Wiggin, and Curator Dave Corrigan of the Museum of Connecticut History at the State Library. They have helped more than they know.

At the Hartford History Center—located on the 2nd floor of the Hartford Public Library—I would like to extend a tip of the hat to Brenda Miller and her staff.

Information about Jennie Hollister's favorite sister, Katie McQueeney—buried in Section 6, Lot 16, at Saint Francis Cemetery, North Providence, Rhode Island—was unearthed by Joan McNulty of the Archdiocese of Providence. I would like to thank her formally for her help.

The staff members of the Cedar Hill Cemetery in Hartford were very helpful in digging out old documents pertaining to the Hollister family. I would particularly like to extend thanks to Executive Superintendent William Griswold, Karen Baker and Beverly Lucas.

The wild doings of the Gilded Age demimonde were recorded in very few places. The *Bridgeport Sunday Herald* was an outlier. The author would like to thank posthumously the paper's managing editor, Richard "Dick" Howell (1869-1932) who chronicled this bizarre—some would say unbelievable—time in Connecticut history. Richard Howell started as a newspaper cartoonist, and later turned to editing. Howell appreciated good caricatures, cartoons, and other art, so his papers were always loaded with top quality line art, making them great fun to read. Howell, a very serious writer, was highly regarded by his peers throughout the state. True, he used the florid style of the day, but he didn't exaggerate. In checking his facts, the author was pleasantly surprised with the accuracy of Howell's reportage.

This, I'm afraid, is only a representative collection of the people who contributed to *Prostitution In The Gilded Age: The Jennie Hollister Story.* For those I have inadvertently missed, rest assured that this book would never have come together without your help. Many thanks.

Bibliography

Papers & Reports

Baics, Gergely. *The Saloons of Hartford's East Side: 1870-1920.* Hartford Studies Collection: Papers by Students and Faculty. Paper 28. Hartford: Trinity College, 2001.

Southworth, Eve. *Drunken Sailors and Fallen Women: The New London Whaling Industry and Prostitution, 1820-1860.* History Honors Paper, 1. (2005).

Newspapers

Anderson Intelligencer, Benham Weekly Banner, Boston Evening Transcript, Bridgeport Sunday Herald, Charleston Daily News, Cincinnati Daily Star, Daily Evening Star, Hartford Courant, Hartford Times, Dallas Herald, Evening Independent, Evening Star, Indianapolis Journal, Irish Felon, Lancaster Intelligencer, Los Angeles Herald, Louisiana Democrat, Marshall City Republican, Memphis Daily Appeal, New York Daily Tribune, New York Times, Pulaski Citizen, Sacramento Daily Union, Saint Louis Globe Democrat, Saint Paul Globe, Salt Lake City Herald, United Irishman

Magazines

Twain, Mark. *Alta California.* September 6, 1868, Section "Hartford."

Jones, Plummer F. *Deserted Ireland: An Account Of How The Irish Abandoned Ireland To Become Americans, And The Consequences To Ireland. The World Today,* February 1906, 286-294, Chicago: The World Today Company, 67 Wabash Ave. Chicago, IL, (Hearst's International, Vol. 10, 2-5.)

Papers & Addresses

Benedek, Thomas D. MD. History of the Medical Treatment of Gonorrhea. (paper) University of Pittsburgh.

Hepburn, Katherine Martha Hepburn. Address given at the National Association of Collegiate Alumni in Philadelphia and published later by the Connecticut Women's Suffrage House in Hartford.

Kerr, Courtney. Geographical History of Prostitution in San Francisco. Journal of Urban Affairs, San Francisco State University, 1994.

Sharpless, Megan. *Unity in Numbers: The Archeology of the Demimonde (1840-1917).* (paper) University of Wisconsin, Senior Thesis, May 2008.

Cemeteries

Cedar Hill, Hartford, CT

St. Francis Cemetery, North Providence, RI

Books

Allis, Marguerite. *Connecticut River*, (New York, G.P. Putnam's Sons, 1939)

Baldwin, Peter. *Domesticating The Street: The Reform of Public Space in Hartford, 1850-1930.* (Columbus, OH: Ohio State University Press, 1999)

Benjamin, Harry M.D. and Masters, R. E. L. *Prostitution and Morality.* (New York: The Julian Press, 1964)

Burpee, Charles W. *The History of Hartford County, 1633-1928*, (Chicago: The S. J. Clark Publishing Co., 1928)

Burpee, Charles W. *A Century In Hartford*, (Pub. by the Hartford County Mutual Fire Insurance Co., 1931)

Cott, Nancy F. (Ed.). *Prostitution,* (Munich: K.G. Saur Verlag, GmbH & Co., Walter De Gruyter, Inc., 1993)

Decker, Robert Owen. *Hartford Immigrants, A History of the Christian Activities Council (Congregational) 1850-1980,* (New York: United Church Press, 1987.)

Delaney, Edmund. *The Connecticut River: New England's Historic Waterway*, (Chester, CT: The Globe Pequot Press, 1983.)

Dudley-Edwards, R. & Williams, T. D. *The Great Famine, Studies in Irish History 1845-52.* (Dublin: Lilliput Press, 1956, Reprinted 1997)
Greenhill, Basil & Giffard Ann. *Traveling By Sea In The Nineteenth Century: Interior Design in Victorian Passenger Ships.* (New York: Hasting House Publishing, 1974.)

Hartford, Conn. As A Manufacturing, Business and Commercial Center. Published by the Hartford Board of Trade, 1889. (Printed by Case, Lockwood & Brainard Co., Hartford, CT.

Hazen, Henry H. *Syphilis: A Treatise on Etiology, Pathology, Diagnosis, Prognosis, Prophylaxis, and Treatment.* (St. Louis: C.V. Mosby Company, 1919)

Hooper & Lewis Browne, *Life Along the Connecticut River*, (Brattleboro, VT: Stephen Day Press, 1939)

Hoyt, James B. *The Connecticut Story*, (New Haven: Reader's Press, Inc., 1961.)

Hyde, Francis E. *Cunard And The North Atlantic: 1840 – 1973, A History of Shipping and Financial Management.* (Atlantic Highlands, N.J., Humanities Press, 1975.)

J.H. Beers & Co., *Commemorative Biographical Record of Hartford County*, (Chicago, 1901.)
    Kneeland, George J. *Commercialized Prostitution in New York City.* A Publication of the New York Bureau of Social Hygiene. (New York: The Century Company, 1913.)

Laxton, Edward. *The Famine Ships: The Irish Exodus To America.* (New York :Henry Holt & Co., 1996.)

Longo, Jerry. *Connecticut State Police.* (Charleston, SC: Arcadia Publishing, 2005.)

Love, William DeLoss. *The Colonial History of Hartford,* (Connecticut: Centinel Hill Press & The Pequot Press, Inc, 1974)

Marquis, Albert Nelson. *Who's Who in New England.* (Chicago: A. N. Marquis, publishers, 1915)

Miller, Eleanor M. and Romenesko, Kim and Lisa Wondolkowski . Prostitution in the United States. (Westport, CT, Greenwood Press, 1993)

Miller, Kerby A. *Emigrants and Exiles: Ireland and the Irish Exodus to North America.* (New York: Oxford University Press, 1985)

Miller, John. *Revenue, Population & Commerce,* London: (Oxford University Press, 1850)

Mills, Lewis Sprague. *The Story of Connecticut*, (West Rindge, NH, Richard R. Smith Publisher, 1953)

Murphy, Kevin. *Crowbar Governor: The Life and Times of Morgan Gardner Bulkeley.* (Middletown, CT: Wesleyan University Press, 2010)

Murphy, Kevin. *Water For Hartford: The Story of the Hartford Water Works and the Metropolitan District Commission.* (Middletown, CT: Wesleyan University Press, 2010)

Murphy, Kevin. *Lydia Sherman: American Borgia.* (Rocky Hill, CT: Shining Tramp Press, 2013)

Murtagh, John M. *Cast The First Stone,* (New York: McGraw-Hill, 1957)

Porter, Daniel L (edit). *Biographical Dictionary of American Sports.* (Westport, CT: Greenwood Publishing Group, 2000)

Préteseille, Landry. *The Irish Immigrant Trade to North America: 1845-1855.* Master's Thesis, (Centre d'Etudes Irlandaises de l'Université Rennes 2, Haute Bretagne)

Rosenzweig, Roy. *Eight Hours For What We Will. Workers and Leisure in the Industrial City, 1870-1920.* (Cambridge: Cambridge University Press, 1983)

Roth, David M. *Connecticut: A Bicentennial History,* (New York: Norton, , 1979)

Sanger, William M., MD. *History of Prostitution: Its Extent, Causes, and Effects Throughout The World.* (New York: Harper & Bros., 1858)

Sharpless, Megan. *Unity in Numbers: The Archeology of the Demimonde (1840-1917).* (paper) (University of Wisconsin, Senior Thesis, May 2008)

Social Hygiene, Volume 4. Ch: The Passing of the Red Light District, Joseph Meyer. (New York: American Social Hygiene Association, 1918)

Trumbull, J. Hammond. *The Memorial History of Hartford County: 1633-1884*, (Boston: Edward L. Osgood, Publisher, 1886)

Vedder, Edward B. *Syphilis and Public Health.* (Philadelphia: Lea & Febiger, 1918)

Van Dusen, Albert E. *The History of Connecticut*, (New York: Random House, 1961)

Weaver, Glenn. *Hartford: An Illustrated History of Connecticut's Capital*, Connecticut Historical Society; (Woodland Hills, California: Windsor Publications, Inc., 1982)

Weaver, Thomas S. *Historical Sketch of the Police Service of Hartford, from 1836 to 1901.* (Hartford: Hartford Police Mutual Aid Society, 1901)

Wood, Sharon E. *The Freedom of the Streets: Work, Citizenship, and Sexuality in a Gilded Age City* (Chapel Hill, NC: University of North Carolina Press, 2005)

Woolston, Howard B. *Prostitution In The United States.* (New York: The Century Co. 1921)

Wright, George E. *Crossing the Connecticut,* (Hartford: Smith-Linsley Co., 1908)

Index

Lafayette House (Columbia House), 35, 46
Lally, James Francis (Officer), 201-203
Lansing, Jessie, 145, 227, 228, 234
Last Chance Gulch, 13
Law and Order League, New Haven, 120, 165, 167-169, 256
Leffingwell, Adelia E. "Ada," 83, 101, 104, 112, 136, 138, 152, 166,
170-175, 223, 230, 231
Lexow Committee, 79, 239
Lind, Jennie, 153
Los Angeles, 58, 129, 205, 236
Louis Phillipe, 26
Louis Napoleon, 26
Louisiana, Alexandria, 176
Liverpool, 23-24, 27, 218

Mahon, Bridget McQueeney, 218, 221
Mahon, Mary Dalton, 218, 221, 239
Mann Act, 236-237
Market Street Police Station, 57-75, 170, 177, 186, 203, 209, 229
Massachusetts, 37, 62, 73, 81, 108, 116-117, 133, 155-159, 167, 174, 192, 231
Mayer, Nathan (Dr.), 147-149
Mayer, Isaac, (Rabbi), 147
McCook, John J., 111
McCormick, Bridget, 193
McGuire, Alexander, 37
McGuire, Ann, 23
McGuire, Francis "Frank," 37, 218-223
McKernan, Edward, 229
McQueeney, Catherine "Katie," 39-40, 49, 138, 220-221
McQueeney, Jane, 25-29, 30, 37, 39-47, 85, 88-89, 218
McQueeney, Timothy, 20-47, 175, 218-219
Memphis, 175-176
"Missouri Kid, The" (see Rudolph, William), 228-229
Mitchel, John, 26
Morris, Luzon (Gov.), 172
Morgan, J.P., 25, 192

National Circuit Trotting, 165
North City Ward, 21
New Haven, 25, 33, 38, 46, 60, 79, 90, 115, 120-123, 144, 165-168,
171-175, 184-185
New London, 33, 38, 89, 175, 186, 246, 249
New Orleans, 13, 127, 206, 258
New York, 23
Nichols, Cyprian, 93-94

United States Hotel, 25, 37, 40, 160-161, 251

venereal disease, 180-182

Waldo, Hubbard and Hyde, 80
Valentine, David and Elizabeth, 235-237
Waller, Thomas, Gov., 38, 81
War of the Rebellion (see Civil War)
Warren, George and Clara, 177-180
Warwick Cycle Mfg. Co., 157
Waterbury (Brass City), 46, 168, 173-175, 186, 200, 221
Washington College (see Trinity College)
Webb, Celia, 41-43
Webster, Carolyn, 91, 171, 223
Weeks, Joseph, 68, 74, 78-79
Welles, Gideon, 40
West, Billy, (born Ernest H. Stetson), 100, 155-180, 203, 216, 228
West, Cora, (a.k.a. Cora Bordeaux), 162, 171
Westcott, Edwin S. (Atty.), 150-151
West Indies trade, 67, 106
Wethersfield and Hartford Horse railroad, 92
Wethersfield Prison (see Connecticut State Prison at Wethersfield)
Wheeler, Ralph (Judge), 246
White Slavery (white slave trafficking), 234-236
Williams, Alexander "Clubber", Capt., 77-78
Williams, John, (Rev. Pres.), 51
Wilson, Annie, "Queen of Omaha's Underworld," 13
Wilson, Charles (Atty.), 224-226
Wilson, James, 108-109
Winslow, Gideon, 191
Wrinn, James, (New Haven police supt.), 167

Yale College, 33, 184, 188, 200-224, 242, 246
Yorkshire, 24
Young German-American Association, 127

www.ingramcontent.com/pod-product-compliance
Lightning Source LLC
Chambersburg PA
CBHW060251100426
42742CB00011B/1706